QUEER MAGIC

QUEER MAGIC
Power Beyond Boundaries

Edited by **Lee Harrington** and **Tai Fenix Kulystin**

MYSTIC
PRODUCTIONS LLC

Notice

Queer Magic: Power Beyond Boundaries

(c) 2018 – Lee Harrington, Tai Fenix Kulystin and Mystic Productions Press

Published in the United States by Mystic Productions Press, LLC
603 Tudor Rd. Anchorage, AK 99503 www.MysticProductionsPress.com

All authors and artists have retained their original copyright, with permission granted to Mystic Productions LLC for inclusion in this project.

Interior and Exterior Layout by Rob River www.RobRiver.com

Image of Lee Harrington by Darrell Lynn www.KiltedPhotography.daportfolio.com

ISBN – 978-1-942733-79-9
Ebooks: MOBI – 978-1-942733-78-2
ePub – 978-1-942733-77-5
PDF – 978-1-942733-76-8

To our queer ancestors and magical
forebearers who illuminated the way

Table of Contents

Introduction: A Journey Into Queer Magic(s)

Queer, strange, weird. Wyrd, the Old English term for fate or personal destiny, twisted through time to say that the Other is that which pulls upon the threads of reality.

As both magical beings and individuals who dance outside the journeys of heteronormativity and cisnormativity, the larger culture has deemed us to be queer, strange, and weird. Our practices and daily lives do not fit into the realities painted as being "normal." Because of this, individuals who fit within LGBTQIA+ (lesbian, gay, bisexual, transgender, queer, questioning, intersex, asexual, agender, and more) have the opportunity to embrace that weirdness, and in turn, their wyrd-ness, and the wyrd of the world.

While we may celebrate and take pride in our fabulous and weird selves, Otherness is often feared by society at large. When we talked with other queer-spectrum individuals, we found that they had also experienced othering and rejection based on their identities or found places where they were overly-embraced. Being placed on a pedestal in pagan communities simply for being queer is certainly not the same as being vilified, but it is yet another form of othering that results in isolation. It is a kind of false visibility, one that praises part of us while ignoring the rest. Even in groups whose pantheons have a diversity of queer and transgender deities, their practitioners often give a confused expression or cold shoulder to their fellow coven-mates, troth-siblings, and fellow journeyers in spirit. In some Asatru groups, for example, racism, sexism, and homophobia run rampant while their followers preach that they bow before Odin, a god who has danced outside of gender norms by both cross-dressing and being a practitioner of seiðr, a magical craft practiced traditionally by women. Women-only Wiccan groups have turned away their trans sisters time and time again, showing the transphobia embedded in a faith that claims to worship all acts of love and pleasure.

In other spiritual traditions – especially those focused on transcendent rather than immanent spirituality – a queer or trans identity held by a practitioner is sometimes viewed as unimportant or unenlightened, a material distraction that they must overcome. This supposed spiritual truth is just one example of spiritual bypassing, or using spiritual ideas to avoid anything difficult or painful to understand or process. In this case, it means ignoring our differences and the way those impact our lives, glossing over that variation in favor of a "we are all one" mentality. This false idea of spiritual attainment is further used to dismiss anything outside of what is considered "normal" as frivolous or a waste of energy that could be better spent working toward some greater spiritual goal. Frequently this is seen in Western or Westernized traditions especially practiced by the most privileged among us who have little to no experience being the Other.

If an individual's queerness or non-normative gender is acknowledged within a spiritual group, it is often assumed to have no bearing on their spiritual practices or experiences. In these groups, all are expected to work within a heteronormative and cisnormative framework for spirituality. These frameworks were developed by straight cis people. Sometimes for the queer practitioner, this means ignoring rigid definitions of masculinity and femininity and focusing on a heterosexual union as the epitome of spiritual experience. This is invisibilizing and challenging at best, though many of us go along with it for lack of a queer-centric option. Those who are often assumed to be cis and straight – especially queer femmes, trans and nonbinary folks, and queer folks in other-gender partnerships – are even more pressured to conform and ignore their invisible identities, lest they get in the way of their spiritual pursuits.

LGBTQIA+ communities have their own problematic issues. Spirit-workers can be lifted up for being the epitome of queer, or ripped down for having any sort of magical beliefs or faith traditions. Just as the spiritual communities are not utopias, collections of people based on orientation or identity can also try to push away or erase differences. Plenty of gatekeeping occurs within queer communities. Those who do not fit into the current queer ideal are often ignored, treated as "not queer enough," and made invisible to their own people, or ostracized for "appearing straight," further perpetuating internalized notions of othering. This is becoming more apparent as our queer communities are being given a chance to face our unconscious (and sometimes conscious) bigotry head-on. After all, pride parades were once protest marches, and the work of Black Lives Matter and Trans Lives Matter are an opportunity to continue to reevaluate our biographies within LGBTQIA+ communities. By doing so, we have the capacity to continue to bring love, pleasure, and justice to the individuals these communities represent, while simultaneously working to end queer erasure, femme erasure, trans erasure, and the erasure of voices of color and indigenous populations within pagan and magical communities.

Having found that others in the world were running time and time again into these challenges, we recognized a very real need to acknowledge and celebrate our wyrd-ness and the ways that our queer identities and our spiritualities inform and encourage one another. From this place of celebration, we put out a call for people to participate in this project. We found that queer flowers of love and beauty are blooming everywhere. We are pushing our way through the cracks in the concrete and carving out spaces for our weird and wyrd ways to manifest. This book is about the blooms that have erupted as a form of resistance. They are a chance to glimpse the diversity of practices and experiences of queer folks that rise above the voices that say that we do not exist. We do exist. We've always existed. We're here, we're queer, and we are magical.

This book represents intersectional populations who are not only queer peoples (self-defined in a broad set of criteria by those participating), but those who practice magic, magick, or magics. We are neo-pagans, druids, agnostics, alchemists, elders, Buddhists, bruja, heathens, diviners, oracles, witches, Jews, atheists, polytheists, and ceremonial magicians. We are practitioners of Santeria, Vodou, Yoruba, Hellenismos, Ifá, Shinto, Huna, tantra, Feri, and Faery alike. We are eclectic beings beyond labels, and deep devotees of mystery cults. We are transgender, two-spirit, queer, agender, drag queens, lesbian, bisexual, gay, non-binary, shapeshifters, kinky, cross-dressers, and radicals who refuse to define ourselves.

We are individuals on the edges of normative culture. We have experienced intolerance, stigma, discrimination, violence, or worse from people who are angry about the many sides of our identities. We survive by turning to each other and lifting one another up. In that tradition, we, invite you to read these words. They contain our hearts and spirits. As you learn about each of us, know the power of your own heart and spirit in turn. This is your chance to channel the power that the larger culture has oppressed and our own queer kin have sometimes pushed aside. It is through projects like this one that we have an opportunity to make magic our own rather than settling. We are beautiful and powerful. We don't have to settle for "good enough." A second-rate status is not our birthright.

In Queer Magic, you will note that there are diverse stylistic approaches taken throughout the book. The reason for this is twofold. The first is to honor queer history by showing the variety of approaches taken throughout the movement for visibility, love, acceptance, and celebration in our queer cultures. The second is an attempt towards a decolonization of language and the false perception that only academic, often white, voices, are the "right" way to communicate information. Our contributors were asked to speak from their authentic voices, their home truths, and in their free and genuine style. By doing so, some authors may resonate more than others. We hope that in this rainbow of voices, there will be some that connect with you on your journey.

Inside Queer Magic, you will find paintings and poster-style art, formal essays, and intimate stories of sub-communities. There are fiction pieces based on life and academic pieces full of citations, comic book pages and poetry. The book includes sigil-art and cartoons, personal stories and how-to rituals, and even interviews with elders who granted us the opportunity to listen from the oral histories of our past. Ours is a multi-pronged approach to finding our spirit and humanity, giving you a snapshot of the diversity of queer experience.

We have been blessed by a wide array of individuals who were able to be part of this book. It has been inspirational to have 43 individuals contribute their passion and convictions to this project. That is not counting our readers, copy and layout editors, distribution team, and the great folks at bookstores large and small who believe in small-press projects like this one. It has been an honor to work with each of you, and to have each of you help bring this project to life.

Our special thanks go out to Butterfly, who listened to late night ramblings from Lee and brought him truffles and sweet kisses, both made with love. To Stian and Kat, who held Tai during the process, offering them snuggles, sympathetic ears, and endless encouragement.

Appreciation must go out to Primal Ordeal, where Tai and Lee brainstormed Queer Magic together, and groups and events such as Black Leather Wings, Living Love Revolution, Dark Odyssey, Keepers Crossing, Primal Arts, Twisted Tryst, Free Spirit Gathering, Turtle Hills Beltane, House Kheperu, PantheaCon, the Sacred Kink intensives, Palimpsest, SW Leather, Paradise Unbound, and the Center for Sex Positive Culture. These events and organizations opened Lee and Tai to the diverse possibilities of exploring queer magic themselves. Thanks also go out to

Sarah McBryde whose keen eye helped us make this work excellent, Patrick Califia, who stepped in to help the magic manifest, and Rob River for continuing to answer random questions on tight timelines and designing our beautiful cover.

Inside this book you will find snapshots of queer mysteries and revelations of dangerous truths. They are deeply personal pieces of the soul laid bare for the world to see the magic within. This is a chance to dance in our collective creativity and be inspired by the work others are doing.

We are the past, and we are the future. We are queer, we are magical, we are wyrd. We are now. Let our words ring out and touch the stars, as well as those who thought they were the only ones. So mote it be.

Blessed be,

Lee Harrington and Tai Fenix Kulystin

February 2018

Hex the Patriarchy

by Inés Ixierda

Inclusive Wicca Manifesto

by Yvonne Aburrow

Inclusive Wicca is not for people who want to stay safe and cosy in their heteronormative cisgender worldview, pretending that oppression is not happening and that racism is a thing of the past. Being inclusive means becoming aware of others' pain, and supporting the oppressed and the marginalised. It means doing some work to make your rituals inclusive and healing for everyone, and understanding your own privilege - the degree to which your reality and worldview is considered 'normal' and 'natural' by 'mainstream' culture or a given subculture; the degree to which you are safe from oppression; and the extent to which your right to existence is not constantly questioned and undermined. Inclusive Wicca is about being inclusive for everyone.

There isn't a competition over who is more oppressed. There is no queue for liberation. We can work on small issues and large issues at the same time. Not all of the concepts and populations mentioned here receive the same degree of oppression in society. They are included in the list because at some point, they have been excluded from some Wiccan circles for reasons related to prejudice. Inclusive Wicca is not a new or separate tradition. It is a tendency within existing Wiccan traditions[1].

Inclusive Wicca began as a way of ensuring that LGBTQIA people are included in Wiccan rituals, but has transformed into an inclusive ethos that encompasses more than sexuality. It also means that we have an inclusive approach to theology by encompassing and embracing polytheistic or pantheistic views, and including queer

1   In Australia, there actually is a tradition called inclusive Wicca, which is unconnected to the inclusive tendency, though it may have similar goals. Founded to include Wiccans from different traditions, they are not specifically LGBTQIA-inclusive, and their website doesn't mention LGBTQIA inclusion, but doesn't take an anti-LGBTQIA stance either.

deities in our practices. An inclusive and egalitarian ethos must include all members, making sure that all practices are inclusive, including queer rites of passage. It also encompasses an anti-racist stance, and inclusiveness of people with disabilities and mental health conditions.

One of the key issues is Wicca's focus on polarity, which is an energetic principle that is comprised of any pair of opposites. There are other ways of making energy, such as resonance (creating energy between two people who are alike) and synergy (making energy with the harmony of a group of people). Cakes and wine, quarter calls, invocations, and consecrations must all be respectful and inclusive. The inclusive ethos embraces all aspects of identity, and the egalitarian approach is a necessary corollary of it. Everyone should have a voice, whether they are a new explorer with an interesting fresh perspective, or a seasoned practitioner with more experience. All aspects of the self, including but not limited to sexual orientation, ethnic identity, neurodivergence, and physical difference are welcome in an inclusive Wiccan circle. Therefore, we reject all attempts to exclude anyone based on their differences by embracing theologies and practices that celebrate and include diversity.

Many people seem to think that inclusive means "I've got some gay people in my coven." That is certainly welcoming – but it is not necessarily inclusive. There is a spectrum of inclusivity. One coven might score 95% and another might score 75%, but it is important to note that different people will have different ideas and priorities. We can avoid miscommunications and heartache if individual covens state the ways in which they are inclusive, and in which ways they are not.

A Manifesto

- **Diversity is important in celebration, theology, and cosmology.** We do not accept the narrative of a goddess and a god interacting at different points of the Wheel of the Year because this reinforces the cisgender and heterocentric gender binary. We explore different aspects of mythology and folklore, including the celebration of queer deities. For this reason, Inclusive Wicca tends towards pantheism, where the divine includes all genders and sexual orientations, or polytheism, where we recognize many deities that have many different gender expressions and sexual orientations. We also embrace deities outside of a heterosexual binary, including deities that have same-sex lovers. We accommodate different theological perspectives, including but not limited to animism, atheism, pantheism, polytheism, and duotheism. Atheist Wiccans are also included in Inclusive Wicca, allowing for individuals who view the deities as archetypes and energies to participate, as long as they can work with those of different theological perspectives in the circle. This applies to those of other theological perspectives.

- **Gender identity, gender expression, sex/gender assigned at birth, and biological characteristics are distinct.** By this, we mean that these concepts are noticeably different, but can be interpermeable and with fuzzy boundaries. Gender is not a spectrum. It's more of a scatter-plot, and cannot be neatly confined to boxes and categories. Queer expressions of gender are creative and beautiful, and break us out of the tired tropes of 'masculine qualities' and 'feminine qualities.' The arbitrary assignment of characteristics such as bravery, nurturing, or creativity to one gender or another should not be sacralised and reified, but rather broken down, challenged, and resisted. Many Pagan practitioners produce visualisations and workings that rely on perpetuating the gender binary, disempowering cisgender, transgender, non-binary, and gender-fluid people alike. In Inclusive Wicca, we push beyond these arbitrary assignments, as we hold that goddesses need not be soft and fertile, nor gods unyielding and violent. Similarly, we also acknowledge and embrace the prevalence of intersex people, which negates the idea that biological sex is a simple matter of 'male' and 'female': there are seven different sex characteristics that make up biological sex, and any of them can vary from male or female, making gender assignment somewhat arbitrary. The social importance that is attached by 'mainstream' culture to biological sex, and the way children get socialised as one gender or the other throughout their lives, means that Paganism should help people escape from these embedded cultural notions.

- **There are many ways to make polarity, as it is simply the tension of opposites.** Bringing a male body and a female body together is not the only way to make polarity. A roomful of people together can be divided into a diversity of binaries: morning people and evening people, cat lovers and dog lovers, tea drinkers and coffee drinkers, air signs and earth signs, fire signs and water signs, people who like Marmite and people who prefer chocolate, extroverts and introverts, and so on. Each of these pairs can create polarity by bringing these energies together. Polarity can be made by two or more people of any gender and sexual orientation, and by two or more people of the same gender. What's more, polarity exists on a spectrum where Person A may be yang in relation to Person B, but yin in relation to Person C. For example, Person A may be more extroverted than Person B, but less extroverted than person C.

- **Energy can be made with resonance.** Resonance is when two or more similar people come together and bring their energies into alignment with each other in order to amplify the signal. For example, two femme people, two extroverts, two people of the same astrological sign, two morning people, two cat-lovers, and so on.

- **Energy can be made with synergy.** Synergy is where the energies of the whole group converge. This happens in circles all the time, such as when the whole group dances in a circle together, or when all members focus on the same visualisation or intention. It can happen with everything from sweeping the circle, to calling a quarter, to invoking a deity. Everyone in the group should focus on what is happening within the circle, instead of allowing their thoughts to wander.

- **The magical concept of fertility is not strictly biological, and applies to creativity.** Wicca is often seen as a fertility religion, causing objections to Wicca from various queer perspectives, but inclusive Wicca shows that Wicca can move beyond the limited belief that fertility only refers to giving birth to children. Even when doing fertility magic, a male body and a female body are not needed to produce magical fertility on a symbolic level, such as when they are blessing crops. It's also worth noting that the notion that Paganism is or was a fertility religion was introduced by an outsider to the religion itself[2]. This makes the idea that Paganism is wholly a fertility religion deeply suspect. The idea that Wicca is a Nature religion is a lot more valid, since much of the Pagan revival has been about recovering our connection with Nature. These opportunities for reconnecting with Nature are as diverse as the people that are welcomed into inclusive Wicca.

- **Women are much more than an embodiment of fertility.** Some Wiccans are very keen on emphasising the fertility of women and their ability to give birth and menstruate. This focus excludes transgender, non-binary, agender, and genderqueer people. It is great to celebrate the body, but inclusive Wicca challenges us to make sure we celebrate all bodies, whether or not they have produced children. Inclusive Wicca does not reduce women to being nothing more than a carrier of a womb.

---

2   J G Frazer introduced this notion in The Golden Bough to discredit Christianity by pointing out its roots in "primitive" paganism. The thrust of Frazer's work was intended to imply that human belief is evolving from animism, to polytheism, to monotheism, to atheism.

- **A deity of any gender may be invoked by a human of any gender into a human of any gender.** The Wiccan tendency to only do invocation where a man invokes a goddess into a woman, or a woman invokes a god into a man, is not consistent with many other occult practices. In just about every other magical system, anyone can invoke any deity into another person. It is healthy to ensure that any one person invokes different archetypes and energies, and is not always invoking the same type of deity, which could cause psychological imbalance by over-emphasising a particular archetype.

- **Ritual roles are not assigned according to gender.** Anyone can sweep the ritual space and cast the circle; anyone can call the quarters; anyone can consecrate the cakes and wine. There is no need for men and women to stand alternately in circle. Men can kiss men and women can kiss women. Consecrating and purifying each other in the circle can be done by any gender to any gender, which includes male, female, genderqueer, non-binary, agender, genderfluid, metagender, postgender, and all other genders. A person's gender does not dictate their ability to perform specific roles, or do specific work.

- **Cakes and wine must be done in an inclusive manner.** Some of us use the symbolism of lover and beloved instead of male and female. We have also developed a wine consecration with two cups, where we pour the wine from one cup into the other, with the words "I fill your cup with love," the empty cup is passed on, and each person fills the next person's cup with these words. Another way to do cakes and wine is with the understanding that we all contain both 'masculine' and 'feminine' energies, or that the ultimate polarity is spirit and matter, or self and other, or the lightning striking the primordial waters, or some other inclusive variation.

- **We accommodate different mental health issues, and disabilities.** These include, but are not limited to, neurodivergence, dyslexia, left-handedness, and aphantasia. It should be up to the individual witch to determine whether or not they are well enough to be in a circle instead of the exclusionary policies of some Wiccan covens. Magical ritual can also be very therapeutic. Inclusive Wicca follows the social model of disability[3], which takes the view that people are disabled by the failure of society to accommodate their difference, rather than being intrinsically disabled from within. One example of ensuring that we are inclusive is by not making people copy the coven's Book of Shadows by hand,

---

3   Leithin Cluan (2015), Do we act justly? Disability, mental illness, and vulnerability. Gods & Radicals.   https://godsandradicals.org/2015/10/02/do-we-act-justly-disability-mental-illness-and-vulnerability/

as this can be extremely discouraging for people with dyslexia and dyspraxia. Another is not telling left-handed people to hold their athame with their right hand. Offering alternatives to dancing for people with mobility issues, making learning materials available in different formats, and being sensitive towards people with body dysphoria are all ways that circles can be more inclusive.

- **We practice openness with other cultures and ethnicities.** We do not insist on a genetic basis for culture (e.g. anyone can worship gods from any culture). We need to be aware of the existence of systemic racism, which is the way that certain ethnic groups are oppressed in areas of employment, housing, access to justice, policing, and society in general. We work magic to alleviate oppression, and engage in resistance to oppression in solidarity with the oppressed.

- **We try to avoid cultural appropriation.** In doing so, we recognise that cultural appropriation occurs where there is a power difference, usually due to a history of colonialism, between the exploiters and the exploited. We should not treat Indigenous cultures as mere commodities and curiosities. Cultural appropriation is when someone from a colonising or culturally dominant culture takes a ritual or sacred or meaningful practice from a subjugated or devalued or colonised culture, lifting it out of context and draining it of meaning.

- **We welcome kink, polyamory, and monogamy.** Safe, sane, and consensual BDSM (and risk-aware consensual kink), is a healthy variant of human sexuality, and can bring about profound spiritual experiences. Both polyamory and monogamy, provided that they are egalitarian and consensual, are also natural and healthy variants of human sexuality. Power-exchange relationships are healthy when they are fully consented to and consciously managed. For both polyamorous and monogamous relationships, as well as Wiccan covens, trust, communication, and transparency are key.

- **We promote consent culture.** In a consent culture[4], the individual is considered to be the best judge of their own wants and needs. Seeking clear consent for social interactions, especially those involving touch or sexual contact, is the

---

4   The concept of consent culture arose out of feminist, BDSM, and LGBTQ approaches to sexual ethics. Although it applies to personal freedom in all areas of life, it is particularly concerned with issues around sexuality and touch. Consent culture emphasises that everyone has the right to enjoyable sex that they have enthusiastically consented to with full knowledge of the risks. It is sex-positive, sets boundaries, and promotes clear and shame-free communication about sex. In a consent culture, everyone values enthusiastic consent. Initiators of contact have the primary responsibility for respectfully seeking consent, rather than it being the recipients' responsibility to fend off predators and others who try to violate boundaries. Consent culture embraces the freedom to say yes and no, and the empathy to honour others' desires and boundaries. Consent can be non-verbal, but when we are on the beginner slopes of consent culture, it's great to practice receiving verbal consent.

expected norm. Because each adult is fully in charge of their own body and mind, it is a violation to try to force them into an activity against their will, or to forcibly prevent them from engaging in an activity they desire (as long as that activity is not harmful to themselves or others). In an inclusive coven, all members must have the right to consent to or refuse all magic involving them, all forms of touch, and all ritual actions.

- **Inclusive Wicca avoids ageism.** We welcome members of all ages that are over 18, and accommodate older members' needs. There is generally a minimum age restriction of 18 years of age in Wiccan covens to ensure that participants have the emotional and physical maturity to cope with the erotic energy and symbolism[5]. We listen to the concerns and voices of members of all ages. We guide individuals under 18 who seek information to useful resources to begin their path.

- **We are body-positive.** Inclusive Wicca does not allow fat-shaming or body-shaming. Bodies come in all shapes and sizes. They are all beautiful, whatever the shape, size, degree of hairiness, scarring, or any other difference they may have.

- **We try to accommodate coven members with low incomes.** This involves arranging events on bus routes where possible, not organising expensive social activities, avoiding a massive and expensive reading list, nor expecting people to buy expensive equipment. Similarly, we do not insist that coven members reach a particular educational level or belong to a particular socio-economic class.

- **We listen to the views of all the members, and value their contributions and ideas.** A new person's perspective can be incredibly valuable, as questions like "but why do we do it that way?" can make a group think and re-evaluate their magical practices. Everyone brings different experiences and perspectives to the circle, and all are welcome.

The simple principle at the heart of inclusive Wicca is empathy and respect. Being inclusive is about respecting and celebrating the experiences and qualities that others bring to the circle, and empathising with their perspective. If you have respect, empathy, compassion, and love, then all the rest is commentary.

---

5   In the UK, although the age of consent is 16, the age at which an older person is no longer considered to be 'in loco parentis' is when the young person reaches the age of 18. Therefore this policy is also legally advisable.

Further Reading

- Yvonne Aburrow (2014), *All Acts of Love and Pleasure: Inclusive Wicca.* Avalonia Books.

- Jo Green (2016). *Queer Paganism: A spirituality that embraces all identities.*

- Yvonne Aburrow (forthcoming), *Dark Mirror: the inner work of witchcraft.*

- Lupa Greenwood (2012). *Talking About the Elephant: An Anthology of Neopagan Perspectives on Cultural Appropriation.*

- www.inclusivewicca.org

Wai-Water

by Adare

This portrait of Mistress JuJu MinXXX, "America's Leather-Clad Sweetheart," captures the healing transformation of water, just as Juju embodies the fluidity of sexuality and gender.

QUEERING TANTRA: A QUEER BLACK WOMAN'S PERSPECTIVE

by Maisha Najuma Aza, MSW

No one truly knows where the mind goes when the body's left to its own devices, but when the mind lets go and becomes a part of the erotic flow, it leads to the mysteries of life revealed.

BLACK GIRL TANTRA

I am an enigma to many, an anomaly, just like many of my friends in the queer world, and in the worlds of sacred sexuality, erotic embodiment, and Tantra sacred intimacy. We don't fit neatly into pretty molds because we are a conscious collection of our connections and experiences; we purposefully choose the way we want to live our lives, and Tantra is exactly that – conscious living.

Tantra is a Vedic/Sanskrit term which literally means "weave" or "loom." A Tantra is also a collection of philosophical systems of ideas created to expand our consciousness. I define it as the conscious co-creation and experimentation of our deeply personal and mutli-dimensional existence, as we weave the energetic and the physical worlds together. There are multiple definitions and traditions of Tantra. This is because it becomes what we become and evolves as we evolve. In its richest, deepest, and most magical form, my evolution in Tantra is a continuous conscious self-discovery because it includes the use of erotic energy; the whole body, mind, and spirit; and the mystical. What I weave into my queer Black Girl Tantra are the intersectionalities that exist within me and within my community of people of all sizes, shapes, abilities, colors, and bodies. My Black Girl Tantra way is sacred, is ritual, is colorful, is fat, is lesbian, is queer, is trans, is fluid, is multi-abled, and is multi-generational. My Tantra is a sensual amalgamation of my eclectic black pagan spirituality, my

Tribal Shaman Priestess training, my black witchery, my massage therapy training, my social work training, my social justice and healing justice background, my Tantra sacred intimacy training, my erotic life experiences, and my hard life lessons.

Most importantly, in order to truly understand Tantra is to experience it and to live it. In my experience of Tantra, our worlds and energy bodies merge, expanding and contracting as we weave in and out of lucid dreaming, ecstasy, intimacy, and the physical mundane world. When we are conscious, we can experience all of these worlds at the same time, while collecting data about our very existence. We can then allow our hearts and minds to expand beyond our concrete ideas and into intuitive knowing.

My life has been very much a Tantric experience, as I've come to know and understand it. I've lived my life exploring, expanding, and experimenting with various ways of being, as well as wandering unafraid (and sometimes afraid) into the mystery of the unknown. I have always been aware that we are all connected somehow, but never fully knew what that meant. I didn't have the language or framework for it until I began to experience that connection through my own spiritual and erotic experiences. My explorations since my early twenties lead me to women spirituality circles, indigenous, and black indigenous rituals, ceremonies and practices from around the world, while simultaneously exploring my sensuality through my erotic adventures in group sex, energetic sex, kink, BDSM and polyamory. This path ultimately led to my awareness and study of Tantra, which I'm still exploring and learning.

I first began noticing the subtle energies of the body when I was in massage therapy school in the late 1990's. As I therapeutically touched my clients', classmates', and teachers' bodies during sessions, I would feel their pulse in my fingers and hands and within my own body. I would feel their life force – though I didn't call it that then – no matter where on their body I touched and no matter how lightly. In fact, I noticed that the lighter I touched their bodies the more I felt these subtle, yet powerful sensations. This feeling or sensing of other people's energy bodies was emerging in me as I began working more and more directly with massage therapy. I soon experienced a deep physical and energetic discovery of feelings and emotions that had been stored deeply in the muscles of my body that led to my own healing. This massage therapy school process began my own personal mind-body- soul connection and it woke me out of a deep soul-slumber that began with sexual trauma in my early childhood. I would continue to wake up, in layers, as my adult life experiences continued. Each time taking in more energetic information into my soul and intuitively developing a more robust and dynamic sense of myself and my subtle, yet powerful energetic connection to others. This kind of awakening is what Tantra is all about. It is more than something you physically do. It is a way of living and engaging consciously with all aspects of the self and the world. Utilizing Tantric practices helps to unlock erotic power and self-healing.

TANTRA BEGAN IN THE MARGINS

Tantra has a mostly oral and experiential history, with only a small amount of written history, which makes it difficult to determine its exact origin. However, common knowledge among tantric practitioners is that it began in the margins of Indic society well over 3000 years ago, and its influence and practices span many cultures and religions from some forms of Hinduism, Buddhism, Taoism, and even Christianity. Some may say that Tantra has no beginning, and that its beginning is not nearly as important as its purpose. Its purpose being, in short, to expand the heart and mind by consciously being aware of our connection to our higher and lower selves and to one another, while practicing balance.

It is important to remember that Tantra originated with people of color and people on the margins of both society and religion. That paradigm shifted once Tantra was brought to the west, primarily to Europe and North America. Over the years, Tantra has become associated with people with social privilege – famous people, affluent people, white people, heterosexual people, thin people, and able-bodied people. This has left little room for people on the margins of our western world – people of color, people with disabilities, people with socioeconomic inequalities, queer people, people of size, and those with multiple marginalized intersectionalities – to think that Tantra is for them.

Tantra in its original form is not about sex, but the practices can be applied to our sexual lives, as it can be applied to every aspect of our lives. That is in fact the purpose, to be conscious in every aspect of our lives. Sex is not a dirty word, nor is it separate from our spiritual selves. In our western form of Tantra, many Tantric practitioners do focus on sexuality a great deal of the time, because of the great amount of sexual repression inherent in our puritanically derived North American culture. There is no shame in understanding that and trying to shift our culture in a sex-positive direction. However, we can do anything in excess and we are a culture of excess, so it is important to be mindful of this and in doing so continue to pay attention to balance when practicing the erotic embodiment aspects of Tantra. It is also important to note that Tantra is not the only sacred sexual practice that exists in the world. Indigenous societies the world over have sacred practices that include the mind, the body – including sexuality – and the spirit.

OUR QUEER INTERSECTIONS

When I first began looking into Tantra, I found that in the western world, it was primarily white, exclusive, heterosexual, hetero-normative, homogenous, and dichotomous in language and practice. It is my greatest desire to teach Tantra in a way that speaks to and embraces everyone and every type of body.

My way of doing Tantra is erotic, is freeing, and is queer because it is a tapestry of my lived experience as a fat, black, queer, kinky, lesbian devoted to social justice and healing justice. It is important that my tantric practice includes and centralizes people within the margins of our self-created Lesbian, Gay, Bisexual, Transgender, Queer/Questioning, Intersex and Allies (LGBTQIA) subculture. This is because even within those subcultures privileges still exist, and therefore the margins still exist. Queer Tantra includes people whose human forms take all shapes, sizes, abilities, genders, and identities. My Queer Tantra focuses on the relationship each individual has with their authentic self, and their authentic bodies, their ancestral lineage, as well as how their bodies and energies can connect with other physical and energetic bodies in erotic community.

My Queer Tantra includes sacred sexual practices, embodiment and self-care practices, power rituals, BDSM, kink, ancestral work, sex-magic, singing, dancing, and other spiritual practices that have become part of my internal tapestry over time. The Tantric practice that I embody is filled with love-consciousness or Eros, along the intersections of our (and our ancestors') privileged and subjugated positions in the world. Many "new age" spiritual practitioners I've met have a reportedly "apolitical," way of viewing the world that is purposefully absent of a thoughtful social justice framework. When I practiced with spiritual groups of people with this ideology, it made it impossible for me to be my authentic self and thrive long-term. So I moved on

I've also experienced being in spiritual community where social justice is purposefully taken into consideration, but the parts that were considered still did not include all of the parts that touch me and my authenticity – again, I felt unable to thrive long-term. The one thing that always gets left out of any of these spiritual groups of which I've been a part of has been race. It appears to be the scariest thing for white people to address and for many of us to address. Sometimes we don't address it, and it begins to erode our ability to connect with one another on a much deeper level. How can our connections remain sustainable if our full selves are not acknowledged or embraced? My black Shaman spiritual community is an intimate sacred community where I feel safe being black.

Sadly, in my experiences in various spiritual communities, some would rather address anything other than race and racism, never mind that all of the social injustices will intersect with race at some point. Racism is the "big scary." It is the "big buzzkill." This kind of invisibility and fear can be heart wrenching and debilitating to someone who experiences racism regularly, and serves to do exactly what it was meant to do: disconnect us from one another. This is one of the many reasons the people of color I know do not choose to exist in white spaces to begin with. But I chose a different road, a difficult road. I chose to exist in these white spiritual spaces, not because they were white, but in spite of that fact.

I've always been called to explore myself and my erotic, spiritual, and physical edges, regardless of who else was in the room. I chose to exist in these spaces because I deserve to be my best self and I believe that we are all inherently good and loving people when we shed our socially-constructed shells. I was privileged enough to find queer erotic spaces where I felt like I belonged. These were spaces where we intimately opened our hearts to one another and where they made a way for me with scholarships and payment plans. I was grateful for that opportunity, and yet scholarships and payment plans are not the only bridge that needs to be built when including people of color, because we are not a homogenous group. The queer erotic spaces have been the places that have actively done their best to be accessible, and they still continue to actively engage in understanding how to do that better. In some ways, I felt lucky. I know that I was privileged to be able to explore my sexual self in erotic queer spaces, which was a beautiful start. Yet, as a black woman in these majority-white sexual healing spaces, I was still missing something. My heart felt it, knew it, longed to see more of myself represented, reflected back to me, and held more closely in deeper and more profound ways.

As I and many quirky, queer, witchy, black and POC folks have learned to do, we sometimes protect or shut off certain parts of ourselves in those spaces – the parts that feel the pain of invisibility, silencing, fetishizing, or otherness – in order to explore other important parts of ourselves. When we can no longer do this we say something, and when our cries of social injustices that we witness or experience, no matter how "big" or "small," go unheard, we move on. When I searched my soul and realized this is what I was doing, I realized that I must go beyond my erotic learning of myself, and that I must also teach so that I can contribute to the creation of inclusive erotic spiritual spaces that re-centralize people of color and people from other marginalized groups. Creating spiritual spaces where we do not have to shut off the parts of ourselves that society ignores or amplifies can be extremely validating, healing, and crucial to our ability to heal. What wonder it would be to take off the projections of others, like clothing, and to just be you. Rather than experiencing something like, "This person is black and therefore they grew up this way, and their parents were this way, and they will respond to me in this way, so I will alter the way I deal with them so that I won't be perceived as racist." I am primarily speaking of black people here because that is the most salient and visible part of me that gets ignored, stereotyped, or amplified. However, this could be applied to many marginalized groups.

When I'm thinking about centralizing people of color, queer people, trans people, people with disabilities, fat people, gender fluid people, and more, it becomes apparent that we are the ones who need to teach each other ourselves rather than be taught by people outside of marginalized experience. I have moved beyond waiting and wanting other people to teach me about myself, in the way that I wish to be taught. I'm discovering that this is an impossibility. While it is certain that people with privileges are able to hold space, and be supportive and even inclusive in some ways, it is important to understand that there is a limit. That the socially-marginalized must teach the other socially-marginalized; because we are able to facilitate, hold space, and support one another from some of our shared experiences. People of color must be in teaching and leadership roles for other people of color. This is one important way that we become centralized.

Queer white people cannot do everything, no matter how much social justice work they have done, or what other subjugated parts exist in them. They will never be able to understand what racism intrinsically feels like, in the same way that I cannot ever know what it intrinsically feels like to experience transphobia. Queer white people can continue to be allies, to make the spaces they run more inclusive, to continue to make more room for marginalized folks even if they choose not to come, and to use their privileges and resources to help open up doors that may otherwise be closed to a person of color. The people with more social and economic privilege can assist while letting go of controlling the outcome, while we on the margins do the work that we came here to do. We each have a part to play in our own liberation as well as each other's. To really affect change, we must have more multi-sized, multi-shaped, multi-abled Queer and Trans People of Color (QTPOC) bodies centralized in sacred sexual spaces. We must also continuously do the work to educate ourselves about our own places of privilege not through fear, guilt, or shame, but, in the spirit of community, through connection and love.

MASCULINE AND FEMININE DICHOTOMY

Due to the fact that Tantra, in North America and Europe, has primarily been presented by white, cisgender, able-bodied, heterosexual, heteronormative, middle to upper class people, there ends up also being a conflation of masculine and feminine energy. The western mind is so dichotomous that it is even challenging for many of us to hold on to the fact that energy, sex, gender, and sexuality are all different concepts. This is because Eurocentric sciences and religions purposefully created the binary, man/woman, male/female, right/wrong paradigm, and this paradigm has spread to other colonized cultures and societies who did not originally have those binaries. One of the principles of Tantra is Inner Marriage – often it is said that this is the masculine and feminine energies within each of us that must be married. Basically, we marry ourselves. When we see masculine and feminine energy though, we end up only seeing man and woman, male and female, especially when you hear the word marriage. But what if we shifted our minds to a non-binary understanding of the poles within us and the ways that the poles must work together to maintain balance in the world. Whether we choose to call these poles masculine and feminine, expansive and contractive, above and below, or within and without, these energies all exist within us simultaneously.

We can call these poles masculine and feminine, or expanding and contracting, or penetrating and receptive, or giving and receiving, because we all experience, and do, all of these things energetically and physically, and often simultaneously. This co-existence is illustrated when we talk about the concepts of yin feminine, and yang feminine, yin masculine and yang masculine energies. They are inherently interdependent. In Tantra, we speak of masculine and feminine energies, but also talk about the weaving of their simultaneous action, existing at once within us all. For example, when I am drinking a glass of water, I am using receptive energy by taking the water into my open mouth, but I am also using active energy to bring the cup of water to my lips. This has nothing to do with genitals, sex organs, gender, or how our physical bodies look. Many heteronormative Tantric classes teach this as though masculine and feminine energy have to do with men's bodies and women's bodies only, purposefully asking that there be a "gender balance" (in this case cis male/cis female) for the class to take place. This is not how I teach Tantra because genitalia have nothing to do with it.

We must remember that we are many things at once in an energetic sense. When the energetic poles that exist in us are off-balance, it can knock us off of our axis (think of the earth's axis and north and south poles) and we can experience spiritual, physical, and energetic upheaval. That is true inside of us and out in the world. This is why Tantric practices – such as conscious breathing, yoga, meditation, and erotic embodiment – and the discernment of what we take in and put out of our bodies are utilized to regain balance. This balance will look differently for each person and each community; it takes us knowing ourselves to understand what it is we need in order to heal. As we attempt to understand these greater concepts and infuse our social justice into our embodied spiritual practices and communities, our approach cannot be "either/or" thinking, but must be "both/and" thinking to account for this diversity.

TANTRA AND SOCIAL JUSTICE

If I want to believe that there are only men and women in the world, and nothing in between, I can certainly do so, but it will be extremely limiting to myself and harmful to others. However, if I know, and can feel and sense that there is more, that we are more, I can choose to embrace what I intuitively know, rather than what I was socialized to believe.

In many heterosexual and LGBTQIA western-adapted spiritual communities, both white and of color that I have come into contact with, it is rare for all of our differences and experiences to be honored, valued, or even addressed. Racism, sexism, misogyny, homophobia, ableism, classism, and more are often left out of the spiritual arena. Sometimes they get mentioned, but not thoroughly explored. Or, depending on the community, the easier issues may be addressed, while the more uncomfortable ones, like race, disability, and misogyny remain at a surface level.

In Tantra, we practice moving beyond the physical world into the subtle world of the immaterial for our healing, both spiritual and physical. What happens when we come back down to earth and we haven't dealt with all of these challenges that still plague our communities, these challenges that separate us from one another? What happens when we ascend spiritually, but our human and sociopolitical prejudices still exist within us? What happens when we continue to unconsciously do psychological harm to one another, even while we are sharing and teaching one another in loving, healing, community? I would submit that we cannot ascended spiritually until we can bring forth what we learn in sacred spaces out into our mundane world. It may take a lifetime of conscious commitment and conscious continuous actions to turn the entire individualistic white supremacist paradigm upside down, but if we are truly seeking change, we must be willing to do our work. That means acknowledging that all of our bodies have been used against us for those in power to maintain social power and supremacy. That acknowledging how we have hurt others, no matter how inadvertently, is our duty to accept and change. Tantra is a beautiful way to further address these inequities and deepen our collective social and sexual healing.

I am human so, I sometimes feel pain, fear, hurt, and closed off. Though I do not often give way to fear when it rises, I pay attention to its message. As you will find as you begin to practice Tantra, all of these parts of ourselves exist and are welcomed – the closed off and the opened up. Denying the parts that we do not like can lead to inauthenticity, and energetic decay, but acknowledging them in loving and compassionate ways, and listening to their message is what leads to healing.

The fact is that no matter how much I would love to sugar coat my reality, I am still not free in every aspect, because we are not all free. We are more powerful and free together. With each of us having some privileged parts and some subjugated parts in varying combinations and degrees, how we support one another is pivotal to our erotic evolution and liberation. We must see the illusions imbedded in our physical body's memories for what they are, and transcend them into who we already were when we came into this world. We must deeply, intuitively, remember that we all deserve to be here and that no one is truly above or below another. That we are all meant to be here for reasons beyond our knowing and understanding. That we all deserve to feel and be free.

It has become clear through this essay, that what I needed to say is the hard stuff which does not get addressed often enough, particularly when it comes to talking about spirituality and accessing spiritual communities. Part of that is probably because we do transcend beyond our social stations in life when we are accessing the spiritual realms, but when we emerge, we still have to live in the world, and deal with its atrocities and its beauty. We can't, in fact, live consciously and deny these realities, because Tantra is all about living consciously.

So, how do we create queer, spiritual, erotic communities and avoid racism, ableism, transphobia, sexism, misogyny, fat-phobia, and elitism? I don't fully know, but I think that the subtle spiritual realm may be the best place to begin looking at new ways to transcend those realities because the intellectual academic way and the action-oriented activist way, though they play a part, are not enough. We've tried it for centuries, and we can lose ourselves in the anger and the pain and the injustices so much that we lose touch with our own spiritual selves, our whole selves. As activists and as healers, it sometimes can become a habit to deny our internal unaddressed, unhealed pain, and to focus solely on all of the pain that exists out in the world outside of our bodies. We must come back to ourselves. We must remember to take the time to connect on a heart-level with one another to heal our own buried pain, while also grappling with social injustices. They cannot be separated lest we continue to be divided, lest our souls be lost to ourselves.

FREEDOM IS POSSIBLE

In a world where you are constantly being told that "you don't belong, you have no right to exist and we are going to figure out every way possible to remind you of that," it is sometimes difficult to believe that anything was created with you in mind. As a fat, black, cisgender girl growing up in a racist, sexist, ableist, classist, misogynistic U.S.A., it is not a surprise to me that many on the margins tell me that they don't think Tantra is for them. It wasn't for me either until I found my queer, sacred, intimate Tantra community.

I was raised in a world where young black girls, like me, get sexually assaulted and used, and are continuously silenced by those closest to us. In my world, family consists of numerous secrets that calcify within the mind and energy body and perpetrators continue to live amongst the children they assault; everyone knows, but no one says anything or warns anyone. One reason this occurs is because we have to survive in a white supremacist world where everyone, including people of color, believes that we don't deserve to exist without white permission and generosity. I come from a world where even other people of color can look at a black girl and be glad that they are not black. A world where people of color from around the world are pitted against one another so that we remain separate and disconnected, even though we all experience oppression in different hierarchical ways. The habit is to take out our pain and oppression on one another, while trying to deal with the pain and oppression hoisted upon us. This has been happening for thousands of years. Our ancestors are telling us, it's time to do better.

Tantra is inner freedom through consciousness, yet freedom is not without pain. Belonging to something greater than ourselves is not without pain. Enslavement via physical, emotional, psychological, or mental means inhibits our spiritual growth and our freedom. This psychological enslavement was designed by the white supremacist regime in which we live, to keep us all shackled. Due to that design, it is imperative that those of us on the margins, those of us who live and think counter to the white cis male hetero-supremacist paradigm, find our personal and sexual freedom in whatever ways we can. We have to take our freedom rather than ask for it. We must access our freedom from deep within and express it by being our unapologetically truest selves, which is the definition of resistance. It has been said, many times over, that the personal is political. I want you to remember that this includes the sexual, because when you own your sexuality you have the power!

Everyone loses when it comes to white supremacy because we do not get to truly experience one another on a deeper level. Often, we find ourselves living by the standards that society has set for us, based on a manufactured social narrative. The minds of most of us are wrapped in chains; our responsibility is to do the work to unchain them.

This work is sometimes painful because those chains have been there for so long that they have been deeply imbedded in our brain-meat and folds; tangled so intricately within the labyrinth of the mind that the tissue has grown around those chains. For our healing, it is imperative that we deliberately remove these chains, often one painful link at a time. This removal process and healing can become frustrating and is often incomplete when we focus solely on healing the mind – through talk therapy alone, or through education and activism alone. It is important that we take into account all of the aspects of the self which need healing. With the help of Tantra and other conscious spiritual and sacred sexual practices weaving in whole body, mind, spirit, and sexual healing, one can loosen the grip that this chain has on the brain with the erotic lube of pleasure, touch, breath, and human connection.

As we open up our hearts, minds, and bodies to one another, we create powerful collective grids across the planet that give us all the potential to be free – the socially-marginalized as well as the socially-centralized. Tantra can be a great tool for creating personal and social healing justice by consciously expanding our hearts, minds, bodies, and energy while compassionately acknowledging the parts of ourselves that are often ignored by society.

TANTRA IS HEALING JUSTICE

From what I've both witnessed and experienced, freedom, bliss, and healing can and does take place during expansive moments of erotic pleasure and embodiment. I believe that it is possible to transcend our social differences and heal our individual and collective trauma and pain through Tantra. This will become more widespread and more expansive as a spiritual movement the more we centralize those on the margins and make it accessible to all. It is magical how the pain rises to the surface and then erotically falls away when our energy, our multifaceted bodies, and our spirits get to learn, play, and soar together as we discover that we all belong here. I'm ecstatically hopeful that we will heal the world through the transformative energy of love and the Queering of Tantra.

The Glitterheart Path of Connecting with Transcestors

by Pavini Moray

Resource. Support. Acceptance. Healing. These are all blessings and goodness available to us from our transcestors, those trans folks who came before us in the world and in our own bloodlines, those who shared similar struggles to those trans folks experience now. For some, connecting with them may feel elusive, or perhaps you just don't know how. Here are some suggestions for connecting with yourself as a Transcestor, the Mighty Trans Dead, as well as the Transcestors of your own bloodlines.

Self as Ancestor: Blessing Transcendants, those Trans Ones Who Come After.

Who are your ancestors? Poet Linda Hogan says "You are the result of the love of thousands." There are so, so many humans who existed before you, and because of the gift of their lives and their sex, now you get to be here. Some of those dead are well, bright and elevated ancestors, ready to support you in your life. What does it feel like to be an ancestor? How do you feel towards your descendants, the lives of those future ones you will love whether or not you procreate? By feeling into who you are as a loving ancestor, it becomes easier to accept the love coming towards you from your well, bright ancestors.

With your eyes tenderly laid closed and your attention focused on the inner landscapes of the unseen world, imagine that you have died. Your body has been tended in all the right ways that you know, and your spirit has used the grief and tears of those you have left to fuel your journey to the Summerlands, the realm of the ancestors. You have been sweetly welcomed by those more ancient than thou, and initiated into this new state of being in which you no longer bound to a body. What does it mean for you to be an ancestor? As you look out across time, you see all the living, and especially illuminated are those who move adeptly on several paths: the trans ones, the mutable, morphable trans ones, the keepers of change.

In this newly not-beating ancestor's heart that is yours, the amount of care you feel for these lustrous and tender spirits is limitless. Feel it now, this well of compassion that rises up in you for your transcendents, those who will come when you have gone. Feel it deeply, you who never die. Feel it with all the protective, hopeful, and inspired love of a very best parent longing for goodness for their child. For once, there can be no disappointment, only the shiny hope and knowing of what the living cannot know; those trans spirits in body are the mysterious ones, the evolution of the human species, the ones for whom magick is the alchemy of the flesh. If you feel that hope without fear, then you know what it is, what it will be, when you become a transcestor yourself. All the ways you will offer help, care, support and blessing when you are in the role of ancestor. All the dreams you will present, all the healing you will facilitate, because you love those who come after you with such wild abandon.

Say this prayer for the yet-to-be-born trans folk of your body, of your heart, and of the world:

Blessings on my transcendents. Blessings on my transcendents. May the learning and work I do be ever in service to your wellness. May the love I feel flow towards you through the stream of time. May you fully savor life's sweetness, through this love-honey I offer, and may my blessing permeate and protect every moment of your lives.

As you practice being a transcestor, notice the effortlessness of offering blessing to those who come after. Feel how it fills you with gladness and joy to do so. Practice feeling this sensation as you move in the world.

Connecting with the Mighty Trans Dead.

Turn your attention now to the Mighty Trans Dead, knowing that this is your eventual path. Those who have gone before you are sending their blessing, through time, to you. When you say their names, the Mighty Dead known by name, and all those more ancient, whose names are forgotten. The forgetting of names can increase the power of ancestors as these spirits lose attachment to human identity, and become forces of goodness and wellness.

Call out their names: Lou Sullivan, Sylvia Rivera, Leslie Feinberg, Marsha P. Johnson! (Add any others you care to name whom you trust are well in spirit.) Old ones! Bright ones! Those beyond name, throughout whole time! Let me know you! Let me feel you wisdom. Whisper in my ear and in my dreams. Please guide me!

The Mighty Trans Dead are easy to know and to feel. You can root in the lineage of their work, their words, and their images. Print out pictures of them, and frame them in tiny, sparkling frames you buy at the thrift store. Put them on an altar you make, and make offerings of glitter and whiskey, of bonbons and poetry. Develop a practice of connecting and relating: talk out loud to them; sing them your songs; and call out to them when you can't figure it out, when you are stuck and hurting, when you feel alone. Read their life stories, their memoirs, their work. Lean into their inspiration. Lean back and feel the activism and the work that have already been done by them for you, sweet transcendent.

Be open to their wisdom as it comes through in dreams, in symbols, or in unexpected synchronicities. You will know them by their continued dedication to the work they began while living. As you fine-tune your awareness and attention to the surprising magick of the Mighty Trans Dead, the relationships will deepen. These are the powerhouses you can call on when you are doing a Big Deal Trans Healing Ritual, have an important political action you are embarking on, or have a critical piece of activism in which you are engaging.

Through connecting to your trancestors, you can know that you are not alone—have never been alone—on this path of queerness, this path of transness. Can you feel the support of those at your back, rooting for your survival, your thrival? Press back, relax back, take a breath, and feel the gravitas of the ancient activist heart.

Ground. Protect. Open.

In your time-travel spell, this is the moment to take it all in: the knowing of yourself as an ancestor who sends blessings forward in time, as well as the knowing of the blessings you've already received from those in the past. To get started, ground the Fuck Into Your Body. When working in the unseen, your body is the safest place to be. Spirit in flesh. Demand the right to be at home in your body. That's why you incarnated. When you fill out your flesh to the edges with you-ness, things like transphobia and oppression have a harder time sliding in under the door. This is not to say that pain and trauma are not present, of course. But still, feel into your bone and muscle, your blood and tooth and fascia, to whatever degree is available. Living inside the body is a practice, and it develops over time.

Are you as present as you're gonna get? Good. Now it's time to protect yourself. Put on layers. Put on a hazmat suit. Imagine a new-age bubble of light or a haze of swamp gas. Whatever it takes so that you feel ultra, super safe. The reason for protection is that all of the dead are not equally well, just like all humans. Some are ancestors. Some are ghosts. Ancestors are the dead who have gone through an initiation process, and are in good relationship with all those that come before them. Ghosts are the dead who have not yet transitioned into the realm of ancestors, and hang around and can make trouble. Adopt a policy of only relating with the dead whom you have vetted to be supremely well in spirit. "Well in spirit" meaning you'd entrust them with your delicate heart, your vulnerable secret dreams, and the safeguarding of your own well-being. Just like when you meet a living human and you feel they are safe and trustworthy, your own intuition is of great importance when relating to the dead.

Connecting with your Blood-lineage Transcestors.

Once you are in your body and surrounded with whatever protection you choose to don, only then do you begin to open your knowing and your desire for connection to your blood transcestors. You will be seeking to connect with those who came before you in your blood lineage, those who were trans, gender non-conforming, two-spirit, gender-queer, hijra, and all the other words throughout time that connote gender fuckery.

Imagine that each of the 37.2 trillion cells in your body has a very tiny door. And as you settle down into your body and your protection, each of those miniscule apertures can start to open. Allow yourself to pretend, to make-believe if you have to, that you feel this somatic softening as you open to connecting.

Invoke your Trancestors of blood. Speak aloud, something like:

> *"Oh sweet, well and loving ones of my blood,*
> *You who transcended the bounds of gender during your life,*
> *You who struggled, you who fought, you who loved fiercely and tenderly.*
> *Please, I'd like to know you.*
> *I am your transcendent. I am your face. I am your breath.*
> *I live now, and face similar struggles as you. I am different. I am special. I hurt.*
> *Please, make yourself known to me, bright and well trans ones of my blood."*

Use whatever words of invocation feel right, but do be clear about inviting in the well dead, the bright ancestors only. Feel free to go beyond those in your bloodlines whose names are remembered. It is often in the more distant past that we find the truly radiant, solidly strong, and profoundly whole in our own ancestry.

In this call from your heart, invite just one of them to come close. Is this one well in spirit? Here is the moment to be a bouncer in your own mystical nightclub. Check their trans-ancestor cred at the door. Ask to be shown the luminous wellness of this one. Ask to see the net of heart-stars they are connected to, all the other trancestors in your blood lineage who are well in spirit, throughout time. Is this one willing to act in your best interest? Does this one have the ability to do so?

Feel your own intuition. Can you trust this one? Awesome, if so. If not, make sure to respectfully say "Thank you" to this one who showed up before moving onward. Alternately, you can also ask if this one could guide you to the one you seek; a shining, bright representative of your lineage with experience with gender complexity. Keep opening to connection with a shining, well-in-spirit transcestor with whom you do feel ease and safety. Just like being discerning about what living people you want to allow in your life, you get to have boundaries with the dead.

Have you found the one? Good. Now be with this one. Ask to receive their blessing, which is your birthright. Are you imagining or is this really happening? Does it matter, if it is supportive? How does this one offer blessings to you? How do you receive their blessing? Let yourself absorb the blessing. Let yourself feel whatever you feel about the experience of not being alone within your blood.

If everything is well, and you're feeling the blessing of trans-ness flowing into you, find that bright light that has always lived in you. For fun, try connecting your glittering heart-star to this larger net of goodness and grace. What happens if you surrender and feel the transcestors catch you?

Once you feel you have fully received their blessing, you can ask some questions of this transcestral guide. Get curious about who they are and how they connect to you. Also, what do they want you to know? What's important to understand? How is trans-ness a specific blessing of this bloodline?

Ask if there are specific actions or offerings they would like that would encourage a healthy ongoing relationship where they would be open to supporting you. Working with ancestors is all about reciprocity; giving and receiving between both the dead and the living.

Ancestors use the energy of offerings to do whatever work they are doing. It's like food for those without a body. Ask them what would be beneficial to them. You get to discern if that's what you want to offer; it's not an automatic yes just because they ask. Sing a song. Sprinkle glitter. Light a candle. Make them a sandwich. Drink a beer for them, or pour a drink in their honor if you don't want to drink. Nourish the relationship with attention just as you would with the living. It's about weaving the relationship/s into your life and not just going to them when you need something. You will find your own rituals to honor and connect with them; rituals that are specific to that particular transcestor and you.

Together with this transcestor, with whom you are developing relationship, you may pray for the well-being of all the trans dead in your bloodlines. Pray that they be well in spirit, lovingly tended by their own ancestors. Do this over time, and the net of heart-stars widens with more and more well trans dead, actively linking together and working in support of the living trans folk: you!

Completing the connection… for now.

At the end of each ritual of connecting with your transcestors, just like you'd say goodbye at a family reunion, say goodbye for now. Gratitude is in order. Make sure you follow up on any agreements you made to them; offerings or ritual actions promised, etc. Don't eat whatever you offered to them, unless you are of a tradition wherein that is done. Feel free to leave offerings out for them on your altar for a few days, and then dispose of them in nature if possible. In time, you may wish to establish an ancestor altar in your home. Tend to the relationships. Think of them during your day. Remember them. Remember them. Blessings on my transcestors.

Blessings on my transcestors.

It's not the End
by Papacon
From "The Initiate," by J. Schwartz

Queer-Fire Witchery:
The Rainbow-Flame that Melts the Soul-Cage
The Emerging Fluidity of Consciousness

by Orion Foxwood

I am a heretic, a witch, of the wonderfully worse kind.
I am a Queer Witch and as such-
I am the eggshell in in the omelet of convention;
A grit that you can't ignore.

Magic and Freedom

The statement heading this essay is one of mine, describing one of the major aspects of my witchery. The power in this thread is one that shatters the links in the chains that bind the mind of the oppressor, much to the chagrin of the oppressor. However, the journey to understanding and integrating the ways of magic (especially this kind) is a slow, intense, personal, and profound one. If a witch (or any other type of magic-worker) is to be healthy, solid, and sane, the unfolding of their magical wisdom and potency must be incremental and preferably within the guidance and tutelage of a more seasoned witch. This need is exceedingly underscored and intensified when regarding a Queer witch, given the intensity of the awakening of two fire-streams of power: Queerness and Witchery.

The brilliant force of being Queer intensifies the magical fire by hundreds of degrees – melting the life pulse surrounding or confining it. The magical instruction and guidance can only take us to the gate. We must choose to walk in. For instance, I was taught and initiated by highly-skilled, wise, powerful, and wonderful teachers. Albeit their talents, my mentors could only reveal, inspire, and direct my efforts. I had to take it upon myself to integrate the skills within me and, more importantly, for me. I had to find the potency – the ways I tap and work through the vessel of my own inner being. This is where the concept of hard work, tilling, inner-weeding, and cultivation of spirit, mind, and body come to light. Let's face it, magic is not for the faint of heart.

To those striving, we must first go deep into ourselves to hear the voice of our constraints; the false identities, the shadow-images and face our fears – find their meaning. Sometimes, we must even resolve our lies and judgments. Then, we tap into the pulse that pushed each of these from the invisible realms into our physical forms. This also requires the unbinding from those falsehoods we've based on what was passed to us, required of us, or permitted to us. We must find our own inner pulse, draw out its power, and do so without setting all the familiar structures of our personality, our external precepts, and our relationships on fire. Doing this work will lead us, and perhaps those we love, to jump out of the metaphorical 'burning building' of our familiar, safe zones and into the fires that forge spiritual transformation. Magical work should come with warning labels. Queer magic should come with a psychic fire-extinguisher for ourselves and a fire-escape for those close to us who do not understand our ways or who live in highly flammable self-shapes.

"The sorcerous tide" is my reference to the journey that, I theorize, is about becoming a force of living-magic where the worker moves through three nonlinear phases: (1) studying the magic (2) practicing the magic and (3) becoming the magic. In this journey, a personal definition of magic arrives as a condensed capsule of wisdom. Operationally, my definition is *"magic is about inner change and outer results, leveraging the invisible to the visible and the visible to the invisible; and, it is the art of conscious creation."*

It seems that the mysterious workings of magic will migrate, morph and adapt as needed and/or summoned. It seems that this Mystical force, and the art of shaping its expressions, is most apparent and important during times of need, when society's fundamentals are lacking and oppression is rampant. Individuals are often drawn to magic when we are tired of being dampened, dimmed, or diminished. When we are emotionally impoverished and spiritually enslaved our inherent self-worth grows a skeletal structure and volcanic ferocity, especially when freedom, justice, and equity are most challenged and restricted.

Inherent worth of the enduring human experience is expressed in the ability to endow power to those feeling powerless, hope to those feeling hopeless, and prosperity to those living in poverty. To decrease inherent shortcomings and increase wellbeing. At all levels, a worker of magic should aim at the larger picture of reducing the presence and power of egregious inequity. Emancipating power, balancing the scales and forging the way for something new like Bayard Rustin organizing behind the scenes to produce the historic March on Washington in 1963.

The Soul's Closet

As a Seer, it is often my task to analyze beyond the simplistic physical appearance because the physical reality is the 'wake of a ship.' The real power and inherent purpose lies within reality's 'underbelly' and it's 'foundations' – out of which comes form comes. In many ways, physical form is the Spirit in drag. However, Spirit is vital, magical, and original consciousness that pulses wherever the mystic force wills or imagines itself. Magic is the consciously created, destroyed, and reformatted self state. Metaphorically, Spirit would be the performer inside life's drag as it expresses itself, forms patterns, and flows accordingly. The performer's stage-adherence represents the vital star-pulse of inspiration and star-flare (similar to solar flares). It is only the greatest of artists that engage in exploring their own creativity through their art. It is an investigative scientist analyzing themself. It is an athlete finding the ranges of possibility by pushing their body to its limits. It is a love-possessed romantic extending their private innermost core. Wooed out of contemplative loneliness into the orgasmic embrace of the ejaculation of galaxies' force. It is a preverbal lotus flower with its innumerable petals ever flowering, each petal drawing out another one while never fixating on finality or a single form of expression. One thing remains consistent – never rest and never conform to a preconceived notion of a final shape. Rather, be more like a river flowing from a vast stream: carving out your own landscapes and ecosystems before experiencing dissolution into a greater oceanic body.

This constant flow of consciousness is where power lies in Queerness. To quote a dear friend and revered Witch-Queen, the late Lady Circe, "never sacrifice your soul on the altar of mediocrity." The mundane nature of antiquated, inaccurate, over-generalized, creativity-limiting, and individuality-stifling beliefs, fears, social phobias, myths and their corresponding religious and social constructs strangle individuality. The same individuality that is the pulsing power of diversity, artistry, and invention that makes us humans.

The Source limited itself to a lowly creature and called itself human so it could spread the color-filled plumage of its beauty and take us on flights to new levels of power. This begs the question, "Why else would it imbed us with a history of forgetting that we are divine and one with the Source, rather than to allow itself to discover its sensual curves and contours?" The Source accomplished this by looking through each of us as windows and mirrors of its own expressed divine diversity. We are its kaleidoscope of creative vitality and the many ways it could love the full extent of its being. The history of forgetting is a type of sleep. Parts of the Source must sleep so it can dream of higher heights and awaken to new sunrises within its eternal unfoldment. Queer people are the exquisite expression of the color-filled filaments of love, the vital sensuality of pulsing life force within each of us.

Look heavenward and claim the pride and beauty that produced your presence here. Queerdom was born by the spirit of inspiration, not one of desperation. You and I are mediators of the rainbow-colored star-pulse. This is the powerful star-fire that inspires humanity to break out of its soul-cage of contrived gender, sexual, and love expressions and release the new, the strange, the innovative, the odd, and the queer expressions from within.

Webster's Dictionary gives us some fascinating insights when we look at the definition of the transitive verb "inspire," *to influence, move, or guide by divine or supernatural inspiration; to exert an animating, enlivening, or exalting influence on; to spur impel, motivate, affect; to breathe or blow into or upon: to infuse (as life) by breathing; to communicate to an agent supernaturally: to draw forth or bring out.*

I particularly love the part of the definition "to draw forth or bring out." As forces of inspiration, we bring human consciousness out of the soul-cage or, one could even say, a closet. The Queer-Fire is an animating, igniting, and illuminating vital potency that has erupted from the plasmatic action of life that continuously births the arriving Earth. This multi-colored flame pulses its way from ancient history through a vivacity that cannot be strangled, bound, trimmed, silenced, or diminished. The invitation from our co-existent co-creators that have shepherded diversity for millions of years is to acknowledge that we are not alone. All of nature reveals the constant unfolding of diversity, the unstoppable, incorrigible Rainbow Flame. Let's face it, nature is Queer. Look at the array of color among the flowers, the plumage among birds, the banquet of beauty in the variances and colors of stones, and the multi-fabric texture of the landscape of nature. All of this confirms, reaffirms, and feeds us. Life is art waiting to happen. We have vast powers that walk with us. As my Spirit-Wife Brigh revealed when I was teaching in an ancient underworld stone chamber in Cornwall, *"You never walk alone. I never walk alone. We never walk alone."*

The River of Blood and Planetary Destiny

All planetary life arrived here on a star-pulse, or as it is called in Faery Seership, "the River of Stars." This stream and its pulsing nature materialized into the beautiful green and blue orb of heaven we call Earth. All life-forms, including ourselves, arise out of this pulse and the continual interplay with the other celestial bodies (such as the sun, the other planets, star pulses, and moon), which we see an illustration of in the system of imprint-translation often referred to as astrology. The concept of "rivers" in folkloric metaphor is a rich way of engaging the constant streaming tides of life, ever-arriving and ever-departing. Humanity is a capillary and contributes to this pulsing steam as we each are extensions of the River of Blood (genetics) that extends from the River of Earth-Light (life-force). This, in turn, extended from the River of Stars. In the inner worlds, I have seen these thresholds change from one strata to another in the great stream. Arising from this stream are forces that do not let anything dock or stay along the banks for long.

The Queer spirit and the forces it embodies are Magic's way of undocking us. Then it proceeds by pushing us back into the true nature of things – fluid and pulsing – especially in terms of the Divine being called human. We are, essentially, the Divine's innate shape-shifting creativity mechanism that does not celebrate the proverbial closed peacock tail, but prefers the spreading array of colorful expression. In every Queer-person is a sorcerer, but it is those born with witch-blood or lineage that must heed the call to decide to become a sorcerer. Please note, that the lore is clear, "the witch-blood is not specific race connected for it is in all of the ethnic streams of humanity." We are, as I previously stated in my rather in-your-face statement to the fundamentalist right wingers that attempted to diminish my wort, the eggshell in the omelet.

Queerness is an aspect of the fire of life, the Queer-fire. The flame of many colors (do you hear Dolly Parton singing that as I do?) dances through its own spectrum, becoming what the life within it desires. If humanity is to become divine presence, our journey must come out of conflict with the desire to make life predictable by making boxes of our own design and then superimpose that it is ordained by nature of God. These contrived and un-natural boxes are what the Seer called "the soul-cage." Talk about a buzz-killer for God's enthusiastic creativity. **As humanity obeys the expressive spiritual fire in its center, it will become a fluid neuro-elastic creatrix machine that communes comfortably in a co-creative eco-life called Earth.**

Nature wants innovation, creativity, and wanderlust from us. Nature requires for us to co-create, commune, collaborate, and coexist: all with the importance prefix of 'Co-,' meaning "together." No dimmed-down, dull versions of the original masterpiece. I am proud to be one of those that are a push-off-force. For you and I who are queer, we have taken on the upper echelon of fluidity in consciousness. We serve as the force that is breaking down the bars of the suffocating 'soul-cage' of conformity – bars made from rigid social roles, stifled dreams, and locked with despair. Our collective fires ignite an array of expressions. Our sexuality, gender, identity, and sexual expression shatters the antiquated, solipsistic forms of how we were trained to convey love, bonding, relations, gender identity, and more. Since this has historically been tied to social and economic control, procreation – even "Godliness" – is a high frequency change-agent. Look at us – we on the fringes have taken this duty on regardless of the challenges, threats to our wellbeing, social reprimands, cultural sanctions, and family abandonment pains. We continue to obey the pulse of "fabulosity," diversity, creativity, and unpredictability. In many ways, that is at the heart of what it means to be human. We demonstrate that we are not humans-being, but rather we are humans becoming.

Sacred Permission and Igniting Magic

We give sacred permission by our liberating presence, to become a unique, fluidic, expansive, and outrageous flower in the garden of life. We must become who and what we are powerfully, beautifully, and uniquely. In doing so, others will be inspired and given permission to break out of their cocoon so they may become their own butterfly. This exalts the human spirit and truly honors the God, Goddess, and Spirit-Source that made us. We are the presence of the Queer-Fire that gives the permission to human-kind to explore the interior landscape and unearth the inspiration at our centers. This rainbow-colored flame is unstoppable. The sacred permission we give to the world is a holy magic, a healing spell cast upon the world that gives wings to the human spirit so we may fly high and exalt, refine, and become the living art we are meant to be. To become anything less is a surrender to the real devil, birthed by man's belief that he cannot trust his desires, which are fueled by his central life-force pulse within. I leave you with these thoughts:

You were born to bear pain and the truth of your spirit, and imprint it onto the canvases of form, not to be trapped in another's painting. In doing so, you give praise, honor, and true service to God, Goddess, All that Is as the supreme Artist. The Queer community is the awakened, uninhibited paintbrush in the

hand of life dipping into colors too bright for the dim, too sparkly for the demure, and too daring for the complacent residents of the soul-cage.

Ignite, and Awaken Unto Life... and Remember your Power.

> One flame unfurls its seven-fold rays.
> Searing the nights – brightening the days.
> The witch one, the queer one, the unfolding fan.
> Awakening the rainbow in woman and man!

For Thou Art Goddess: Creating Affirmative Goddess Community

by Susan Harper, PhD

I will never forget the first time I saw and fully understood the phrase "womyn born womyn only" attached to a Goddess Spirituality event. I was in my early 30s and had been practicing Feminist Goddess Spirituality – what had been euphemistically called "Women's Spirituality" throughout the 1970s and 1980s – for more than a decade. In that time, I'd spent countless hours in circles of Goddess women, reclaiming our bodies, organizing for social justice, and communing with, in the words of Patricia Lynn Reilly, "a God who look[ed] like [us]." Goddess Spirituality had been for me, as it was for so many of my circle-sisters, a refuge from abuse, from patriarchy, and from religiously backed misogyny as well as a site of personal and political transformation. The rituals we did, the magick we made, the spells we wove, and the relationships we built were all part of a larger shift we hoped to bring about in both our personal and the global consciousness, a reawakening of the Feminine Divine that might help to fundamentally change the world as we knew it. Women-only spaces were a key part of what we hoped to create – spaces that ran by different rules, where the male gaze was not the default, where women and women's power and creativity were what ruled the day. And while I was a generation younger than many of the Witches and Priestesses and Goddess women I circled with, and thus too young to have experienced the heyday of "Women's Culture" in the 1970s, there was still much in these women-only spaces that fed my heart and my spirit.

Looking back now, from the vantage point of 25 years, over a decade of graduate study in gender and religion, and extensive study in feminism, I can see my own naiveté and that of my sisters. We never questioned why our circles were overwhelmingly, if not entirely, White. We never questioned the adoption – read "appropriation" – of Native American and African practices, symbols, and deities. We never questioned the class privilege that allowed so many of us to purchase expensive ritual tools or attend weekend long events. We never questioned that we knew what it meant to be a woman, what a "women-only space" entailed. We never questioned who might be excluded when we talked about the global sisterhood of women unified by a set of biological processes.

Many of us never realized who "womyn born womyn" was leaving out.

It is in some ways tempting to make the easy excuse that we didn't think about who we were excluding from our sisterhood because we were speaking in, and being spoken to in, the language of Second Wave feminism – a feminism which was and is rooted deeply in the gender binary, and even more so when we're talking about the Radical Feminism which underpins so much of Women's/Goddess Spirituality. This language didn't talk about the inclusion of people whose gender doesn't fit within the easy gender/sex binary because, as far as those writers were concerned, there were no such people – or, if there were, they represented pathological deviations from the norm. Many of us had never met, to our knowledge, a trans or nonbinary person. Our world, including our spiritual world, was neatly divided into the distinct categories of women and men, and that made it easy to know who was allowed in and who wasn't.

It was only after meeting my first trans (and later, nonbinary) friends that I began to question these neat categories. Once I began to have close and meaningful relationships with trans women, I realized that they were being excluded from the Goddess-centered spaces in which I had found so much empowerment, healing, and community. It was then that I finally started to ask those hard questions. Now, after nearly 20 years of education in anthropology and Women's and Gender Studies, it's easy to see how naïve a binary understanding of gender is – even though it's the understanding that pervades Western society.

A rehashing of the arguments for and against the inclusion of trans and nonbinary people in Goddess-centered spaces is beyond the scope of this essay, and is, in my opinion, fundamentally unnecessary. The Goddess Craft that I practice is intended to be inherently affirming of all individuals, and as such I come from the non-negotiable standpoint that trans women are women, trans men are men, and nonbinary people are nonbinary. All genders and gender expressions are worthy of affirmation, respect, and honor. Those who are interested in the arguments for the exclusion of all but cisgender women from Goddess Spirituality spaces are encouraged to seek those out, read them, and consider them. However, this essay is concerned not with arguing for the inclusion of trans and nonbinary people within Goddess Spirituality spaces, but with the how of creating spaces that are not simply inclusive of trans and nonbinary identities, but which are explicitly *affirming* of those identities.

A Note on Author Positionality

I base this essay on my own experience as a cisgender, or cis, facilitator of Goddess spirituality spaces, with almost two decades of experience. I also draw on my experience as an academic whose scholarly work focuses on the intersection of gender, sexuality, and religious identity, chiefly within Goddess Spirituality and NeoPagan spaces. That said, I feel it's vital that I recognize my own social location as a cisgender, enabled, bisexual, White woman in doing this work. I come to my work both in Goddess Spirituality and in creating this essay aware of the fact of my cisgender privilege, and encourage readers to seek out transgender and nonbinary voices on this topic rather than taking my assertions and recommendations as some sort of final truth. I write from the perspective of a cisgender ritual specialist, speaking chiefly to other cisgender ritual specialists – and as such, realize that my recommendations and understanding of the issues involved in creating trans and nonbinary affirming Goddess Spirituality spaces is necessarily incomplete.

Affirmation vs. Inclusion

I have intentionally chosen to focus both my work in Goddess Spirituality spaces and in this essay on *affirmation* rather than *inclusion* because, following Lasara Firefox Allen in *Jailbreaking the Goddess*, I believe that inclusion simply does not go far enough. Allen asserts that inclusion involves inviting people to spaces that are already created, and encouraging them to find a place within an already existing structure. While inclusion can be a vital step towards opening spaces to those who have been marginalized, I agree with Allen that it ultimately cannot catalyze the transformation we wish to see. Rather, I contend, along with Allen, that we must become co-conspirators rather than allies, and seek to co-create spaces that are radically different and transformative.

As such, I have chosen to focus on creating spaces that are *affirming*. Affirming spaces do more than just say "You can find a space here where you are welcome." Instead, they are actively co-created spaces that recognize, honor, and actively celebrate all identities and intersections. The reality of these identities, of these lives, of these experiences, is intimately woven into the very fabric of the space, the ritual format, and the magick and ritual performed. Most importantly, affirming spaces are co-created with the people they seek to affirm.

Through my own experience as a facilitator, and through conscious consultation and deep listening to the trans and nonbinary people in my life, I have assembled a toolkit of Affirming Best Practices which I share in the remainder of this essay. I invite other ritual facilitators to borrow freely from these practices and apply them to their ritual spaces, to build upon them, share what you have built with others, and to leave behind those practices which do not benefit your communities.

Listen Deeply

Whereas inclusive spaces are often created by those with privilege and then opened up to the marginalized, affirming spaces necessarily must be co-created in consultation with the people they are being designed to affirm. There is no one-size-fits all approach that will affirm every trans or nonbinary person who may come to your ritual space, of course – people are complex, messy, beautiful intersections of identities and experiences, which is part of what makes us magick! As such, I encourage cisgender ritual facilitators who seek to create affirming spaces to consult trans and nonbinary people in their spiritual communities, to read widely what trans and nonbinary practitioners are saying about what constitutes affirming spiritual community, and to reflect critically on the things they themselves take as given (dare I say "gospel truth") in their spaces and traditions.

With the notable exception of explicitly trans-exclusionary radical feminist (aka "TERF") spaces, most of the Goddess Spirituality and NeoPagan spaces I have been in are not *overtly* transphobic or exclusionary of trans and nonbinary people. In fact, many of these spaces state explicitly that they welcome people of all genders and sexualities, and may even include spaces such as a "Rainbow Camp," or may feature rituals and workshops addressing and celebrating gender diversity. It must be said, though, that most spaces I have been in do a considerably better job of affirming gay, lesbian, and bisexual/pansexual identities than trans and nonbinary identities. While trans and nonbinary folks can also be gay, lesbian, and bisexual/pansexual, on the whole the spaces I have been in are still on a steep learning curve when it comes to affirming trans and nonbinary identities even when they are quite progressive in creating affirming spaces for gay, lesbian, and bisexual folks. Some spaces, such as Pagan Spirit Gathering 2017, have made great strides in inclusion and affirmation, and may provide models moving forward.

While overt transphobia or trans exclusion is rare – though not unheard of, particularly in more stridently Second Wave Goddess spirituality spaces – there is often subtle transphobia or trans exclusionary rhetoric and practice that goes on in even the most well-meaning space, especially in spaces where Wicca is the template for practice or where there is a focus on the male-female gender binary as the template for human relationships. The same is true of Goddess Spirituality spaces which are predicated on Radical Feminist rhetorics about Nature and the embodied experience – even those spaces which are open to trans women and nonbinary femmes may still fall back on language about the womb as the source of power, on "women's natural inclinations," and so forth. Even when this language is tweaked to include those who fall outside the binary, who may have been assigned a sex other than female at birth, or who do not have a uterus, this language becomes the default liturgical vernacular, unquestioned even by those who would absolutely stand up against overtly exclusionary language. It's covertness or unintentionality does not ameliorate the hurt that such language causes trans and nonbinary people when they are in a ritual space where it is used.

I admit that I didn't think about this piece when I started creating my Full Moon Circle which was, at the outset, inclusive but not yet affirming, though I didn't know that at the time. It wasn't until I spoke with several trans and nonbinary practitioners within my immediate circle that I realized that even with the tweaks I made to the language – talking about "womb space" or making it clear that one need not be born with a uterus to be a woman – I was still creating a space that was not affirming of these people's lived experiences. I am glad that these individuals felt both safe enough to attend my nascent inclusive circle, and empowered enough to come speak to me about what they felt wasn't working. I am grateful that they were honest with me, so that I could get on with the business of creating what I set out to create – and that they have continued to co-conspire and co-create it with me.

Best Practices for Creating and Facilitating Affirming Spaces

Based on my own deep listening to trans and nonbinary practitioners in my community, what follows are some practices, techniques, and strategies I've applied to my own Goddess Spirituality spaces to take them in the direction of affirmation.

The first "best practice" that I recommend, and the one that does more to move your space from inclusive to affirming than anything else, is listening, and moreover, *listening deeply*. Following Women's and Gender Studies scholar AnaLouise Keating in *Teaching Transformation*, I define *deep listening* as the practice of listening with vulnerability, openness, flexibility, and awareness of each person's unique, specific, and intricate history and lived experience. Moreover, deep listening requires listening to *understand* rather than listening to *respond*. When we listen deeply, we are required to put aside our need to tell our own story or to counter what we are hearing, and instead we put ourselves in the transformational space of simply being present. Listening deeply can be challenging, but being willing to listen deeply to the trans and nonbinary people within your circles and communities is vital to the creation of affirming spaces.

The caveat that I will give is that it is, of course, never the job of marginalized people to educate those with more privilege. Deep listening in this case does not mean asking (demanding) that every trans or nonbinary person you encounter engage in this conversation with you. Rather, I encourage cis ritual facilitators and community leaders to invite trans and nonbinary folks within your immediate community, or within the circles of those you trust, to have this conversation with you. Before you have these conversations, I further encourage you to educate yourself on trans and nonbinary identities so that the focus of your discussions in community can be what constitutes affirming spiritual spaces, not Trans and Nonbinary 101. Seek out writings, podcasts, and other materials by trans and nonbinary practitioners as well – there is a wealth of such material online which has proven useful to me in my own growth as a facilitator in this area.

Deep listening cannot be a single conversation or a one-time thing. It must be ongoing, with the realization that as cisgender facilitators we will never be able to know all there is to know, and that we will always see things through the filter of our cisgender privilege in one way or another. Cultivate an environment where practitioners in your ritual spaces can approach you with feedback about what you are doing well and what you could be doing differently to create affirming spaces. Most importantly, *be open to that feedback*. Remember that your goal is not to have your ego stroked, but to create the ritual space that affirms and empowers the greatest variety of people!

Choose Deliberate Language

When I first started facilitating my Full Moon Circle in 2015, I knew from the outset that I wanted it to be open to both cisgender and transgender women. This wasn't even a question for me. It was an easy choice, as I created that first Facebook event, to title the event "Women's Full Moon Circle" and then included in the description "This event is open to all women, whether cisgender or transgender." I felt that this description conveyed the intent of the circle: to be a space for women to gather and celebrate community. I had noticed in looking at advertisements for women's rituals in my city that none of them included language stating explicitly that trans women were welcome, and the few facilitators I contacted to ask said they either had not considered the issue, or that their rituals were open to "womyn born womyn" (that dreaded phrase) only. I also knew from trans friends of mine that they were uneasy going into anything advertised as "women's space" if there was not an explicit statement of inclusion, for fear of encountering TERF sentiment or worse.

This language worked well for me until – and I bet you can see where this is going, Dear Reader – a nonbinary femme friend of mine asked if they could attend the next Full Moon. My first instinct was just to respond, "Of course!" and leave it at that. Instead, I chose to ask my friend why they might think they were not welcome. "Well, I'm not a woman. I mean, I was assigned female at birth and have experienced women's oppression, so I feel very comfortable in women's spaces, but I just wasn't sure…."

Lightbulb moment.

In consultation with several nonbinary people (femmes and non-femmes), I finally arrived at the blurb which takes prominent place on the event page of anything I facilitate: "This event is open to all women – cis, trans, or otherwise – and nonbinary individuals who find their homes in women- and femme-centric spaces."

Yes, it's clunky to read, especially out loud, but it's clear and deliberate. It makes clear from the get-go both who is welcomed and what the intent of the space will be. It works and it's welcoming to the broadest array of people while still keeping the spirit of the space we're creating intact. Might that language change again in the future? Absolutely. For now, however, it conveys much more clearly the type of affirming space we are co-creating than simply "women's circle" ever could[1].

Choosing deliberate and clear language can be work, as my experience above shows. Especially when we are working in English, the gender binary is everywhere. It can

---

1   Some readers will question the need for a gender-segregated space at all, even if that space is broadly defined and affirming. That's another question for another essay, one that I hope someone will write. In the meantime, I can only say that as a facilitator I am drawn to co-create spaces that affirm and empower women and femmes, but that I also do not ask for anyone's gender history or make judgements about whether someone is "femme enough" to be in ritual space with me. If someone has found the event invite and made it to the event, I assume that they know better than I do if they belong.

be hard to remember to think beyond that deeply ingrained binary. And cisgender folks can easily fall into the trap of thinking that any trans or nonbinary person who knows us knows our heart regarding inclusion and affirmation, and thus we don't need to come right out and say it.

We do need to say it, though. We need to say it clearly, loudly, and often.

Choosing deliberate, clear, and affirming language goes beyond your event invite or announcement, but that's where it has to start. A further best practice for those of us who either facilitate "women's" rituals or who work within Feminist Spirituality/Goddess Spirituality is to avoid the creative spellings so common to our community: *womyn*, *wimmen*, *wombyn*, and so forth. While they were not intended to do so when they came into usage, they have become dog whistles for transphobia, trans exclusion, and TERFy politics within the Goddess Spirituality, and to some extent, the larger NeoPagan community.

Perhaps the most challenging and the most important shift for ritual facilitators to make – especially those of us who facilitate ritual spaces centered on women and femmes – is to change the way we speak in the moment. Simply shifting from binary phrasing – "women" – to broader language – "women and femmes" or, as I often say, "women, femmes, and people who walk the world and are read as women" – goes a long way towards creating an affirming environment. These subtle language shifts may feel a little strange in your mouth at first, but ultimately they not only communicate to trans and nonbinary folks that they are welcome and part of the circle, but they also establish for other cisgender members of the circle that the space is inclusive and affirming. I use this language even if I don't have anyone in circle who I know to be trans or nonbinary – it is now simply a part of our liturgical vocabulary.

One of the subtlest – and, I will admit, most difficult! – shifts for me to make as a facilitator was to not speak of "women's experience," "we, as women," and similar concepts. Because my spaces are women- and femme-centric, the focus is often on experiences common to women, femmes, and AFAB people – sexism, gender discrimination, sexual violence, and more. I think it's incredibly important to call these out and heal them through ritual. Universalizing these things as "women's experiences" not only erases their impact on people of other genders, it erases people in the ritual space who are not women but who have had these experiences. Instead of talking about "women's experiences," I find myself more often using language that explicitly names the experiences themselves – "people who experience sexism," "survivors of sexual violence," "people who give birth," "people who menstruate," and so on. I find that these language shifts not only include and affirm identities beyond cis women, but also can be a catalyst for magick and healing by naming the specific experiences, positive and negative, that people are navigating and seeking to affirm or heal. I imagine my language will continue to shift and evolve, as I listen to people name their own experiences – many of the shifts I have made are the result of deep listening and mirroring people's language back to them.

Establish Inclusion and Affirmation as a Norm

Rather than only changing your language and practices when you have someone you know to be trans or nonbinary in the space, establish inclusion and affirmation as the norm for your ritual space or community. This starts with establishing that your event is open to trans and nonbinary folks, and should be woven into the fabric of every ritual or event.

The simple practice that I've incorporated into my Full Moon circles, and on which I've gotten the most positive feedback, is making a "pronoun share" part of the start-of-circle ritual of introductions. At the start of each of the rituals I facilitate, after the circle is cast, we go around the circle and introduce ourselves (in good feminist fashion). I always go first and model the way we do introductions, and as part of that I give my name, my pronouns (she/her/hers, for the record), and a couple facts about me. Even though many people in the circle are already aware of this information about me, I feel it's important for me to model the form and set the expectation that pronouns a) are not to be assumed – there are no inherently "female" or "male" pronouns, and everyone has the right to choose those pronouns which best reflect who they are; b) will be respected; and c) do not fall on the binary. This method also avoids trans and nonbinary folks having to single themselves out – since everyone is offering their pronouns as part of the ritual protocol, it makes it a natural part of the space. What has been most surprising to me – in the best of possible way – is that even cisgender women who are not familiar with nonbinary identities or the concept of diverse personal pronouns, after perhaps a moment of pause, get on board with the pronoun share.

One important thing about using the pronoun share is to make sure people know that they can choose to state their pronouns or not. People may at first be hesitant to out themselves as trans or nonbinary if the rest of the circle seems to be composed of cis people. While I model the pronoun share by giving my own pronouns, I also never call someone out who doesn't state theirs. The goal of the pronoun share is to establish the norm that people use pronouns beyond the binary, and that those pronouns will be respected – not to put anyone on the spot.

Decenter the Concept of "Biology"

Especially in Goddess Spirituality spaces or "women's" spaces, there can be an over-reliance on the concept of biology, most obviously expressed in the conflation of "born with a uterus" with "woman." This is underpinned by the fact that celebration of bodily cycles and events such as menstruation, childbirth, and menopause are central to much of feminist spirituality writing and ritual-making. While I do think it is important to celebrate these events for people who experience them and want them honored ritually, I also contend that we have to recognize that not all folks who experience these bodily events are women, and not all women will experience these bodily events. Both cisgender and transgender women alike may have bodily experiences which differ sharply from the stereotypical "women's experience." This can be due to genetic factors, medical conditions, life events such as early hysterectomy, or choices they make about their bodies, including choosing to be childfree. It can be incredibly easy to fall into language conflating biology and gender, given that it permeates the literature and liturgy, not just in Goddess Spirituality but in Wicca and Wicca-adjacent forms of NeoPaganism.

We can, and I think we should, still honor bodily experiences in our spiritual spaces, but in order to create affirming spaces we must not conflate gender with a particular bodily configuration. As is probably becoming obvious, the way I've chosen to deal with this is to use precise language – instead of "women," it's "people with uteruses," "pregnant people," "people who menstruate" – when we discuss bodily experiences. Some facilitators I have spoken with have wondered if they should remove all references to uteruses, menstruation, childbirth, and the link from their ritual spaces. I think this is unnecessary, and it ultimately doesn't solve the problem of erasure. It is not necessary to ignore the fact that there are bodily experiences that are central to people's lives and which are so often stigmatized by the culture – and that one of the main goals of Goddess Spirituality is to reclaim those. We can, however, honor them in a way that also affirms a diversity of bodily configurations and experiences.

Challenge Transphobia, TERF Ideology, and Nonbinary Erasure – Always

The final best practice I want to share is the one that's perhaps the hardest for cisgender ritual facilitators and community members, but the one that does the most to create affirming spaces and communities.

Challenge exclusion and erasure, wherever you see it.

In the context of my Full Moon circles, I state clearly that I decided to create a space that would be open to trans women and nonbinary people because I couldn't find one in my local area. Sometimes cisgender women who come to my circle have no idea that this is an issue within the Goddess Spirituality community, and so this opens up a conversation. It also makes clear that any ritual space that I am facilitating will not be a forum for TERF ideology, exclusion, or erasure.

It can be intimidating to challenge TERF ideology, transphobia, and trans and nonbinary erasure when we see it in our communities – especially when it's being endorsed, even casually, by our elders and people who are our teachers and mentors – but we must. When we see a Goddess Spirituality space that has explicitly trans exclusionary policies, we must push back by refusing to attend, letting organizers know why, or by attending and being a vocal advocate for change. In the online sphere, we have the responsibility to challenge transphobic and erasing comments when they come up, and to state that such ideology disenfranchises people who are important to us. While we never want to play the "Cis Savior," one thing I've come to realize is that, in a space where trans and enby folks are explicitly not welcome, it is incumbent on cis folks to have these tough conversations. It's only through this work that we move the culture forward on a large scale, where we move from individual and discrete affirming spaces to a Goddess Spirituality and larger NeoPagan culture which is truly affirming.

Bear Woman
by Malcolm Maune

The Queer Gods of Alchemy

by Steve Dee

Strange Beginnings

"We are unraveling our navels so that we may ingest the sun.
We are not afraid of the darkness.
We trust that the moon shall guide us.
We are determining the future at this very moment.
We know that the heart is the philosopher's stone.
Our music is our alchemy."
– Saul Williams, *Coded Language* (2001)

I was always a bit of a strange child. In the midst of my family moving to the other side of the planet (from the UK to Australia), I was busy beginning a journey into the depths of my internal world.

Due to my Mum bravely enduring some pre-natal yoga while carrying me, we had a couple of volumes on the topic in our family's small book collection. I can clearly recollect the bemused looks my working-class Dad gave me as I valiantly sought to recreate the black and white images of the speedo-clad yogis. However faltering these attempts may have been, I was intoxicated by the idea that I could use my body and movement as a means for exploring who I was. While concepts like faith and belief were quite foreign to me, having not come from a religious family, I was able to connect to the idea that there were physical practices that provided tools for navigating this strange inner terrain.

At the same time, as I began to experiment with yoga and meditation practice, I had also begun meeting people who wouldn't stop talking about Jesus. While I was regularly chanting mantras and performing sun salutations, I also kept bumping into some fairly wide-eyed Christian surfers who were keen to tell me that I was a sinner worshipping false Gods.

At fourteen, the confusion about both my sexuality and spiritual identity were worrying enough that I felt that I needed to be rescued from myself. This rescue came in the form of "going forward" at an evangelical Christian rally by "accepting Jesus as my personal friend and saviour." Although I was consistently unconvinced about their claims of exclusive truth, the lure of forgiveness and the sense of belonging that this form of church had to offer were enough to bring me into the fold.

Looking back, I can see that during those early years as a believer, I was definitely in a child-like state. I wanted to be fed certainties that would calm the turmoil that I was feeling. My faith undoubtedly did this for me, but I came to learn that the suppression of the core drives and central aspects of the self rarely come without serious consequences:

'If you bring forth what is within you, what you bring forth will save you. If you do not bring forth what is within you, what you do not bring forth will destroy you."
– The Gospel of Thomas

The awakening that I eventually experienced came during an under-graduate degree in theology at a conservative seminary a few years after my family had returned to the UK. My certainty of Faith was replaced with confusion, anxiety, and eventual hallucinations due to the extreme psychological stress I was experiencing. Unsurprisingly, my psyche began to give way.

The slow process of my healing came by way of lots of tea drinking, silent meditation, and my discovery of that great wizard Carl Gustav Jung. In contrast to the faith-based approach to belief that was suffocating me, Jung's rich psychology plunged me deep into the subversive world of heretical Gnostics and tinkering alchemists. Part of what drew me to the genius of his vision was the way in which he creatively engaged with Western alchemical traditions. He saw them as a means for exploring how we might more consciously create Soul through the use of visual art (e.g. Mandalas) and also as a means of paying greater attention to our dream lives.

From a personal perspective, Jung also introduced me to the idea of a contra-sexual self that, when recovered, would enable a greater sense of wholeness. While I now view the language of the anima and animus as being overly binary, they still provided vital keys for re-accessing gender-fluid aspects of my identity. For this bisexual introvert, such an awakening meant the beginning of a search for tools that were less about having "the answer" and far more about finding an approach that would allow playful curiosity and a chance to reconnect to my own fey, liminal Queerness.

Jung's ideas concerning the collective unconscious and synchronicity had gently nudged me outside the confines of mainstream Christianity. Some tentative explorations of Tarot and Hermetic Kabbalah provided me with glimpses of the type of direct knowing or "Gnosis" that I longed for. The next couple of years were spent desperately trying to hold on to a belief system that could no longer fit me, but Deep inside, I knew that I needed to pursue a path of Magic in which true awakening was valued over adherence to creedal dogmas.

As I began to walk a magical path, I had the good fortune to make friends amongst Druids, Rune Masters, and Witches. Through each of them I learned so much about these rich forms of Pagan spirituality. My own practice was undoubtedly shaped by these approaches, as my current path could be described as a heady fusion of Witchcraft and the anarchic style of ritual experimentation known as Chaos Magic.

This form of freestyle ritual magic seeks to reinvigorate the dusty pseudo-masonry of many magical orders by injecting them with a dynamic combination of punk rock energy and quantum mechanical insights. Chaos Magic is far more interested in exploring techniques that induce change rather than getting invested in a prescribed set of metaphysical beliefs. It is not particularly polite, with many critics viewing its embrace of Postmodernism reflected in its consumerism and potential shallowness. Much has been written about the nature of Chaos Magic, and for those wanting to understand it more fully, I would recommend the works of Pete Carroll, as well as Phil Hine, and The Book of Baphomet by Nikki Wyrd and Julian Vayne. The brilliant Julian Vayne and I have also co-written the book *Chaos Craft* that explores the topic in depth.

Strange Gods

The more deeply I explored my own work as a Witch and Magician, the more I found myself attracted to those depictions of divinity that embody something of the alchemical processes that I seek to pursue for myself. As Magicians, we are individuals who are willing to get our hands dirty in our attempts to explore Mystery. Rather than trying to find easy answers that seek to reduce complexity, we seek transformation through actively working with the tensions and dualities that we experience in the universe and ourselves.

Famously, when asked this question, Carl Jung answered that he didn't believe that there was a God; rather, he "knew" there was. Familiarity with his biography enables us to know that Jung was a fairly seasoned Gnostic explorer at the time that he made that comment. Based on his reception of *The Seven Sermons to the Dead*, it is unlikely that his deity of choice was of an orthodox variety.

In contrast to either creedal formulations or some distant "unmoved mover," for Jung the God that seemed to encapsulate the endeavour of the Gnostic explorer was that strange bird Abraxas. Abraxas is one of those Gods whose queer visage keeps popping up in esoteric lore, while at the same time being very difficult to categorise. Research provides some insights into the roles that he played/plays within a whole host of occult traditions - this strange cockerel (and sometimes lion) headed being with its serpentine "legs" is viewed as an Aeon (a positive force) by some, and as an Archon (a negative force)or even the Demiurge (an imperfect creator God) by others. His number (using Greek Gematria) being 365, along with his association with the seven classical planets, connect him to both the round of the year and the physical cosmos.

For Jung, Abraxas represented a movement beyond dualism. No longer is the divine image split into a good Lord and an evil Devil; rather, the mysteries of godhead are held within the complex iconography of Abraxas:

> *"Abraxas speaketh that hallowed and accursed word which is life and death at the same time. Abraxas begetteth truth and lying, good and evil, light and darkness in the same word and in the same act. Therefore is Abraxas terrible."*
>
> – Stephan Hoeller, *The Seven Sermons to the Dead* (1982) Translation by the Author

When meditating on the most commonly found cockerel headed form of Abraxas, we are struck by the bizarre chimera-like quality of the image. The body of a man is topped by the head of a solar cockerel (possibly symbolizing foresight and vigilance), while from under "his" concealing skirts, strange chthonic serpents wriggle forth. This cosmic hybrid holds together the transcendent and immanent, solar and night side. Viewed through my late-Modern lens I am both awed and unsettled by the sense of internal tension that this God seems to embody.

My own attraction to strange gods is hardly new territory – the monstrous hybrid Baphomet has long been jabbing at my consciousness as I've sought to make sense of life's "Solve et Coagula" (dissolving and coming back together). Baphomet is a God whose myth and imagery are gathered from fragments and rumors. When we start exploring the alleged object of veneration by the Knights Templar that

A Gnostic Gem depicting Abraxas, 3rd Century C.E.

may have had links to the mummified head of John the Baptist, we are entering decidedly strange territory. Even the name Baphomet is probably linked to a historic mishearing or misunderstanding of the name Mohammed. Whatever historical conclusions we eventually draw, for me, contemporary magical engagement with Baphomet seems to reflect the creativity of our human struggle to locate meaning. Both Baphomet and Abraxas represent something of the core paradox that many Queer-identified individuals experience in trying to make sense of the world.

Most attempts at constructing "big theories" or metanarratives are designed to make sense of the universe that we live within. The success or failure of any such world view seems to be largely determined either by their followers' ability to manage nuance and complexity or, conversely, their naivety and willingness to block out new information. For those of us who are seeking to promote some form of cognitive liberty, it is almost inevitable that at some point we are going to have to develop deeper strategies for managing complexity, paradox, and the types of uncertainty that such realities often give rise to.

Through my own magical work as both an individual and within a group magical context, the alchemy of my own exploration was compelling me to find tools for understanding the evolving, unfolding nature of the divine. In many ways these iconic images of Abraxas and Baphomet provided tools and powerful means for awakening. The juxtaposition of apparent opposites and the sense of movement that they contain speak to me of dynamism and process rather than fixed Platonic certainties. Whether via weird cosmologies or shape-shifting iconography, these gnostic riddles push us to the edges of comprehension and certainty. In seeking to engage with these ideas, we often experience a profound unease, and yet for the intrepid explorer, such discomfort can trigger the types of "strange loops" that arguably enable the evolution of consciousness.

This circular use of myth and paradox leads us away from certainties that cannot bear the weight of new insight. We are asked to engage in an unfolding process of becoming of both ourselves and our perception of the numinous. For me, this is a Process Theology that sees our understanding of the divine as being part of an unfolding story profoundly influenced by our human experience of life. Revelation or the incoming of new religious information comes both within a human context and also always in response to it: "God grows with the world, always in process" (Alfred Whitehead, *Process and Reality* 1978)

Baphomet, from *Eliphas Levi's Dogme et Rituel de laHaute Magi*

Humanity's religious expressions, be they tribal deities, anthropomorphized monotheisms, or Lovecraftian terrors, all mirror our collective journey through history. For me personally, to see value in this type of process-focused theology is not to imply some removal of mystery; rather, it glories in religion as an art.

One such example of openness and evolutionary fluidity is the brilliant aeonic litany contained within the *Mass of Chaos B*, which provides us with a vivid example of how such evolution continues to occur:

> *"In the first aeon, I was the Great Spirit.*
> *In the second aeon, Men knew me as the Horned God, Pangenitor Panphage.*
> *In the third aeon, I was the Dark One, the Devil.*
> *In the fourth aeon, Men know me not, for I am the Hidden One.*
> *In this new aeon, I appear before you as Baphomet.*
> *The God before all gods who shall endure to the end of the Earth!"*
> – Peter Carroll, *Liber Null and Psychonaut* (1987)

The images of both Abraxas and Baphomet provide vivid pictorial depictions of the cosmic balancing act that we are engaged in. Humanoid bodies mutate with animal heads and transgender bodies, as arms point at balance, or bear the whips and keys of our deliverance. For me, these glyphs are road maps for becoming; the path of the demiurge is a journey through the reality of our lives, not simply away from them. As much as the realm of matter and the body may provide challenges and obstacles, this is the place we find ourselves and where our work needs to happen.

The Magic of the Queer Self

To engage with Magic is to engage with the whole of life. It is art and it is science; it is both acceptance and change. The very nature of the magical path will mean that it is unique to the magician pursuing it, but it seems to be a common requirement that we embrace a heroic pursuit of curiosity and a willingness to question almost everything we thought was true of our lives and selves.

Whatever else Magic may or may not accomplish, it is clear that it aims to transform our own awareness so that we become more effective human beings. By self-willed mimetic infection, the change that we seek becomes more likely as we sensitize our perception to the themes and opportunities around us.

When I enter the circle or cast a spell, it means lifting anchor on what I thought I knew about myself. When we do magic, whatever the scripts and stories that we have inherited about what our lives should look like, we are called into question as we sail Queerer, more uncertain seas.

"Queer is by definition whatever is at odds with the normal, the legitimate, the dominant. There is nothing in particular to which it necessarily refers. It is an identity without an essence. 'Queer' then, demarcates not a positivity but a positionality vis-à-vis the normative."
– David Halperin, *Saint Foucault: Towards a Gay Hagiography* (2001)

Personally I think that Queerness and Magic are a bit of a chicken and egg situation. It's hard to know whether Magic's strange ways are innately attractive to the fey, liminal shape-shifters within a culture or whether it makes the curious even Queerer. As a lover of strange loops and circularities, I'll take both. My Queerness drew me to the experimental playfulness of magic, and magic asked that I listen to who I really am.

My own magical journey demanded a deeper acceptance of my identity and sexual longings. As much as my past Evangelicalism had tried to dampen my awareness of who I was as a bisexual and gender-fluid person, these truths were far too apparent to truly deny. Such transformations are ongoing and are often felt in the body before they make sense in the mind. As with my love of hatha yoga as a child, my own adult explorations of BDSM and Leather sexuality challenged me to experience a deeper level of authenticity in connecting to different ways of experiencing and working with my body.

For me, the Queerness of my magic is far more than a set of meaningful self-descriptors and sexual lifestyle choices. Queerness also embodies the role that we as magicians play as edge-dwellers who question oppressive categorization and help to pull our culture forward.

While some may view the conscious deconstruction of category as being overly hip or labored, for those of us who find liberty within Queer's punk rock attitude, our Queerness challenges us to experience relationship and uncertainty in new ways. Rulebooks that rely on clear categorization and the safe assertion that problems are held by "the other" can no longer be true. This Queered Magical project of awakening is far from some form of self-righteous superiority; rather, it asks that, while pursuing our individual emancipation, we also send out complex tendrils of connectivity between self and other. For me, this Witchcraft is a liberation theology that asks us to move beyond Magic as a form of consumerist wish fulfillment and that we take the risk to become the answer we long to see in the world.

The Sabbat of the Queered Christ

I'm sure I'm no different from most of people in trying to make sense of the paths I have walked and what they reveal about the core aspects of who I am. When I consider the differing traditions that I have worked within, I'm often struck by the commonalities in how I have approached them. While I might admire the dignity of a scripted ritual rubric, I personally love music, dance, and drumming. This type of embodied, ecstatic leaping about was once part of my teenage Pentecostalism, and now strongly connects me to the shamanic archetype of the Witch and the nightside mysteries of their craft.

The Witch often receives the shadow projections of those cultures that they are part of. They are the hags and the shape-shifters whose messy bodies both arouse and unsettle us. They are the scapegoats onto whose heads the repressed longings of society are spoken.

Within the collective psyche of Europe, the Witch has often acted as an icon of disturbance and freedom. The projected fantasies of clerics and folkloric imaginings often allude to something dark, disturbing, and subversive. In bearing the weight of such dangerous passions, the Witch often holds a position on the outer edge of social and ethical evolution.

If our magic is to mean anything, we must be willing for it to Queer and haunt us. The certainties that we cling to must be placed on the altar as our Gods and ancestors draw us to the crossroads at which the sacrificial cost of true change must be weighed.

My own work with the Witches' path induced a profound sense of unease. Have you ever felt haunted? Haunted by an idea or a person who, despite all your best efforts, seems to be lurking at the edges of your vision and prodding your unconscious to give them a bit more space? This was a phantom of my own history pointing towards past explorations and adventures that were still unresolved.

In my seeking to more fully appreciate the connections between the Witch trials and medieval Christian heretics, I became aware that the figure haunting me from the shadows was that old trickster Yeshua Ben Joseph (Jesus to his Greek speaking friends).

In relation to my own journey, I have already sought to describe how my initial flight into Christianity was largely related to my adolescent confusion about the fluidity of my own sexuality and gender identity. While I now feel that it was necessary to take leave of Christ due to the type of self-suppression that seemed innate to my faith at that time, I am still able to appreciate some of the Queer liberation that I experienced via the androgyny of Christ.

While owning my own needs and bias, I eventually encountered in my reading of Jesus a blurry ambiguity that that provided me with an alternative mode of being. Yes, this was the Jesus who cleared Temples and overturned tables, but this was also the Jesus who blessed the gentle and sought out the one lost sheep.

In a personal world where the versions of maleness, certainty, and force made little sense to me, my own gnostic encounter allowed access to a gentler, more mysterious experience. This Christ became a mirror through which I could view myself more closely. Such a perspective can be far from comfortable, but over time it allowed me to engage with deeper truths about who I needed to become. This magical process of engaging with the Christ myth allowed me (somewhat ironically) to become accepting enough of myself that I no longer wished to call myself a Christian.

To follow the path of the Witch or the Gnostic explorer is to pay heed to those incoming messages bubbling up from the unconscious. In the same way that I couldn't adhere to the exclusivity of a Christianity at odds with my Queerness, neither can I turn away from the insights still offered by the Christ-spark within.

In chapter 10 of the Gospel of John, Jesus describes himself as "the door," and the Christic myth still provides a doorway via which I can explore greater self-understanding. Walking through this doorway asks that I leave behind the child-like sentimentality of my past beliefs. I choose to risk this path as if offers freedom from claustrophobic certainties and the possibility of breathing in fresh insights.

For all of us, I would pray that we might access true gnosis as we listen to the Wisdom of our Queer ancestors and Gods. Let us take heed of their counsel that we may be brave enough to pursue the uniqueness of our path towards greater wholeness and freedom.

So Mote It Be!

Interview with Clyde Hall, Shoshone Two-Spirit Elder

by wolfie

wolfie: we're here interviewing clyde hall, shoshone elder, and one of the founder of gai, the gay american indian caucus. let's start with basic background information, clyde. when and where you were born, how you grew up.

Clyde: I was born in 1951 in Pocatello, Idaho. I was born in a time when something had just been invented called an "incubator," because I was born a month or so premature. If it wasn't for that I wouldn't be here talking to you today. It was a little metal box with a heat lamp in it, a high wattage lightbulb.

wolfie: so then, your childhood was spent on the reservation at fort hall?

Clyde: Yes. I lived in a one-room house, log cabin, with my grandmother. And later on with my sister. It was a good life.

wolfie: so we talked a little bit about this in previous conversations, because normally one of the questions with these interviews is, "what is your coming out story?". but you don't really have one? […]*

Clyde: It was just like Laine Thom [another Shoshone walker of the old ways], he didn't have a coming out story either. We're the people that were raised by traditional people. Because of the values our people have, they observe you when you're born and what your preferences are and what you like and, traditionally, they encourage that, because everyone is valued. Nobody is thrown away in tribal cultures. Even today, that, for the most part, is still the case. There's always something, some ability or some skill that people have that can be integrated into the survival of the band or the tribe.

wolfie: that's a culturally historical way that that happens, so it's not a like, sudden realization. i would assume that at some point you did have the realization that you were gay, but it wasn't a, "oh my god, this is this thing i either have to hide, or tell people."

Clyde: […] It was just the way I was, and I just went along with the flow. I mean, the word "gay," I didn't know it.

wolfie: even post-stonewall?

Clyde: Oh there were other words. Like "homosexual" and things like that. But, it was just a sense of being who you were, and I was encouraged by the old people. […]

wolfie: can we talk some about the different nature of the magic you grew up with?

Clyde: Well, it isn't separate from life. It's integrated. It's not like, "Oh I'm gonna do something magical." Indian people believe that that's always around you. That power is always around you, those things are always around you and it's integrated into your life, what you do from day to day. The way you live, the old people have a saying—"at this time." And for a long time I wondered what we meant by that, "at this time," and it's because that's literally all you have, is at this time—past, present, future, revolving around that moment in a circle, because Indian people believe that all things are in a circle, everything. And the universe, everything, moves in a circle.

wolfie: i remember you said something about there's a phrase or something about how all of nature is circular, except for rocks.

Clyde: All power lies in a circle. There are no straight lines in nature except for the rock, who has angles and points and has the power to create or destroy, which is related to the thunder and lightning beings. Everything is like that, everything is round in the world, according to Indian philosophy, and what you call magic, which we call 'bo'ha',' and Sioux call 'skunskun.'

Bo'ha, that's the power that moves. You know, it's in everything from the way the galaxies and everything move to the shaking of the leaves and trees in the wind, or how you walk about the earth and talk, that's all part of it, that's a manifestation of it. So Indians live with the realization of that power, 24/7.

wolfie: witches are very into setting aside their "sacred space," and i've always had the thing with them of "well, isn't all space sacred, all the time?"

Clyde: Yeah, all space is sacred all the time, but if you want to do something special, then you can create that space right then and there. Creating a container if you want to call it that. But we liken that to a medicine wheel. You're in the center of that medicine wheel, you can create that medicine wheel any time at any given moment, just be thinking about it, just by calling in the directions or calling in things or having a smoke and praying with the smoke. It can be a cigarette or burning cedar or sweetgrass or whatever, right then and there it's created.

wolfie: there's been a lot of writing in what i tend to term the gay revisionist historians about how 'two spirit' is the same thing as 'gay.'

Clyde: No. (loud laughter)

wolfie: can you clarify that and then we can go into more of the history of the term two spirit. you've said that there was sort of a diaspora, for lack of a better term, of old ways and two spirit and then the modern day.

Clyde: There's words in the traditional languages for people who had different roles that they played within the tribal structures, within the bands of people that lived together. I don't think they would recognize the word 'two spirit' or even 'gay,' you know. Take for instance in Sioux the word Wankan Tankan. Now what does Wankan Tankan mean to you?

wolfie: the best translation i remember learning was something like "great spirit/ all that is" kind of thing?

Clyde: It doesn't really necessarily mean that. Wankan Tankan was part of a hierarchy of powers or gods that the Sioux had, spirits that the Sioux had, but it wasn't necessarily the godhead. Wankan Tankan became the godhead I think due to colonialization when the missionaries came amongst the Indians and then they were trying to shove Christianity down their throats, that's when Wankan Tankan became foremost, so the kids during that period of time, turn of the last century, when they would talk to their older people and use the word Wankan Tankan in that context, the old people would look at them like, "What you talking about?" […]

wolfie: let's talk a little bit about the origin of the term "two spirit." that was born out of your involvement with founding the gay american indian caucus, yes? can you talk about how that came together?

Clyde: Gay American Indians was founded by Randy Burns and Barbara Cameron originally at Stanford University, because they were both going to school there at the time. A lot of Indian people came to the Bay Area under a program called "Indian Relocation." It was a plan that the government had to get the Indians off the reservation, train them up for some kind of vocational or tech skills, or go to college or some kind of trade or what have you, and they would provide transitional housing and supplemental income when you were going to these trainings and then hopefully place you in some kind of job when you were done. So there was a tremendous influx of Indian people into the San Francisco Bay Area and also to places like Chicago and Albuquerque. Different places around the country, to see if they could get Indians to transition. The ones that went to San Francisco went for a unique purpose because San Francisco was known at that point as kind of a gay capital. Things weren't completely on the out and out, but that was the place where particular and peculiar men congregated.

wolfie: (chuckles) and it still is. so, when that group started getting together, was it social, or was it political?

Clyde: It was purely a social group, because there's people from all over who came to the Bay Area. It was considered a social group originally and then it morphed into a political group. That's the way it went because, of course, we wanted a place at the table. You know, with the up and coming gay movements and things. It was a tremendously exciting time to live in San Francisco. In the late 70s or so, we started discussing a name because "Gay American Indians" was fine for us, and we were the first group ever in the world.

wolfie: when we talked before, you talked about how the actual coalescing with the word 'two spirit' happened around the first march on washington in 1979.

Clyde: Was it that far back?

wolfie: mmhmm.

Clyde: Time is like a river, I don't know, I can't remember.

wolfie: we did talk a lot last time about how linear time is sort of a western notion.

Clyde: We were involved in the early gay freedom marches, or pride parades as it's called now, in San Francisco and it was a very exciting time, but things were all about politics and making statements back then. And it would always end up on hippy hill in golden gate park, that's where the marches ended. We started talking about "gay American Indians," which it was ok for our group, but as a national thing, you needed something that was much more encompassing because, number one, gay was mainly connoted with males, and Indians have many traditions about the subject, many ways and viewpoints that have been practiced for thousands and thousands; millennia of years, and so, we thought, how do we incorporate the old traditions with something new and be encompassing and inclusive?

So we tossed around a number of words and descriptions and it all kind of congealed when we got to Washington, DC, that was the first time that Indians came from all over including Canada and different places. We had a meeting of what to call ourselves, And we decided on the term "two spirit," so, that's where it was decided on. Coined there, and then later on I think it was in 1990 at the American Anthropological Association convention in Washington, DC, we all gave a number of papers and speeches on the subject, which are collected in a book called Two Spirit People by Sue Ellen Jacobs, Wesley Thomas, and Sabine Lang. So that's when it was decided that the old time words that the early explorers knew, like the word "berdache," which is a French word as far as my understanding of it, would only be used in a historical context, that anything from that day forward, the word "two spirit" would be used, so that's when it was cast in stone. In the meantime, from the March on Washington there was a group that decided that they would hold a two spirit encampment, or gathering, which was held in Winnipeg, I think, that year.

This urban myth was told about this woman that went up, I don't know if she was a lesbian or what, but she went up and got this inspiration that that should be the word. I'm not saying it didn't happen, it probably did, I don't know, but that's not where it all started. […] There are many encampments now, about 32 of them a year, there's about 32 to 35 groups around the country. I found it amusing that I helped start those two spirit things, and then never got around to going to them until about four years ago.

wolfie: and what was your experience going to them after such a long time?

Clyde: Well, I was kind of curious to see what they did, and you know, they're nice gatherings. They have a sacred fire that they keep and they have pipe ceremonies and a drag show and a little pow-wow and there's different workshops where they talk about things that are unique to two spirits and get HIV testing done there and so it's very supportive of two spirit Indians in this day and age. I like them.

wolfie: so to further clarify, we talked about how two spirit is more a role within the culture.

Clyde: Well it's a role, it's a contemporary role, and not all people identify, not all Native American people identify with the words two spirit, they feel it doesn't describe them.

wolfie: yeah, two spirit is a modern construct.

Clyde: It's a very modern construct.

wolfie: for the people who lived in those old ways or even those who might identify with the modern construct, my understanding is it had nothing to do really with who you had sex with or who you married or who you slept with.

Clyde: No, it didn't have anything to do with who you had sex with, who you married, any of that. It was a vision, those old time people had a vision that was equally valid as any vision and should they choose to act on it, then they did.

You know it was just like the contraries, for instance, the contraries did everything backwards. When they washed their hair, they washed their hair with dirt. When they went someplace, they'd say goodbye when actually they were saying hello, and there was all of that. And the old time with their heemaneh or that type of thing, well then that was acting on your vision too and bringing it into this reality, whether that meant wearing a dress and doing women things, those people could also do men things too—it just depended on what they wanted, how they wanted to be at that time.

wolfie: so then, the people who would follow the old ways, followed their vision. what roles did they often take in society?

Clyde: They served all kinds of roles. With Native American people, they were the vanguards, the ones who went out and explored something new. They were the ones who met the explorers because they were interested in what kind of people were coming to visit them and they were judges and they were people who held the traditions and the stories and the medicine ways and all these things. They were matchmakers, and they were the persons who took care of the elderly and took care of the children, and plus they had certain talents they could do too, to do with roots and herbs and things that were unique to those kinds of men and women. Because you know, there is a great power in-between, I think we talked about the heemaneh, in the Cheyenne stories the original heemaneh was a big giant being who had its feet on the ground and it went up into the sky and therefore was a part of both and that was the big heemaneh spirit, the original heemaneh spirit, you know, because it was the great power in between this and that applies to European tradition too. It's the concept of the crossroads or having one foot in the water and one foot on the land, and there's a great power in that because it's somewhat nebulous. It's a neither fish nor fowl kind of a thing so there's a big power with that. […] So the Native American tribes recognize that power for the most part, with these people. They were also the namer of names for children and so forth.

wolfie: so you're talking about the past and how people understood the in-between as having great power, but what about how you think our current society, let's say, united states, western culture, views the in-between?

Clyde: Well, those old time people did not know the concept of Christian sin. That explains a lot about how things are now, as compared to a long time, years ago, decades ago. They did not know the concept of Christian sin. Old men for instance, could walk through the camp with a big hard on, no pants or leggings or breech cloth or anything, and nobody thought anything of it. It's just the way he was and the way he wanted to be at that moment. And there was no judgment or saying, "Oh, that's terrible, you should cover yourself up you nasty old thing," like that, and of course when the missionaries came amongst the tribes, the first thing they did was see these men and women in male attire and female attire and they considered that the worst abomination. That was the first thing to go underground or attempted to be destroyed, and it was almost completely destroyed. Things went way deep underground, you know.

I think we talked about Hosteen Klah. Hosteen Klah was a Navajo man, and woman. Some people say that he was…

wolfie: intersex?

Clyde: Yes, intersex. He had the power to do both feminine and masculine things. He conducted sings with the Navajo ways and religion. […] Most people, most traditional Navajo people, consider themselves lucky and accomplished if they mastered in their life one ceremony or sing, with all the sand paintings and the songs that go with it; but Hosteen Klah at the time that he passed on he had mastered something like 10 or 15 of these things which was unheard of. He was also a master weaver, and weaving is only done by the women. He wove rugs and things like that.

wolfie: did he create whole new techniques?

Clyde: He created a whole new tradition where he took the figures that were in the sand paintings, the sand paintings of the sings, and he translated them into woven rugs.

It was previously unheard of. You know, you had the Yeibichai figures portrayed and things like that always in Navajo rugs now, they weren't necessarily there before. He was the one who was responsible, he was the only one who could translate those things into it, otherwise it was very separate, you didn't portray those beings in something like a rug, you couldn't recreate those sand paintings based on those beings. So he did all that, he was able to do that, and he worked with a lady, a lot of his things are at the Wheelwright Museum [Now called The Wheelright Museum of the American Indian]. But Hosteen Klah was responsible for helping establish that museum and his weavings and recordings are still there today. So that's kind of a story about him. And the old time people could do that kind of things. They could innovate new songs, they could innovate changes in ritual, and all of that because they knew that it was within their power to do those things, but also to change them and transcend and remove them in a different way, should they choose.

wolfie: doing so from a very solid foundation, though.

Clyde: From a very solid foundation, yes. Because they were the keepers of the song, they were the keepers of the ritual kinds of things and so they could either preserve it the way it was or change it a little bit. Or a whole lot. […]

wolfie: so, we talked about two spirit being a fairly new construct, and so is "queer" as a construct. it doesn't seem like in native american traditions that sexuality was ever separated out the way it's separated out in western culture.

Clyde: No, it's just something that's woven in the thread of life, and it's the Christian concept of sin that's made it something that could be thought of as dirty, and in this country because of the people that were empowering this country, the puritans and things like that, we still carry as a country this puritan ethic that didn't exist in Indian society at all. For us all of sexuality was just part of the weave of life, something that just ran, and it wasn't considered anything isolated or it wasn't considered something you did in the dark, or that was bad, or anything. It was just part of what you did in living in your day-to-day existence. […]

wolfie: when you brought the dance for all people [the ceremony of renewal and racial harmony based in the great plains traditions] to the radical faeries [a radical queer spirituality movement] for the first time… would you say there was a qualitative difference in how it flowed having a majority of the people in circle being queer?

Clyde: I was curious on how it was going to work with Radical Faeries because I understood that they did earth practices with that among other things, and also I've always had this thought or belief that most of what you'd consider gay people in this country are like sleeping spiritual giants, should they be awakened. It's just the way that our society has funnelled all those unique talents and abilities and things of the in-between person into something that fits in these little boxes and you don't dare get out of these little boxes. I was wondering how would it work if these people were awakened to this particular way and how it would move with them. It was a grand experiment, and it worked wonderful in a lot of ways because again, like we were talking about, in Native American society two spirit people are the vanguards, they're the ones that move and change things, they're the ones that do all this kind of the stuff. And what I found at Wolf Creek [the Radical Faerie sanctuary in Oregon] is for the most part, it's like a, like you're saying, a cauldron, and some of the things that they've done at Wolf Creek have ended up in absolute disaster, but other things that have worked, have worked very well and the other dance communities emulate them. If it works at Wolf Creek, it'll filter through the other communities, but it was Wolf Creek that was in the vanguard.

wolfie: last night, there was bundle opening ceremony and when i was standing there at one point i looked around and counted the people who were there and i noticed that probably 75% of those people were queer people – and so this ties in i think, could you talk a little bit about that, not just how the faeries changed the naraya [the dance for all people], but how the naraya is changing the faeries and queer people who come to the ceremony?

Clyde: It is because they become more focused and they have become able to acknowledge their own inner power and strength. See, my intention when I brought the naraya to New York, was to have it focused on queer people and women, because we were disenfranchised ones, just like the Indians, we're disenfranchised too, so to give that power, that spiritual ability back to those people, you know, and I think it's moved in wonderful ways through the year, but that's where the focus of the naraya has always been, is with those people. It has evolved that way, the naraya. The way I look at it is something that started out with this tradition, but is it necessarily that anymore? It's evolved into its own thing, its own being and having mainly women and queer people, that's the whole purpose of it. Why it's coming to be and why it manifested when it did is becoming more and more clear as we get along in these decades because the naraya, the last time it manifested was in 1890 and that as a time of much turmoil and trouble with the Indian people and their world was rapidly changing, and now our whole world is rapidly changing, not only Indian people but everybody, we don't know where it's going to end and whether it's going to end for better or worse or what, and so hopefully, it's coming kind of clear to me why the naraya is back in the world again right now, and that's the thing, that's why in December I got all those elders together in New York and we had about 1000 years of experience in that room.

We were there to come up with a group statement, how is the naraya going to help us to continue and how is the naraya going to help us to keep this world on some kind of even keel or at least pick up the pieces later. And it's all becoming very concrete on why it's in the world right now, why it's afoot. Because our world is changing for better or worse right now, and that's why it's here and that's why it's here mainly for women and mainly for queer people, so it will give us some way of being spiritually strong and good.

wolfie: can you articulate what you see as the difference between a queer experience of magic and i don't know whether to call it straight magic or cis magic or what. language is so limited.

Clyde: Well, you can say this, is that you know, a lot of European magic and even Indian, Indian spiritual ways, are based on a duality of feminine and masculine. Like last night, when we were in the bundle opening, well, that's how we open the bundle, there has to be a woman on one side and a man on the other, and you know, men sit on one side, women sit on the other, and with the queer magic it's across the board because it's an in-between type of magic and that's really where the greatest power lies, in any magic practice, is that in-between. The point that's not fixed.

wolfie: one of the ways that we talked about this was going into the discussion of essentialism and social construction, and is there an essential feminine and an essential masculine, are they beholden to biology?

Clyde: It doesn't have anything to do with biology, it's just the way that the world moves for procreative purposes, I mean that's the way it is, for a manifestation of life.

Up in Blackfeet country there's the Matoki Society, that's exclusive woman society and they get together once a year and they build this lodge and they have their secret doings in there. And I hear about maybe 10 years ago, 15 years ago, they invited this man in who identified as being feminine and they invited him to be a member of that society. Unheard of, but they did, and he's still a member of that society today because he views himself as a feminine person.

That's one wonderful thing about Indian beliefs and other beliefs is you can't get dogmatic about them, people say 'oh the Indians are doing things like they did in their age old traditions a thousand years ago, it's the same'... It's not the same. You know, you draw inspiration and you do things as an honor to that, but it's not the same because it has to fit the people who are living now otherwise if you're just going through the motions of doing something you did, it's going to be meaningless to the people who live now and are practicing it. [...] It's a living tradition rather than an ossified one.

wolfie: i wouldn't exactly call modern society integrated, but to the extent that people from lots of different traditions are coming together and talking about and sharing; what do you see as the role of queer people, in terms of how things are going to continue, both magically and socially.

Clyde: I should hope that the world is going to evolve, that spiritual beliefs are going to evolve, because I think with queer people, they have such unique gifts and viewpoints of the world, should they choose to do so, I'm not talking about the Log Cabin [Club] Republicans, that they could probably benefit the world a great deal with what they know and the powers that they have, should they choose to embrace and explore those powers. [...]

wolfie: within the monotheistic structure, everything is so fixed, that's what I see as one of the powers of queer/two spirit/epicene, whatever we're calling it, is that there is not just a fluidity but a mobility with that.

Clyde: It's like water, and you know with the Native American traditions of course, the sun and the eagle is the masculine, the light, and the eagle is the messenger and the doer, and here on the other side you have the moon, and you have the owl. And the sun and the eagle is all about. That rigidity, and the moon and the owl are all about secret things in the night, and also about the water, the water is part of that too, so. You have that, all again on that concept of a circle, you were asking me about what, in Shoshone tradition, was there a two spirit being in the...

wolfie: in the iconography.

Clyde: There is, indeed. Coyote is the one who was that. He could change himself into a man or a woman, you know, with all the qualities thereof ... and he was also, in his most highest aspect, he was the bringer of light and knowledge into the world by stealing the fire, you know and again, only a two spirit being could do that. Could bring that light into the world and consequently knowledge, and so there's many other stories with Native American traditions too. Like we mentioned the heemaneh, about heemaneh being this big giant being who had his feet in the ground and his head and upper torso in the sky, so you know there's all kinds of things that acknowledge that circle as the way things go.

wolfie: and if i remember some of my stories, part of why coyote would change from male to female was based on who he was attracted to at that moment.

Clyde: Who he was attracted to at that moment or some purpose that he had, that would work better with him doing that, so there's that too.

wolfie: just in the discussion of moving forward as a species, where do you see that fluidity being beneficial? that's kind of an obvious question.

Clyde: All change comes from that fluidity. For better or worse, it all comes from that fluidity. People have to get back to the concept that all of those things, all those ways of being are within the circle. It was Christianity that made it bad in this western culture. In other cultures, in other traditions, it was dependent on how long the civilization lasted. It went through waxing and waning periods. That's the natural flow of things.

wolfie: and it's not in any hierarchical sense.

Clyde: No, it all flows together.

wolfie: that's been one of the problems with talking about this in the neo-pagan community. people get defensive and say, "well, you're saying that queers are better!" and it's like, "this is not a supremacy game."

Clyde: No, it's not a supremacy game, that's a very western concept, supremacy over, I'm better than you, blah blah blah, you know, no, it all goes together.

When we started this conversation, about how people in Indian nations recognize that there was a unique talent that everybody had within the tribe, whatever that talent was, was incorporated into the tribal structure to enable the tribe to survive, everybody had a unique talent, everybody had a unique gift and it's part of what made things go around. […]

wolfie: thank you so much.

Clyde: You're welcome, this was wonderful!

* Interview conducted on February 12th, 2017. Original interview abridged for length. Complete inteview can be found at www.MysticProductionsPress.com/queermagic

Protect All Queers sigil
by Inés Ixierda

Walking With Mystery

by W. L. Bolm

I have always existed between worlds, never quite belonging in any community I've found because my identities are not easily defined. I'm a Floridian who spent my childhood in the Upper Peninsula of Michigan and became a Yankee-Southern hybrid when I moved back to Florida. I grew up as a Lutheran who didn't believe in God, transitioned to living as a witch without a coven, and converted to Reform Judaism in college. Now I practice a spirituality shaped by ritual honed through years of practice that combines the mystery of a Jewish god that cannot truly be known with the natural awe of the British Romantics, a cadre of poets known for their connection to natural, wild places and exploration of supernatural themes.

This same dichotomy of belonging and not belonging is something I experience in the QUILTBAG (Queer/Questioning, Undecided, Intersex, Lesbian, Trans, Bisexual, Asexual, Gay/Genderqueer) community as well. I am pansexual, but I often call myself bisexual because of society's need to assign gender to a binary system. I label myself queer because it gives me the room I need to be my most authentic self, but I still show up at bisexual events, lesbian events, and gay (the most nebulous of all terms) events. I am demisexual—somewhere between asexual and hypersexual—with the caveat that I need to find people I connect to on an emotional level before I feel anything akin to sexual stirrings, and, as a sex positivity activist, I often feel like I don't belong in the very crowds I help organize because of my lack of desire is often read as repression or a sexual hang-up. When you add in the fact that my pronouns are they/them and the gender of my soul could be best described as "genderless blob," my inability to be categorized in easy ways makes it hard to find a group to belong to within rigid definitions often ascribed to alternative communities.

Through the years, my queerness has shaped my religious beliefs. Through rejecting gender and the gender binary, my eyes were opened to the idea that god doesn't fit the projections people use to anthropomorphize the divine. As I learned more about myself and who I was, I started to break free of seeing the divine as two halves of a gender binary. I also learned how to intentionally break the gendered rules that were being passed down to me through the pop magic texts easily available in the early to mid-nineties. In doing so, I began to learn more about myself.

There were two false beliefs I held in high school.

The first was that I was a straight woman. This was easy to dispel as I moved from high school into my adult life and began to meet a more diverse population of women, as well as when I explored anthropology classes and online communities centered around people who were no longer trapped by a gender binary system.

The second was that I was a chaos magician. All of the books that I read, and all of the pagans that I knew, either addressed the god and goddess equally out of a sense of balance, or they focused on the goddess and the much-ignored feminine divine in their practices. Calling myself a chaos magician was my first step toward breaking away from the divine binary.

I was a weird kid. I sat in trees and read books during family reunions. In my head, I constructed a male avatar for myself. He went on daydream adventures and was the side-kick of many of my favorite television and movie heroes. These fantasies definitely prepared me for visualization during spellwork later in life. I thought of myself as one of the guys.

In high school, as my sexuality awakened, my inner world changed. My avatar became a brooding goth girl with long black hair. I discovered books by Scott Cunningham, Starhawk, and Silver Ravenwolf and started to replace my uncertainty with my family's Lutheran beliefs with uncertainty over pagan beliefs. Except, I could see my spellwork working in my life, for good and for bad, mostly through love spells that entangled me in relationships and glamours that gave my chubby teenage self-confidence.

The books I was reading had a universal theme that there was a god and a goddess, two parts to the divine. Many included laundry lists of deities to invoke for specific purposes. There were lists upon lists of colors and elements and flowers and gems and how they related to the different divinities and my goals, but none of these gods and goddesses resonated with me. I dabbled, looking for a place I belonged amongst ancient cultures and pantheons, moving from the Nordic gods to the ancient Greeks to the Egyptians and finding bits and pieces of lore I found fascinating, but no true belief or sacred caste system to ground me. My magic became dispassionate, more like putting together a recipe for curry than contacting the divine. Even though my spells were working, I started cutting the invocation down until I was no longer invoking the god and goddess suggested for the situation I was dealing with. Thus began my identity as a chaos magician, a label I chose because my rituals were bare bones in form and appealed to no deity beyond a wild, undefined spirit I could not yet truly grasp.

It was December 31, 1999. My mother was out for New Year's Eve, and I was at the dining room table preparing a spell. I had long ago given up on invoking the goddess that had once graced my makeshift altar. Her likeness was a light-up Mother Mary Christmas tree topper I had dressed up with some random swag from my room, her veil transformed into a cloak with the addition of a lone earring, and her blue satin dress decorated with red magic marker. I had transformed her from saint to goddess then abandoned both before my graduation from high school. She sat neglected on a shelf, her invocation replaced with a silent appeal and visualization of white divine energy. She was the nameless replacement for a deity I could not name.

I thought the world was going to end for Y2K; I was seventeen and was a news junkie, so I hoped that I and witches like me could at least tip the world back towards a technological future, even if the computers we already depended on failed us.

For the bulk of my ritual, I counted on visualizations and prayer. I prayed that the world be okay, that we would be protected. I envisioned a white bubble of protective energy surrounding me, expanding to envelop my house; then the neighborhood, city, state, country, and finally the world. I would fall back to this visualization over and over again throughout the years to come, whenever my young world seemed out of my control.

The clock struck midnight, and nothing happened aside from the turning of the year. Planes weren't falling from the sky the way I had feared. People were celebrating on television. I could hear the sound of firecrackers going off in my neighborhood. The world continued, and I had crystallized the beginnings of a skeleton that would slowly become the foundation for my ritual work as an adult.

I came closer to forming a god of my understanding through conversion to Judaism when I was almost finished with college, close to a decade later. In Jewish theology, there are male and female aspects of god, but the modern Jewish concept of god is of an unknowable mystery, not really male or female. As with every religion, Jewish followers split off into different paths of ritual and belief, but the two constants are that god is a mystery, and you must study not to discover the ultimate answers, but to build a connection with god even though so many questions remain.

The first rabbi I studied under often said that the more he learned, the more he felt there was to learn. The emphasis on ritual and arcane knowledge is what first attracted me to Judaism, but when I discovered that Judaism allowed mystery without concrete answers, that it prized independent study and lively debate, and that it was a religion that was still evolving, I knew that I had found a religion that fit my inability to believe that any religious doctrine holds all of the avenues to truth.

There is a saying that if you get two Jewish people together in one room, you'll end up with three opinions, and I've found this to be true. The Jews I have met throughout the years have been very diverse. Jewish hippies. Jewish Buddhists. Jewish soccer moms. Jewish witches. Orthodox Jews. Jewish feminists. Jewish gamers. Jewish stoners. Jewish musicians. I've heard rabbis discuss the pagan origins of holiday rituals. I've heard heated debates on whether or not prayer works, on whether or not god exists, and on whether or not the Bible was really handed down by god. Judaism is messy and loud and a vibrant community, one that I was willing to put in two years of study in order to join.

I have experienced two Jewish rebirths in my life.

The first was when I floated in the Gulf of Mexico, enclosed in a makeshift *mikvah* (a ritual bath) in the ocean, experiencing the Jewish version of baptism. I floated in warm Florida waters at Clearwater beach inside of a symbolic womb as trusted members of my community witnessed my emergence into the Jewish tradition.

In those moments that I was surrounded by undulating curtains on a floating, cobbled-together frame in the Gulf, bobbing in warm water, surrounded by love and support, I had never felt closer to the divine feminine. In those moments, I felt safe. After we said our prayers, I emerged out into the larger ocean to join my new community. Yet, even though the energy that surrounded me felt feminine, I recognized in the moment that god is larger than this experience and my perception.

The second time I was reborn was when I cast off a bad marriage to begin my life anew.

I stared at the invitations I'd ordered from Scriptura, a local New Orleans printing company. They were pale blue with a green oak tree in the background. They were invitations not for my wedding but for my divorce. I had invited a handful of close friends to come witness the ritual I had written with my rabbi, so I could finally let go of my ex and the baggage that came along with the bad memories of a marriage that had dragged out for too long.

When the day came, I walked down Esplanade Avenue to City Park and the wind chime tree, the one place in the world guaranteed to bring me to a place of calm and serenity. The wind chime tree is a massive oak next to one of the park's lagoons, and the chimes are tuned to the same frequency so that natural music is perpetually playing in its branches.

We recited a blessing to Adonai, a placeholder name for the Jewish god, a god that is often called "Lord." The constant tension of reconciling the gendered language of Hebrew with the genderless ideal of the Jewish god flared in my mind. This was even after years of queer Jewish study with teachers who accepted modern interpretations of texts as well as citing pagan origins of teachings, texts, and rituals. Even though all mundane words in Hebrew, from chair to sky, are gendered, being reminded of a male god in ninety percent of Jewish texts and prayers, of god as king or father or lord, was a source of dissonance in my mind.

Surrounded by friends, I made a temporary peace with the tension and said blessings to Adonai then threw breadcrumbs into the lagoon, reminiscent of the ritual Jewish people around the world practice on Rosh Hashanah, casting away their sins. Instead, I was casting off an old skin, a life and relationship that no longer served me.

This was my ritual; I had written it into being. I had pored over suggested texts and books and come up with something meaningful for me. Though Judaism is an ancient religion, modern progressive Jews often cobble together their own hymns, services, and rituals based on their own needs and the meanings they draw from life. As I sat down to break bread at the concluding picnic under the windchime tree, I was part of that long tradition, though I was still frustrated with the confines of a gendered language when I didn't see myself concretely represented by either gender. Appeals to a male god are often habitual even when deeper teachings and studies bring up so much more gender variance and interpretation. A few years into my Jewish conversion, I was having growing pains. I was still searching for a way to put into words my experiences with a deity that could not be defined in terms of male or female, man or woman.

It wasn't until I started working on my master's degree in English that I really found a text that succinctly describes what I believe, and I found it in the works of the British Romantics.

"The awful shadow of some unseen Power/ Floats though unseen amongst us; visiting/ This various world with as inconstant wing." Percy Bysshe Shelley penned these words in *Hymn to Intellectual Beauty*, which speak so clearly to me of what god is; God is inconstant and fleeting. It is through ritual, meditation, communing with nature, and our connection to other people that we are able to touch the divine. Each of us is left to figure out how to touch this power in our own way. To me it seems very American that I am a genderqueer Jew who practices magic and whose philosophy on god comes from a British atheist who died almost two hundred years ago.

Shelley's views on god as an unknowable, natural force are very Jewish, and very pagan. His poetry is a beginner's template for entering god-space. He gives no path for holding onto a connection with the divine, but that is where ritual provides framework. Simply going into sacred natural space can create a sense of divine awe, but casting a circle, calling the quarters, and building energy all work toward ensuring a connection with the divine. As Shelley writes in *Mont Blanc*, "the wilderness' has a mysterious tongue/ Which teaches awful doubt, or faith so mild,/ So solemn, so serene, that man may be,/ But for such faith with nature reconciled." It is not a named god or goddess that creates open-minded reverie, the energy needed to do magical work, but a connection to the natural world that helps us bridge to higher planes. With my exposure to Shelley's writing, my understanding of god shifted; I no longer had to hold a picture of god, even a shifting picture, in my mind to work my magic.

I sat cross-legged on the floor in my new basement office and art studio. A book I'd picked up from the library on art and design had inspired me to claim this space. I was breaking it in, consecrating it, and introducing it to magic and to myself. A circle of white, protective energy surrounded me. I was deep in meditation. Psychic roots flowed from me down into the ground, and sparkling, gem-encrusted branches grew from my crown and out into the room. I was prepared. I had evoked the divine that is everything. That was enough.

A candle I used regularly for centering meditation sat before me, as did a sacred journal, a special pen, and an ornately carved glass bowl. I began to write on a page of the journal. I wrote about my old life and the things holding me back. I wrote about fears and people hundreds of miles away who no longer served my life. And then, with spoken intentions and a blessing, I ripped the page out of the book and held it to the candle's flame. I dropped the paper into the glass bowl so that it could safely burn out.

Then the smoke alarm went off.

I laughed, and the smoke alarm was close enough to be inside my circle and within waving distance, so I picked up the book and used it to fan the small amount of smoke in the room away from the smoke detector, so it wouldn't wake my roommates. The fanning became part of the ritual, a last use of energy before finishing the rite and grounding. That humorous moment made grounding in child's pose easier, my forehead pressed against the floor, the image of the energy flowing out and into the world behind my eyelids.

I channel energy through meditation and ritual, chanting and intention. Emotion and repetition. I have learned how to visualize energy, to raise it and hold it, to work it as it manifests. In my path, the anthropomorphization of the divine is a tool, but it can also be a barrier to growth and knowledge. The eventual goal is to be able to reach the divine in Mystery, broken free of my own preconceived notions.

Everything is sacred. Everything is holy. Everything that exists makes up the whole of god, and therefore, god encompasses all and nothing, male and female and neither.

My path has been a winding one, and because of its twists and turns, I often find myself on the outside looking in. I have a pagan foundation and a Romantic Jewish philosophy that sets me apart from other neo-pagans and from other Jews. Just as I find myself apart from those who can see themselves clearly in one gender or another. Though I walk my path alone, I have found where I'm meant to be at this moment.

Creation: Step One
by Adare

Gregangelo is a queer Whirling Dervish, emulating the infinite prowess of the universe in both his dance and his otherworldly production *Velocity Circus* in San Francisco. Through his revolving dance, Gregangelo embodies the reality of an eternally rotating multiverse, from the micro-swirl of subatomic particles to the macro-spiraling of majestic galaxies.

Living in Attunement with Sensation Rather than Identity

by Z Griss

This place we are from, the bodies we live in… I sense they hold some understanding about our common humanity if we can give our bodies our full attention. What if we could live from sensation and soul purpose rather than social identity? What happens to our humanity if we don't acknowledge our sensations or express our relationship to them?

Belonging

Belonging is often based on a social identity. I belong because I'm…a woman, an artist, queer, white, black, brown, pagan, an activist, an entrepreneur, a submissive, an intellectual… I'm curious how these social identities might impact our ability to track bodily sensations or to track our soul purpose. **Is there something to see that I can see more clearly when I'm not attached to my identity?** I want to distinguish the difference between social location and identity. Your social location is something assigned to you whereas your identity is something you co-create. Your identity may be how you navigate your social location and how you choose to define yourself. **How can that support a deeper inquiry and self intimacy where we attune to our sensations even when they don't align with our social identity?** If our sense of belonging depends on an identity, it can be difficult to connect with the sensations that defy that identity. James Baldwin wrote an incredible untitled piece about a young white boy attending his first lynching. The boy was starting to feel nauseous and sick at the sight of this murder, but the adults in his life were demonstrating that this was acceptable behavior. So the young boy started to discount his own ill sensations as evidence that what he saw was wrong, because the boy wanted to belong to the white adults who are raising him. He started to tell himself that he must have been getting sick and that his nausea didn't have to do with a response to the lynching.

It's so common for us to choose our identity and our desire to belong over choosing to feel the truth of our sensations. **Every time we trust our sensations and dare to communicate about them, we move towards liberation. We give permission to ourselves and everyone around us to belong simply because we exist, not because of our identity.** If we can find the courageous experience of belonging simply because we exist, then we can be free to move through sensations and identities in a dynamic, nuanced, and expansive way. When we focus on our physical sensations and not on our social identities, we can have a felt sense of ourselves without needing to "other" someone else. Sometimes it's valuable to deconstruct our social identities so we can connect more to the heart of what we want and who we are.

What Sensations are with You Now?

Where is your body in space right now? What is the most relaxed part of you? What is the most protected part of you in this moment? How much of your attention is engaging with the thousands of nerve impulses in your body right now? What parts of you are in contact with surfaces of support (like a chair, a bed, a floor, or a lap)?

Many of us are putting our attention in places outside of our felt sensations. Consider all the sensations you can track right now. Is there muscular tension in your tongue? Is there tension in the crease at the fronts of your ankles?

Have you ever feared that if you acted the way you are truly feeling that you would be killed or that people would be shocked? Which sensations could you express and still feel seen, safe, and accepted in the social space you are in? Perhaps feeling tired with a yawn. Perhaps feeling happy with a smile. Perhaps moving towards the bathroom because you feel the sensation of a full bladder. All of these are fairly safe sensations to feel and express.

How many of the sensations you are feeling in this moment would be challenging to express? Rage. Deep grief. A strong sensation of arousal. What happens to these sensations if you do not express them?

Sensation is the Rawest Form of Experience

Our sensations precede our thoughts and emotions, which motivate social identity. Building our capacity to stay present and accept our uncomfortable sensations can ground us when expanding beyond our social identities. **Sensation anchors us through the death and rebirth of who we are and who we are to each other.**

Alito Alessi of *Danceability* would say "at any moment there are tens of thousands of sensations happening in your body, but the brain only registers a few." Imagine what is possible if we start to expand our attention and willingness to feel unfamiliar sensations, uncomfortable feelings, or even feelings that make us fear social rejection.

The Sensations that Connect to Gender

Some of you reading this, like me, have experienced gender dysphoria. Or perhaps you know someone who has. This simply means that we lose sensation in part of our anatomy that doesn't reflect our gender identity. For me, I lost sensation in my breasts, which have a history of being extremely sensitive and easily aroused. Just breathing warm air while hovering your lips an inch from my nipples could make me cum. But when I started to connect more with the sensations of my energetic cock, I started to feel a numbness and aversion to receiving touch on my breasts. If you are new to the idea of an "energetic cock," is simply means that I don't have a physical cock but I have a strong felt sense of a cock that can get aroused and penetrate as if it is a physical part of my body. It was challenging to stay tuned in to my cock sensations and my breast sensations simultaneously.

This numbness in my breasts was incredibly humbling for me as someone who identifies as an embodied being. I used to assume that if people just did more yoga, dance, or meditation, it would enhance their connection with their bodies and they wouldn't have gender dysphoria. I was clearly wrong. I didn't know how long this would last. I didn't have an explanation for my lovers. What I gained was a deep compassion and empathy for other people with dysphoria. Body, you humble me and remind me to surrender to things I may not understand but am willing to accept. I started to soften, as this frustration became a sense of awe. Where do these sensations come from?

I can imagine that if you've had this experience, reading about the value of sensation could feel quite overwhelming. If I could go back in time and speak with myself during that period now, I'd say, "be gentle and curious about the lack of sensation and simply focus on what you can feel. Be open to the possibility of your body and mind shifting. Oh yeah, and I've since met lots of people who've had a similar experience. You're really not alone. It's ok to tell lovers that you prefer to not receive focused attention or touch on your breasts. It might even feel better to say 'chest.'"

On some level, my identity could not reconcile that my sensations in my cock and my breasts were happening at the same time in a way that made me bigger than either man or woman. **My social identity was not big enough to contain the amount of sensations my body was feeling.**

I remember the exact conversation I had last summer when my sensation in my breasts returned. I was speaking with Meagan Murphy, director and producer of the Breast Archives, a documentary about women's relationships with their breasts. She shared with me that 85% of women are unhappy with their breasts. It hit me that small and large breasted women alike were socialized to feel flawed. Here I was, with petite breasts, living my whole life feeling I wasn't woman enough. Now that I was starting to present as more masculine, several close friends who were getting top surgery were envying how flat I was. It was quite a mind trip. That's when I became aware I had internalized a sense of inadequacy in my relationship with my breasts that was actually true for the majority of women. In that moment sitting with Meagan I realized I was no longer willing to let this social conditioning interrupt my relationship with my breasts. I was ready to accept them just as they are. That's when my breasts started to feel again

Women's Circles

For 15 years I offered women's circles exploring sexuality and spirituality through dance. During this time I identified as a woman and I thought I was welcoming the other women to show up in their full expression. **I realized that my women's circles had made the assumption that I still see in many women's embodiment practices: if a group of women explore embodiment they are exploring feminine energy.** I remember one time I was teaching a group of women cancer survivors in Washington, DC. When I asked everyone to share their intention for coming to the workshop a woman said she came to explore her feminine energy. I paused. I asked her why that was important to her. She was so surprised and said nobody had ever asked her that before. I said if her intention to explore feminine energy was really coming from her that's great, but if it's coming from an assumption that an embodied woman should be feminine, or that I as the teacher was invested in her feminine energy, she could let that go. The next day she wrote me.

> *"That point freed me up to not "try" to get what I thought I should get out of the workshop, but to be open to whatever comes organically…*
>
> *I could feel a kind of energy rising up through my belly, and it almost felt like my ribs were gonna crack open as I breathed deep and expansive in my chest. My eyes began to flutter uncontrollably, which they've never done before in my life… my heart exploded, and my body went into full outburst and I saw like a kind of gold river break out of my head through the crown and gush all over these 2 people, like a blessing on them to just be who they are, freely. I cried and screamed in release. I felt like I was quaking the walls with uninhibited blessing for those 2 people… I felt this amazing experience where I reconnected with my deepest passion in terms of what I want for humanity, that this experience and expression could be more than just about me…I felt like I reconnected to my ministry, to my passion, to compassion, to something greater than myself, to causes. Afterwards, I found myself walking the streets of DC without resentment."*

What is More Constant than Our Identity?

Many of us discover a new way of being, dressing, and acting, and we like it. But we don't allow ourselves to be different and to let go of who we used to be. Letting go often means recasting our life and letting relationships transform with the people who have been close to us but who cannot companion us in our new way of being. It means being willing to be misunderstood, especially by those we used to feel kinship and empathy with. It's also possible that many of these same people will expand and continue to companion us. But the depth and sustainability of our relationships depends on being present with what's truly alive as a felt sensation now, not just recreating the familiar.

Letting go of an identity does not mean losing our sense of purpose. In fact, sometimes purpose is the anchor that guides us as we transition through multiple identities. Our life intention, our soul purpose, lives in a realm of who we are that is not based in identity or limitations. We have the honor and opportunity to move this knowing of who we are from visionary reality into physical reality through our bodies. When we are in alignment with this soul purpose, we know it because of the vital sensations that arise in us.

My purpose is to expand people's capacity to feel at home, ecstatic, and whole in their bodies so that we can create social change from an emotionally resourced, imaginative, and awe-inspired way of being. Early on in my journey, the identities of woman, yoga teacher, meditation teacher, and dancer were all easeful ways to live in my purpose and make it easy for people to find me.

Over the years, I listened to the sensations in my being. I felt far more sexual energy than I used to feel comfortable expressing. I felt a quality of strength and rootedness in my movements such that when I taught birthing dances to women, I was told I was too masculine to teach these feminine art forms. I felt a dark desire for intensity, surrender, and dominance that revealed my lack of innocence and either attracted similar mischief-makers, or created distance with "light clingers." My identities had to expand.

I didn't anticipate being a kink educator, a sexual empowerment coach, or a gender-transcendent magician… but these new identities grew from me living the truth of my sensations. They continue to serve my purpose to expand people's capacity to feel at home, ecstatic, and whole in their bodies so we can create social change from an emotionally resourced, imaginative, and awe-inspired way of being.

Me Too: A Call for Healing

In 2018, the #metoo movement, started by Tarana Burke in 2006, is shaping American culture in a big way. The media is featuring the voice of many women calling out men for sexual misconduct. Women are taking power by speaking their pain, by setting the record for the largest march in U.S. history, and by running for political office in unprecedented numbers. Debbie Walsh, director of the Center for American Women and Politics at Rutgers, has tallied 390 women[1] who say they will run for seats in the House of Representatives.

If we look at what is happening on the level of social identity we may reduce the #metoo movement to a fight between women and men, or between victims and perpetrators. But if we are open to attuning to our sensations rather than these identities we may discover something more liberating. The collective is ready for a healthier relationship to sex, gender, and power. If we invite a gender transcendence or a letting-go of the binary we can see that a lineage of trauma is coming into the light so we can acknowledge how pervasive it is and we can heal it in solidarity.

We want to be respected *and* we want to heal. Sometimes our pain makes us more invested in blaming than healing. Sometimes the media exaggerates this and tells the story in the language of victim and perpetrator and focuses on celebrity men as they

1   http://cawp.rutgers.edu/potential-candidate-summary-2018

get called out. **But when Tarana Burke started the #metoo movement the focus was not about disclosure but what happens after disclosure. The purpose was to decentralize perpetrators and decentralize white powerful men so we could put our attention on the people who experienced a violation. We are called to create something more inspired and sustainable than "victimhood wearing the cloak of social liberation,"** a phrase created by kink educator Om Rupani.

How do we expand our capacity to feel and heal the sensations that arise from injustice? These sensations may feel enormous because they connect not only to our personal pain, but also to the pain of our communities and of our ancestors. **The body wants to *heal*. The spirit wants to *heal*. The parts of us that are ready to feel and heal are not very interested in who might be to blame. The practice of attuning to our sensations rather than our identity could not be more vital than it is now. Our healing thrives when we can focus attention on our sensations. Our healing does not depend on what happens to the people who have been called out. As much as we may want them to "get it," or to be held accountable, our healing does not belong to their remorse or awareness. Our healing belongs to us.** No matter what the media focuses on we can prioritize putting attention on our healing process rather than being distracted by blaming or seeking revenge.

Our body is a sacred compost system for our sensations. We can use our breath, sound, movement, and compassionate attention to transform our sensations. The body can transform our pain, anger, and grief into resilience, creativity, connection, clarity, and commitment. **The body returns us to a truth, based in our sensations, that is more nuanced and dynamic than a social identity.**

Some of the clients I work with are healing from a past sexual trauma, often a violation that occurred with a family member or loved one. It's common for them to identify as a victim or survivor. This identity can make it difficult for the healing process even though they are not at fault for the event. The identity of victim can alter or limit the ability to perceive healing because it positions the healing as dependent on an acknowledgement, action, or apology from another person who committed the violation. I purposefully do not want to use the nouns "perpetrator" or "oppressor" because we cannot reduce someone's identity to an action they took in the same way that we do not want to reduce someone to a "victim." The nervous system simply wants to heal. It is not preoccupied with blame, or who is suffering more, or why this happened. **There is an innocence and simplicity to the body's appetite to heal and we can choose to partner with it.**

One of my clients has been on an incredible healing journey from a childhood sexual trauma and has generously volunteered to share some of their experience.

"For much of my life I had so many stories about what it meant about me if I felt big emotions. I was 'choosing victimhood,' 'being weak,' 'inadequate'. As a result of this shame story, I had a lot of trouble allowing emotions to move through me. I felt I had to hide them and avoid them. Working with Z, I've learned to partner with my body to experience an internal place beyond story. I have been able to experience and move through emotions that I had repressed for many years. I notice how becoming tuned in to the subtleties of sensations inside me allows them to shift. They evolve on their own. I simply create a container to be with what is here."

Healing Leads to Expansion

It's a mystical experience to be fully present. "Mystical" meaning it creates awe, possibility, healing, and connection. Gender is more than a conversation about pronouns and bathrooms. **Gender is an invitation to make beauty out of our dynamic self-alignment.**

People are not stagnant beings. Inclusion is permission to be whole, to be in the expansive experience of being human. Inclusivity cannot only be based on social identities such as equal access to the identity of being a woman. Inclusivity recognizes that we as human beings can access multiple identities.

The expansiveness available in our internal experience does not have a familiar narrative. The clearer we make it, to ourselves and to each other, that all of us are welcome, the more we will expand. **The compost system of the body is not only about healing.** It's about expansion. We are in the midst of expanding our identities – a vulnerable, courageous, and revolutionary act.

Gender happens to be at the forefront of this expression. Gender is deeply ingrained in us on erotic and visceral levels. Some of the most profound mystical experiences that I have had access to have been around the doorway of gender.

There's something very natural about living beyond the binary. I see such curiosity and creative self-expression when children are not limited to being a boy or a girl. Let's follow their lead and join the call to creativity for all of us.

It's vital for us to find people with whom we feel safe and respected when we are expressing our truths. **The company we keep impacts our feedback loop with our body. The more we are around people who give us permission to express**

ourselves with love, the easier it is to feel our truth. Some of us may be living in areas where we have to put more effort into finding people who can really see and affirm us. Fortunately, there are more online opportunities today for building our support systems.

As we move beyond the binary of gender, sexual orientation becomes irrelevant. What sex is, why we do it, the purpose of our genitals... these are now all up to us to create. It opens us to a much larger experience of intimacy that we can have with ourselves, with each other, and with other forms of life. **Coming back to sensation grounds us in the present, in the body, in the experience our nervous system is having not just the experience our mind is curating.** Often we may oscillate between our sensations and our thoughts.

Letting Go in the Physical Body

The physical embodiment of expansion involves shaking and trembling. If you have tight hamstrings and you are leaning forward over your legs, you may feel a quivering in the back of your thighs. It's your body asking, "Do I hold on? Do I let go? Do I hold on? Do I let go?" This is the sweet spot where your voluntary and involuntary nervous systems intersect. In this moment, your hamstrings surrender to length and suppleness in the presence of your deep breath and masterful attention to sensation.

Our eros is part of full embodiment and letting go. An orgasm is also a muscle spasm on the physical level. The pelvic floor muscles contract, release, contract, and release... until the voluntary rhythm of contraction and release gives way to the involuntary flutter that becomes orgasmic expansion. **This trembling and shaking is how transformation and expansion express themselves in our physical body. It's also what releases trauma from our nervous system.** When we do not feel and express our sensations, they become wound up in our system, waiting for us to release them.

What is Trauma?

Trauma is not the result of a specific event. Multiple people can experience the same event and some of them may feel trauma while others do not. **Trauma is when the nervous system goes into fight, flight, or freeze, and sensation can no longer be tracked, integrated, and responded to with clarity and ease.**

This distinction comes from Peter Levine, the founder of Somatic Experiencing. Releasing trauma in the body allows integration when the thoughts, feelings, sensations, and expression are in communication and sync.

My favorite part of how Levine relates to trauma is that our primal self is well-equipped to release trauma. Animals do it all the time by shaking. At its simplest physical level, if you are feeling overwhelmed, put on music you love, breathe deep, and shake. **The emotional and spiritual body will let go just like the physical body.**

Letting Go of an Identity

If you have had the opportunity to visit another culture or country, you may notice that when you come home, there is a reverse culture shock. You can suddenly see things with more perspective, things that you used to take for granted. Or after you lose a loved one and you remember how precious being alive is, there is a renewed sense of attention to the details of your life. Your attention zooms in to the brilliance of the blue sky, the sound of your mom's voice on the other end of the phone, the taste of the kale you eat most mornings, the gentleness of your breath after an orgasm… but there's a deeper awe and appreciation because it's no longer taken for granted. **You connected with something beyond the familiar that decentralizes your experience of "normal" and heightens your ability to feel.**

It's really helpful when doing yoga or dance to try a move on one side of your body several times and then to pause and notice the difference between the two sides. The asymmetry allows your attention to track more information because there is no "neutral." I've been teaching *Pelvis: Basin of Power and Surrender* for years. We always open half of the pelvis and then pause. I ask people to breathe, engage their pelvic floor, and move around. Everyone in the room notices a sensation that is different between the two sides, and sometimes it's a new sensation they've never had before! While they may not have language for what to call the new sensation, they notice that something has changed.

A physical letting go looks like contract, release, contract, release…. let go. An "identity spasm" in the emotional and spiritual body could look like "I'm a woman, Who am I? I'm a woman, Who am I?… Let me discover who I am without using 'woman' as my point of reference." This opens access to more possibility of sensation!

Receiving New Sensations

When I let go of being a woman I had a big download of new sensations, mannerisms… I had access to a new movement vocabulary. I started to have dreams where I was in multiple bodies with different gender expressions at the same time, and sometimes they interacted with each other. Where did this come from? I didn't realize how my identity as "woman" had blocked these other parts of. I don't feel any less of a woman now; I just know there are so many other parts of me that are now welcome because I've let go of that identity.

Deep laughter, grief, orgasm, and trembling in fear are all similar vibrations in our nervous system. They reorganize our sensations so we can have different thoughts, feelings, and consciousness. While we might consider these to be involuntary, they are states that we can invoke! Try laughing right now. It may start out forced but it's possible to find some real joy. We can start with the physical expression of laughter, grief, or orgasm, and the emotional experience often follows. It's a delicate balance of initiating the physical experience and being willing to fully feel it.

The Power of Sex and Grief

What if one reason sex is taboo in our culture is that it gives us a profound resilience, reboots our nervous system, and expands our capacity to know ourselves beyond a social identity? It gives us access to spirit, and to feeling the force of our life in a way that is more constant than any identity.

When my fiancé and I separated, I started grieving more than in any other time in my life. I grieved her presence in my life. I grieved the dream we shared of getting married and having a baby. I grieved the false hope that our partnership would somehow protect me from ever feeling isolated in a way that haunted my soul. During this time, I started to attend rituals with Sobonfu Somé of the Dagara Tribe in Burkina Faso. **I started to have a taste of what it feels like to be in a community courageous enough to not only name, but to feel and transform, the sensations that come with our personal and collective histories.**

One night I sat with Sobonfu and asked, "why is it the more I cry, the less I experience gender?" She looked at me with such grace and simply answered, "because grief dissolves your limitations and opens up possibility." Grief also opens our hearts and our sense of belonging. Sobonfu taught us that making the world a sustainable place is deeply connected to our ability to grieve together, because this is what creates sustainability for the human soul.

Resilience: Trusting Our Ability to Integrate Our Sensations

What if we could create a new way of relating to sensations as ways the universe tells us that we are alive? I was recently facilitating a tantric kink retreat that included a scene where a man about three times as big as me was flogging me with all of his life force. He guided me to stand in the middle of a room where there was no physical support to lean on. My body started to create a stance similar to tai chi; soft bends at my ankles and knees, my hands were open, elbows gently bent. My breath exhaled at the height of each thwack and a sound moved through me like a wave. After the retreat, I was checking in with one of the participants. She told me she was mesmerized watching this moment and could only conclude that I was connecting to something larger than my own physical body. She asked me how I was doing that. I said, "You're a doula yes? Why are you a doula?"

She answered that the most resilient she has felt was when she was giving birth. I smiled. "You know this state because you've felt it too. You help other women to find this state of resilience through your birthing work and that's why you recognize this state." I consider resilience a form of remembering that **we belong** simply because we exist and **we trust our ability to integrate any sensation moving through us.**

Casting a Spell for Us

My dream is for each of us to deepen our ability to track our own experiences and sensations with care by creating time each day to notice what we feel. For this care to become more important than the social identities that create "us" and "them." For us to cultivate an exquisite ability to voice our sensations and express them in safe and affirming company that demonstrates we belong simply because we exist and feel. For us to strengthen our ability to observe and reflect the responses of each others' nervous systems so we can better tune in to each others' experiences at the rawest level of sensation, which is deeper than stories, emotions, and identities. For our creative gender expression to give us permission to feel and move beyond the limitations of the woman/man binary. For us to lead with our soul-purpose and allow the complexities and transitions of identities that best serve this purpose. For us to know the felt sense of living in complete alignment with who we are meant to be and to take action consistently from this place. To have the courage to witness, voice the truth, and take authentic action each time we do not feel the sensation of alignment with our soul-purpose. For us to connect with our sensations as an opportunity to shift from the identity of victim to a dynamic state of healing. For us to experience our resilience as we gain trust in our ability to feel and integrate our sensations. Living in attunement with sensation rather than identity gives us the opportunity to accept ourselves, to express our truth, to heal, and to belong unconditionally.

Umsnúa: Ergi and inversion in Old Norse magical practice

by Abby Helasdottir

The Old Norse word *umsnúa* means to 'turn upside-down.' This concept can be found across a range of Icelandic magickal techniques that utilise what is arguably a particularly queer focus; a focus one that is indicative of the matrix of meanings associated with terms such as *ergi* and *trolldómr*. These techniques share ideas of passing between boundaries, of turning the world upside down, and of the breaking down of conventions.

The earth would turn before my eyes

The history of Icelandic settlement known as *Landnámabók* contains a story from the valley of Vatnsdalur in Northwest Iceland about a witch called *Ljót* and her encounter with Þorsteinn and Jökull, the sons of Ingimundr inn gamli. The two men were engaged in attacking Ljót's son Hrolleifr when she was seen leaving her house and walking in a peculiar and contorted manner: *"Þá var Ljót út komin ok gekk ǫfug; hon hafði hǫfuðit millum fóta sér, en klæðin á baki sér"* ('Ljót had come out and was walking backwards; she had her head between her legs, and her clothes over her back'). Jökull responded to Ljót's disconcerting attack by throwing Hrolleifr's decapitated head at her, causing her to lament that she was unfortunately too late, otherwise *"nú mundi um snúazt jǫrðin fyrir sjónum mínum, en þér munduð allir ærzt hafa"* ('now the earth would turn before my eyes, and you would all have gone mad').

The same account is retold in more detail in the late thirteenth century *Vatnsdæla* saga, which provides more information about Ljót's appearance: *"hon hafði rekit fǫtin fram yfir hǫfuð sér ok fór ǫfug ok rétti hǫfuðit aptr milli fótanna; ófagrligt var hennar augnabragð, hversu hon gat þeim trollsliga skotit"* ('she had thrown her clothes forward over her head, and was walking backwards and had stuck her head back between her legs; she had an ugly expression in her eyes with which she seemed to be shooting magical glances at them.')

There is something fundamentally queer in Ljót's actions, with all its attendant anatomical transmogrification and use of backwards and inverted imagery. The events of the sequence and the description of Ljót's contorted form find an almost perfect fit with Carolyn Dinshaw's classic definition of queerness as a disruptive, consciousness-altering paradigm.

"Queerness works by contiguity and displacement, knocking signifiers loose, ungrounding bodies, making them strange; it works in this way to provoke perceptual shifts and subsequent corporeal response in those touched… It makes people stop and look at what they have been taking as natural, and it provokes inquiry into the ways that "natural" has been produced by particular discursive matrices of heteronormativity."[1]

Within Dinshaw's definition is an uncanny description of the mutable body displayed by Ljót. Her distortion of form disconnects her from conventional bodies, and, to use Dinshaw's term, this *ungrounding* of her body creates a metamorphosis of uncertainty that is extended to the very ground itself. From the uncertainty created by her actions comes the potential for the landscape to itself enter a similar state of inversion and flux. In the case of Ljót, the perceptual shift is her own. Her act of queerness facilitates a change of consciousness, and when her queer eye perceives the world inverted, with it comes the danger of this vision moving beyond the individual and affecting everyone around her. It is counteracted in the narrative by another act of perception, with the male gaze of her enemies overriding her act of queerness by seeing her before she sees them.

This sense of otherness is compounded in the *Vatnsdæla saga* version of the sequence in which the inversion of reality is associated with transformation into animals: *Hún kvaðst hafa ætlat at snúa þar um landslagi öllu - "en þér ærðizk allir ok yrðið at gjalti eftir á vegum úti með villidýrum, ok svá myndi ok gengit hafa, ef þér hefðið mik eigi fyrr sét en ek yðr."* ('She said that she had intended to overturn all of the landscape —"and you would have all gone mad and turned into wild boar out on the tracks with the wild animals; that is what would have happened if you hadn't seen me before I saw you."')

Here Ljót's actions are shown to have further associations with the alterior. The overturning of the landscape not only ungrounds the causal world but transforms its unwilling inhabitants into creatures of Utgarðr, the outland, of the wild and the

---

1   Dinshaw 1995, p. 76-77

wilderness. The inverting of the land is, thus, associated with the danger of loss of control, with the image of wild animals suggesting both a return to a primal mindlessness and the risk of animalistic lust unfettered.

The same magickal procedure occurs in a similar account from the fourteenth-century *Þorskfirðinga saga*, where another powerful old woman appears, here simply named Kerling ('old woman'). In a similar attack on a house, the saga describes how Kerling went *"um völlinn at húsbaki ok hafði klæðin á baki sér uppi, en niðri höfuðit, ok sá svá skýin á milli fóta sér"* ('around the grassland at the back of the house and had her clothes up on her back, and her head down, so that she could see the sky between her legs'). While there is no mention here of Kerling's gaze inverting the landscape, there is a sense of this act of maleficia breaking conventional order because it is understood that her performance is preventing the attacker's weapons from biting their opponents. The order of things is only restored, and the weapons bite again, when Kerling's act is interrupted by another woman, Þuríðr drikkin, who attacks her in her vulnerable state, ripping flesh from the nape of her neck.

Andsælis: twirling backwards

The Icelandic sagas document another magickal technique that, although not as evocative in imagery as that of the inverted Ljót and Kerling, still contains the themes of liminality, reversal, and an undoing of the world. Categorised by Gunnell as the 'goatskin twirl,' the rite involves waving a skin towards the wilderness or a mountain to affect geological or atmospheric change.[2] While the material that is twirled is not always the same—being in some instances a hat, shawl, or other item of clothing—what is consistent are themes of alterity, with the procedure usually emphasising a stepping out of the house, and thereby into the wild. This is emphasised still further by the practitioner facing mountains or the wilderness as they invoke its outland forces.

Vatnsdæla saga describes one example in which a woman called Gró, who was being forced to leave the area, was seen by a shepherd as *"hon gekk út ok gekk andsælis um hús sín ok mælti"* ('she walked out and went widdershins around the house'). Looking up at the mountain, she waved a goatskin or cloth within which she had knotted some gold, said "May things go as they have been prepared," and then returned inside and closed the door. As a result of her actions, a rockslide came down on the farm, killing her and everybody inside the stead, and the site was subsequently abandoned.

---

2   Gunnell, 2012, p. 136

In a second example from *Vatnsdæla saga*, the procedure does not have a negative intent or effect and instead calms a storm. Conversely, it causes bad weather in *Víglunda saga* and *Reykdæla saga*, and brings fog or darkness during the day in *Njáls saga*, *Reykdæla saga,* and *Harðar saga*. In all of these examples, though, there is a suggestion of ultimately disrupting nature, of turning the world upside down for good or for ill.

This is exemplified in some of the rituals which emphasise the idea of going against the flow. In both of the examples from *Vatnsdæla saga*, for example, there is an association with walking *andsælis* (widdershins), literally meaning 'against the sun.' Similarly, in *Víglunda saga*, the material is twirled towards the east, implying once again an adversarial movement against the sun, or alternatively, towards the world of the giants and the trollwives of the Ironwood.

The Body as Landscape

The transformed bodies of Ljót and Kerling are mirrored in the landscape which they seek to overturn, creating that intersection so beloved by queer theory of the corporeal and the ecological. As Judith Butler notes: *"Bodily contours and morphology are not merely implicated in an irreducible tension between the psychic and the material but are that tension."*[3]

The association of Ljót with the landscape is an ironic inversion of a common practice in skaldic poetry from medieval Iceland and Norway in which land is kenned or glossed as a woman, and vice versa. The most frequent use of this trope occurs in a conventional form of woman-kenning in which a woman's appearance or work is associated with the land. For example, a woman could be kenned as *línvangr* ('linen-field'), as *fold mens* ('earth of the necklace') or as *grund hringa* ('ground of rings').

A significant contribution to this practice was the identification of women with Jörð, the giantess and mother of Þor, who was seen in Norse mythology as the personification of the land. Óðinn's relationship with Jörð is suggestive of what Emily Osborne refers to as a 'cosmic colonisation.' This conquering of land and claiming of ownership is mirrored in *Hákonardrápa*, where the skald Hallfreðr vandræðaskáld Óttarsson draws an analogy between Hákon Sigurðarson's conquest of Norway and the somewhat coercive tryst between Óðinn and Jörð.[4]

In the case of Ljót and her sisters in witchcraft, this association with the land is already subverted by their pre-existing untethered status. Ljót, with her single

3   Butler, 2011, p. 36
4   Osborne, 2015, p. 28

name devoid of patronyms, represents the land breaking away from the controls of sovereignty and patriarchy even before she steps outside her house. This is true of other Icelandic female spirit workers, such as the goatskin-twirling Gró, who are predominantly mentioned without patronyms, appearing as autonomous, almost autochthonic, beings with no allegiance to a male forebear, or often any forebear for that matter. This autonomy is compounded in Ljót who, despite having a son, is not placed in relation to the child's father, of whom there is little mention. Indeed, in *Vatnsdæla saga*, most references to Hrolleifr's spear side of the family occur as a way to distinguish him from it. His uncle Saemund, for example, makes a point of telling Hrolleifr that he is more like his mother than his other kinsmen.

There is a mythic dimension to Ljót's actions, with Terry Gunnell noting that her ritual can be seen as an attempt to break down the barriers between the conventional world above and the upside-down world of Hel below. This is a place that he describes as "a world of rock and darkness which is ruled by a woman and where women (the valkyrjur) are the ones who wear armour, ride on horses, and make the decisions."[5] In her attempt to make Hel on earth, Ljót is seeking to undermine not just the physical landscape, but all the accepted morals and norms of heteronormative society. This association with Hela is compounded in Ljót's troll-like son, with *Vatnsdæla saga* having Ingimundr warn Þorsteinn that Hrolleifr is no ordinary man, but rather a Heljarmann ('man of Hel'). It is almost as if Ljót's trafficking with Hela has gifted her a son, one endowed with malevolence and *heljar-afl* ('strength of Hel').

It is easy to see in this confluence of wild animals, turbulent landscapes, and the ungrounding of bodies, additional mythic resonances evocative of another of Loki and Angrboda's monstrous and gender ambiguous children, the World Serpent. Ljót's inversion of the landscape recalls the cataclysmic transformation of the land that occurs at the conclusion of Ragnarök when the World Serpent rises and, as the völva who narrates *Völuspá* describes it, stars fall from the sky and *"sigr fold imar"* ('earth sinks in the sea.') This description has a poetic precedent in *Hymiskviða*, where Þórr attempts to fish up the World Serpent, causing an undoing of the land: *"Hreingálkn hrutu, en hölkn putu, fór in forna fold öll saman. Søkðiz síðan sá fiskr í mar."* ('Giant monsters staggered, steep crags reverberated, the ancient earth was all ashudder - until that fish sank back into the sea.') In this way, Ragnarök can be seen as a queer act, as a version of Ljót's simple world-altering performance wrought large on a cosmic scale.

---

5   Gunnell, 2012, p. 147

As Gunnell notes, the undoing of land during Ragnarök or in Ljót performance has parallels elsewhere in other acts of destructive magick, such as the *Buslubœn* ('The Curse of Busla'), from the fourteenth century legendary saga *Bósa saga ok Herrauðs*. In this spell, spoken by Busla, the fostra of the titular hero Bósi, landspirits are instructed to lose their way, and this is effected by the world going mad and the land being disrupted: *"verði óðæmi, hristist hamrar, heimr sturlist, versni veðrátta; verði óðæmi"* ('may terrible things take place, the cliffs shake, the world go mad, the weather worsen; may terrible things take place').[6]

Ergi and Trollskapr

The themes of alterity in the story of Ljót make it suggestive of that other Old Norse term for the aberrant or the Other, *ergi*. The word remains problematic in Old Norse studies, providing no clear meaning but carrying various associations with outlaws, homosexuality, effeminacy and lust. Ármann Jakobsson provides perhaps the simplest interpretation by consistently translating *ergi* as 'queer' throughout his work, finding within the word a breadth of meaning and evolving interpretations comparable to the equally diverse *ergi*.[7]

While Ljót's acts are not explicitly referred to as *ergi*, the accounts use the somewhat analogous word troll, which has many of the same associations with encountering the border, and of going beyond the everyday into the areas of otherness that sit outside the realms of societal convention. When Ljót looks at Þorsteinn and Jökull, her queer gaze is said to be *trollsliga skotit* ('cast trollishly') while her sorcery is referred to as *trolldómr*. Even her contorted form inevitably makes one think of the mythic and metamorphotic bodies of trolls.

As a word used predominantly to refer to female beings in the mythic period, *troll* carries with it an inherent sense of the Other. To act in a trollish manner was to connect with the alterior world of the supernatural trolls, and, in so doing, such a person could pass beyond being human and become a troll themselves. In the case of Ljót, she enters this world by leaving the Midgard of her home and stepping out into the wild. This is compounded by walking backwards, thereby entering the alterior via the posterior; just as Kerling in *Þorskfirðinga saga* is seen going around the back of her house. As Jakobsson notes in association with Ljót's trollish behaviour, "there seems thus to be an undeniable link between a troll and the rear end or the 'queer' end."[8]

---

6 Gunnell, 2012, p. 146
7 Jakobsson, 2013, p. 209
8 Jakobsson, 2013, p. 103

This intersection of *ergi* and *troll* is found in contiguous uses of the terms in *Gísla saga Súrssonar*, which gives an account of a male witch called Þorgrímr nef. The saga tells how Þorgrímr nef had been hired to perform a maleficent act against the saga's eponymous hero. This *maleficia* is referred to as *trollskapr* and while the exact details of the rite are never explained, it is stated that he "performed this magic in the most *ergi* and devilish manner."

In his summary to a thorough investigation of the various meanings of trolls and *trollskapr*, Jakobsson argues that *troll* does not simply refer to a particular race or species, or for that matter to a human witch or sorcerer. Instead, it relates to a fluid state of being that can be entered into, unrestricted by human limitations. It is this interpretation which enables Jakobsson to align *troll* with *ergi*, with both words being essentially cosmological, creating subversive zones or states that *"both encapsulate that essential quality of magic as turning the world on its head. In magic, everything is upside down or inside out, and that can be described as ergi or trollskapr."*[9]

The Backwards Way

Ljót's consciousness-altering ritual, with its inversion and undoing of norms, aligns it with what Kenneth Grant described as the Backwards Way, or the Way of Resurgent Atavisms. This path he associated with all manner of symbols redolent of witchcraft including the Sabbath, the numbers seven and thirteen, the moon, various animals, the widdershins and back-to-back dance, the anal kiss, and the witch mounted on the besom handle.[10]

The correlation between the witches of the Icelandic settlements and the witches of sixteenth-century Europe are particularly noteworthy in relation to these themes of inversion. Gunnel notes that Ljót's posture has a parallel in the depiction of a naked witch looking back between her legs in one of the works by the German artist, Hans Baldung Grien.[11] The *Three Witches* of 1514 is a mass of entangled limbs, with the lowest witch looking through her legs, effectively directing her trollish gaze at the viewer. Her two companions stand above her, legs and arms spread in various directions, with all three bodies seeming to merge into a single Ljót-like agglomeration.

Charles Zika argues that the sixteenth-century depictions of witches in the works of Baldung Grien and Albrecht Dürer defined their power through references to

9   Jakobsson, 2013, p. 118-119
10   Grant, 2013, p. 203
11   Gunnell, 2012, p. 143

sexual and gender inversion. When witches were depicted riding backwards, as in Dürer's engraving Witch Riding Backwards on a Goat, it conveyed an idea of people who had *"threatened the sexual balance and order of the community, had confused roles, had failed to maintain the gender identity and honour necessary for moral order."*[12]

As with their distant sisters Ljót and Kerling, these continental witches were effectively undoing society and turning the landscape on its head with their queer actions and their queer bodies. In this way, possessing a queer body becomes in itself an act of magick. There need not be a ritual procedure to follow or an incantation to utter, rather, simply existing provides a way to enact Dinshaw's queer promise of knocking signifiers loose, ungrounding bodies, and provoking perceptual shifts.

References

- Butler, Judith. *Bodies that Matter: On the discursive limits of sex*. New York: Taylor & Francis, 2011

- Dinshaw, Carolyn. "Chaucer's Queer Touches/A Queer Touches Chaucer." *Exemplaria*, 1995

- Grant, Kenneth. *Cults of the Shadow*. London: Starfire Publishing Ltd., 2013

- Gunnell, Terry. "'Magical Mooning" and the "Goatskin Twirl": "Other" Kinds of Female Magical Practices in Early Iceland.' *Nordic Mythologies: Interpretations, Intersections and Institutions*. UCLA Centre for Medieval Studies, UCLA Los Angeles, 27-28 April, 2012

- Jakobsson, Ármann. *Nine Saga Studies: The Critical Interpretation of the Icelandic Sagas*. Reykjavík: University of Iceland Press, 2013

- Osborne, Emily. 'Grund gulls [ground of gold]: The Trope of Woman as "Land" in Skaldic *Poetry from the Tenth to Fourteenth Centuries' Scandinavian-Canadian Studies*. Volume 22, 2015

- Zika, Charles. *The Appearance of Witchcraft: Print and Visual Culture in Sixteenth-Century Europe*. New York: Routledge, 2007

---

12   Zika, 2007, p. 28

I grew up in North Mexico and became an adult in South Texas.

Religion was inescapable, as was its rejection of who I was.

It was the era of The Minutemen militias, of "One Man, One Woman" laws, and of Bush the Second.

La biblia es la verdad- léela

I drew pleasure from the cities I lived in. Street lamps sparkling in the inky night, like stars encrusted in the earth.

I craved a religion that rejoiced in my weird, queer parts, that embraced my heritage rather than colonize and sanitize it.

(That made me feel half as wonderful as I did when I looked down at the city glowing in the dark.)

I read some intro books.

A lot of them presented cities as a place to endure rather than enjoy, awful and unnatural.

MAGICK 101

(The opposite of how I felt about them, basically.)

In the end, I opted to construct my own religion.

(One with less heteronormativity, too.)

Psh.

MAGICK 101

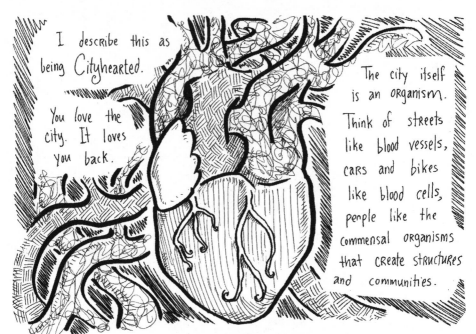

The Passion of Agdistis:
The Gender Transgression, Sexual Trauma, Time Travel, and Ritualized Madness in Greco-Anatolian Revival Cultusess

by Alder Knight and Rocket

Dea, Magna Dea, Cybebe, Dea Domina Dindymi,
Demitte me tuo furor parvu, obsecro, ut furor magnum pertransit me.

Goddess, Great Goddess, Cybele, Lady Goddess of the Mountains,
Visit your small madness upon me, I pray, that the great madness may pass me by.[1]

It began, as so many myths do, with rape.

Cybele, mother of the gods, was slumbering atop Mount Dindymon[2] when Zeus came upon her. Cybele woke to the unwelcome amorous advances of her own son, fighting him off as he persisted in forcing himself on her. In the end, two things happened: one, Zeus stumbled away and, with his own hand, spilled his semen onto the rocks; and two, the goddess Cybele, greater than the mountains and more powerful than volcanoes, felt a little piece of herself fracture off from the force of this too-common trauma.

The consequence of both actions was Agdistis.

"In the tenth month, Acdestis [sic] is born, so called from [their][3] mother's name. In [them] there was insuperable strength and uncontrollable ferocity of disposition, a lust mad and furious and arising from both sexes. Violently [they] plundered, laid waste,

---

1   Prayer by Rocket, adapted from Catullus 63, 91-93
2   Mount Dindymon is now called Mount Murat, situated in the Gezi region of Turkey.
3   Authors and translations vary on what pronouns are appropriate to use when discussing Agdistis. A few sources describe Agdistis as a goddess or an early form of Cybele, and, accordingly, use "she" exclusively, or "he" before the transformation and "she" after it. The most common sources, including most direct translations of Arnobius, refer to the daemon as "he," while others use more dehumanizing pronouns like "he/she" or "it." In this piece, for the sake of consistency and respect, the singular "they" will be used throughout.

wherever [their] monstrous spirit led [them]. [They] cared not for the gods nor men, nor did [they] think anything more powerful than [themself]; [they] despised earth, heaven, and the stars."[4]

The story of Agdistis survives primarily in Arnobius' *Adversus Gentes*, but their name can frequently be found at the center of a complex web of syncretism, polytheistic colonialism, and multivalence. They are always, in one way or another, associated with Cybele. The Great Mother goddess Cybele was incorporated and syncretized into the Greek and Roman pantheons as her Anatolian cult spread from Phrygia (in what is now Turkey) through Greek colonization around the 6th century BCE. By the accounts of Hesychius, Strabo, and Pliny the Elder, Agdistis is either simply an epithet of Cybele, or else they were transformed into Cybele through their later ordeal at the hands of Dionysos. Both Pausanias and Arnobius, however, identify Agdistis as a discrete entity: a mad, lustful, and nonbinary-gendered daemon born of Zeus' accidental fertilization of the earth itself.

The furious lust described consistently by all sources that address the story of Agdistis also rendered them dangerous. Mortals who came into contact with their body or bodily fluids invariably went mad themselves and frequently died; a vector for sexually-transmitted and bloodborne madness, they rampaged across the land, leaving a trail of corpses and broken minds in their wake.

The correlation between Agdistis' gender and the trauma that conceived them, as recounted by Arnobius, parallels harmful modern narratives pertaining to transgender identity and trauma. While it is possible that Arnobius intended to imply that Agdistis' transness is a direct result of the violence from which they sprang, a critical reader can resist this reductive narrative. While gender nonconformity can and does attract violence, and many trans people are indeed traumatized - a phenomenon with which the latter portion of this essay will grapple - it is inappropriate and inaccurate to state that gender variance is necessarily a result of trauma. This theory of causality has its basis in transphobic assumptions, rather than in research, which assumptions may have influenced period writers and secondary sources. A more nuanced understanding of the complex interrelation between gender identity and gender-based violence will inform this paper's treatment of Agdistis.

Much of this work will address the relationship between Agdistis and Cybele, and specifically the hypothesis that the trauma of Zeus' sexual violence against Cybele caused her to dissociate a part of her divine self, which became embedded in the stone

4   Arnobius of Sicca. "The Case Against the Pagans, Book 5." *The Ancient Mysteries: A Sourcebook of Sacred Texts.* Ed. Marvin W. Meyer. (1987). Philadelphia, PA: University of Pennsylvania Press.

of Mount Dindymon and grew into Agdistis. That examination, however, hinges on an understanding of the dramatic, lustful, and violent relationship between Agdistis and Dionysos. Like their creation, Agdistis' ordeal is addressed briefly and ambiguously in most recorded versions of the myths: that the Olympians were threatened or disgusted by their gender, their lust, and their power, and that to contain or punish them, some agent or agents of Olympus castrated them, possibly killing them.

While most accounts briefly describe the maiming of Agdistis as a collective decision and action by "the gods" without naming any individual actor, Arnobius attributes the act to Dionysos at the behest of the pantheon, the rest of whom he describes as reluctant to approach Agdistis at all. Dionysos' own account clarifies that his desire to be accepted on Olympus motivated him to carry out their orders.

"I was very young. They told me conditions — I was hazed to be accepted as a god. I was not alabaster like most of the gods. They reflect, but I change to my own taste. They are more purely idea and less material, and so they are shaped by perception. I was dark and small and foreign-looking and curly-haired and young in a way they don't have to be young. Aphrodite was born a grown woman. I got to Olympus and I was not welcome. I was given conditions and I tried. What happened changed a lot of the ways that I behaved. I had not yet known madness.

"Madness is liberation from the expectations of sanity."[5]

Lynn E. Roller draws parallels between the pantheon's motivation and the story in Plato's Symposium (more recently entered into popular culture by way of the song "Origin of Love" from the musical Hedwig and the Angry Inch). Specifically, Roller points out that the gods are threatened by the immense power and resistance to control exercised by entities which embody both masculinity and femininity. They seek in many stories to mutilate those entities, thereby rendering them only male or only female, and stripping them of that unique power.[6] Indeed, in Raven Kaldera's retelling of the myth of Agdistis, agents of Olympus approach them and offer them a choice between manhood and womanhood, which they defiantly reject.

"So they went to Agdistis and spoke to hir. 'Agdistis,' they said, 'you must choose what you will be. If you choose to be female, we will cut off your male parts. If you choose to be male, we will sew up your female parts. Choose, Agdistis.'

And Agdistis said, 'Fuck you.' And split."[7]

5   Dionysos. (2016, Nov 11). Channeling through Alder Knight as transcribed by Rocket.
6   Roller, Lynn E. (1999). *In Search of God the Mother*. Oakland, CA: University of California Press.
7   Kaldera, Raven. (2008). *Hermaphrodeities: The Transgender Spirituality Workbook*. Hubbardston, MA: Asphodel Press.

Kaldera's depiction is supplemented by channeling and psychography:

> *"Everyone was hungry for them — that's what scared Olympus. They saw Agdistis and all they felt was mad, uncontrollable hunger. Imagine how that made Apollo feel. Imagine how that made Hera and Athena feel. It couldn't be their fault and so it had to be the daemon's fault, and the daemon refused to be diminished."*[8]

Arnobius describes Dionysos' act in yearning and lurid detail, lingering on the tenderness with which Dionysos touched the body of the sleeping Agdistis. "I should like, however, to see — were it granted me to be born at those times — [Dionysos], who overcame the fierceness of Agdistis," he writes, "...who carefully introduced his hands, handled the members of the sleeper, and directed his care skillfully to the parts which were to perish, so that the hold of the nooses placed round might surround them all."[9]

Divination and gnosis supplement this story and bring into greater focus the tenderness and eroticism wrapped into this brutal act. As Dionysos recounts the story to a scribe:

> *"They looked ferocious, breathtaking, as they slept. I wanted to run my hands and mouth over every inch of them. I wanted to touch their sex. I wrapped string around it tightly. They fidgeted and moaned. The blood pooled. Their knee was bent. They were curled up. I remember the soft hair of their shin, their stomach. I wrapped the string around the arch of their foot, their toes. I bit my lip. Their toes turned purple. I hadn't slept in two days. A creature startled them. They woke suddenly. It tore them to pieces. They howled. It was not a quick death. I came to them. I tried to fix what I had done but I could not fix it. I remember being covered in their blood as they howled like a wounded dog. They looked me in the eye, the most beautiful thing that had ever existed, and they died. I destroyed them."*[10]

Through his own words, Dionysos' role is clarified as the infatuated and reluctant agent of the pantheon's trans panic. He describes what he refers to as the death of Agdistis, but we might refer to that moment as their traumatic splintering, through which he finds himself infected by his own actions with their uncontrollable blood-borne madness. This madness catapults him into a journey that ends with his own initiation into the cult of Cybele, atonement through self-castration, service as one of Cybele's transgender priestesses, the Gallae, and his aspect as Thelumorphos, or "Womanly One."

8   Dionysos. (2016, Nov 11). Channeling through Alder Knight as transcribed by Rocket.
9   Arnobius, *supra*.
10   Dionysos. (2016, Nov 11). Channeling through Alder Knight as transcribed by Rocket.

This insight also extends to the ongoing relationship between Dionysos and Agdistis: the trauma and madness, and the dance of fury, pain, desire, and sex that has bound them together through the centuries.

> *"When you taste him, you taste me as well. My madness is in his. When you drink of him, you drink of me."*[11]

From the moment when Agdistis' blood came into contact with Dionysos, the two entities – young, lost, thrice-born, half-human half-god and uncontrollable, terrifying, murdered daemon – were inextricably connected. The myth doesn't have a tidy end; the Olympians are appeased, but Dionysos and Agdistis are each destroyed in their own way, finding themselves with unfinished business.

> *"I had to undergo the same ordeal as Agdistis. The Mother brought me in and handed me a sharp stone [for ritual self-castration]. I did not use the stone. I used a string. I joined her rites and wandered with her across lands I'd never seen. I remembered who I was and what I'd done. You danced with the Mother, shrieked with the Mother, bled with the Mother, and the Mother helped you heal. I recovered myself eventually. I returned. Then I was grown. Until then I was just a little boygirl in a dress, fucking with things I didn't understand, killing something beautiful just because it was there."*[12]

It is impossible to discuss queer spiritualities without discussing trauma, and it is impossible to discuss trauma without discussing time travel, explicitly or otherwise. Both of these overlaps have been the subject of academic focus which will not be fully recreated here. However, a brief sketch of the landscape of the interplay between divinity and ancestor work, trauma theory, and time travel is a necessary step before bringing the lens of that interplay to bear on the story of Cybele, Agdistis, and Dionysos.

A marginalized body is a traumatized body, to begin with. The protracted experience of moving through the world in a body that is the constant object of spiritual and psychological violence, derision, and destruction has an unmistakably traumatic effect, even absent discrete and identifiable traumatic interactions.

The experience of trauma as a body-based, rather than purely psychological, phenomenon is one of the bases of the interdisciplinary field of somatics. A touchstone of somatics is the epigraph, "Memory lives in the muscle."[13] A traumatic incident, in the somatic framework, can be described as one which fractures the self,

---

11   Agdistis. (2016, Dec 5). Channeling through Rocket as transcribed by Alder Knight.
12   Dionysos. (2016, Nov 11). Channeling through Alder Knight as transcribed by Rocket.
13   Strozzi-Heckler, Richard (1993). *The Anatomy of Change: A Way to Move Through Life's Transitions.* Berkeley, CA: North Atlantic Books.

segmenting or quarantining a shard of the self, which then resides in the body, trapped in an endless loop of continually experiencing and re-experiencing the trauma. For every traumatic event undergone by an individual, a part of that individual remains stuck in time, and in moments where that part is touched (read: "triggered"), it floods the individual's experience, overwhelming them with somatic memory.

To be a traumatized person, then, is necessarily to experience time non-linearly - to contain suspended pockets of time inside one's body between which one moves involuntarily. To be triggered is to be punted from a linear ("present") experience of time into a stalled ("past") one, a state that lies dormant in the matter of the living body until activated. A trauma trigger is thus a form of time-travel.

The mechanism of the human body, further, possesses an extraordinary capacity to metabolize and heal traumatic experiences. There are a variety of tools used to effectively process trauma, two of which are of particular note here. One is connecting and being present with others to process memories while simultaneously being conscious of current experiences and sensations. The second is creating circumstances in which the body can have new experiences that fundamentally contradict and heal the helplessness, rage, and collapse that result from trauma.[14] This provides enough space and safety to be able to reintegrate that shard into the rest of the self, healing the break that occurred at the moment of trauma. The effect of these tools is to extract these traumatized shards of self from their time loops. Such extraction and reintegration, as well as the processing of memories, effectively transform the time-travel of the trigger from an involuntary experience into a voluntary one.

In this somatic framework, a living human body is a necessary tool to process, transmute, and heal trauma. Processing stalled traumatic memories requires orienting oneself intentionally in the flow of time using the sensory capacities of a living human body. Non-corporeal entities such as deities, ancestors, and other spirits that have unprocessed trauma are unable to somatically metabolize it themselves, and therefore need to connect with the living to do so. This can be part of the mutuality that characterizes relationships between spirits and the living and renders that relationship equitable rather than coercive.

In some forms of work with spirits, including ancestor work, devotion can take the form of offering up a living body to process the stalled trauma of the ancestor or other spirit at hand. The devotee works to extract the spirit's traumatized shards

14   Van der Kolk, Bessel, M.D. (2015). *The Body Keeps the Score: Brain, Mind, and Body in the Healing of Trauma*. London, UK: Penguin Books.

from their time loops, allow them to express their pain and have it heard and held, and give them space to experience safety through the senses of a living body. Tools for processing trauma can be offered through the living body as devotion to and care for a traumatized spirit or ancestor.

"Pray for the dead, and fight like hell for the living."[15]

Death does not eliminate trauma; it stays with the spirit. Furthermore, the experience of death itself can compound the trauma carried by the deceased if they reach death unprepared for it, whether by lack of understanding or by sudden violence.

The violence inflicted upon Agdistis by the Olympians reverberates into the present day: as in the myths, modern individuals who transgress hegemonic rules of gender are often punished. Today, transgender and gender nonconforming (TGNC) people, trans women of color in particular, are subject to brutal early deaths at rates far exceeding the general population.[16][17] Without belaboring those facts, which are of significant enough importance that delving into them shallowly here would only do them a disservice, traumatic deaths bring about traumatized spirits.

All ancestors are people who have died, but not everyone who dies becomes an ancestor. There are various reasons that a spirit might not become an ancestor, including unresolved trauma at the time of death. Such individuals can become enmired in spiritual miasma and unable to move on, and are known as restless or troubled dead. In the case of those who have been violently killed, restlessness after death is overwhelmingly common. As such, the TGNC dead are disproportionately troubled, forgotten, unattended, and unable to move on, compounding suffering in life into suffering thereafter. These restless transgender dead can be brought to peace through the living bodies of members of their line.

While most traditional forms of ancestor work address the veneration of the practitioner's blood ancestors, i.e. those with whom the practitioner shares genetic material, the techniques of ancestor work can also be offered to lines of ancestors of the practitioner's spirit. The line of TGNC ancestors carries the reverberation of ancestral trauma, and can be venerated, elevated, and transformed into a source of support for the living descendants of the line in the same manner and using

---

15   Mary Harris "Mother" Jones

16   National Coalition of Anti-Violence Programs (NCAVP). (2016). Lesbian, Gay, Bisexual, Transgender, Queer, and HIV-Affected Hate Violence in 2015. New York, NY: Authors: Emily Waters, Chai Jindasurat, Cecilia Wolfe.

17   Schmider, Alex. (2017, Apr 24 updated). Doubly Victimized: Reporting on Transgender Victims of Crime [Web log post]. Retrieved from http://www.glaad.org/blog/glaad-calls-increased-and-accurate-media-coverage-transgender-murders

the same tools as a line of biological ancestors. Veneration of the line of TGNC ancestors can involve the offerings of ordeal, emotional release, and trauma processing, as well as fighting like hell for the living.

Not only are these offerings works of compassion, but further, they are works of self-preservation for living transgender people. Trauma further up the ancestral line has repercussions all the way down it. Scientific research bears out the concepts of trauma genes, PTSD in the living descendants of enslaved people, and other forms of intergenerational collective grief.[18] [19] This is especially true of blood relations, but the pain of those who are ancestors of spirit also reverberates through their living successors. These forms of trauma reside in the bodies of the living and persist until neutralized, ideally at the source.

Agdistis' refusal to compromise their truth, and their subsequent encounter with the violent enforcement of gender norms, rings true to many experiences of gender nonconformity from antiquity to present day. Whether experienced consensually, through elective gender affirming surgeries, or through deliberate violence, the act of being "de-sexed" is common to TGNC experience and, in all cases, invasive and potentially traumatizing.

In considering the work of honoring the lineage of TGNC dead and ancestors, Agdistis stands out as a member of that lineage. Neither fully human nor fully divine, they inhabit the liminal space of daemons, demigods, and heroes, and seek such honor and veneration from the descendants of their TGNC line.

Part of this honor and veneration is in the form of *katharsis*, a category of ritual which uses ordeal to cleanse or expel an emotion or experience that is toxic or harmful. *Katharsis* plays a significant role in the mystery cult practices of both Cybele and Dionysos, as well as in the manifestations of ritual and gnostic practices incorporated into the work contemplated herein. When used in conjunction with other tools, it can function to address and heal both individual and ancestral trauma.

What Agdistis endures at the hands of the entire pantheon, and Dionysos in particular, is a trauma which continues to bear repercussions through the line of TGNC descendants alive today. As in the case of the ancestral trauma that plagues genetic lineages, everyone down the line suffers for the original act of violence. To tend that original wound is to care for Agdistis as a troubled and traumatized

18   Thomson, Helen. (2015, Aug 21). Study of Holocaust survivors finds trauma passed on to children's genes. Retrieved from https://www.theguardian.com/science/2015/aug/21/study-of-holocaust-survivors-finds-trauma-passed-on-to-childrens-genes
19   DeGruy, Leary, PhD. (2005). *Post Traumatic Slave Syndrome: America's Legacy of Enduring Injury and Healing*. Portland, OR: Uptone Press.

predecessor. Their *katharsis* can integrate them into the host of ancestors and supportive spirits for the living and dead members of their line, and can help to spread healing and peace throughout those pasts, presents, and futures.

The first step in working with the trauma of Agdistis, however, is to begin with the trauma of Cybele. Long before being subject to their own gender-based attack, Agdistis had that violence as a core component of their being, having been created from an act of violence against the Mother of the Gods.

Contextualizing the experiences and the relationship of Cybele and Agdistis in modern trauma scholarship requires an examination of the story of Zeus' rape of Cybele, which can also be found in the work of Arnobius. According to Arnobius' recounting, Zeus, overcome with lust which Arnobius described as "detestable," "wicked," "shameful," and "execrable," approached and touched Cybele as she slept on Mount Dindymon. When she awoke and resisted him, he responded violently, but because of her resistance, "having striven for a very long time while she is unwilling," he found himself unable to attain climax. Instead, he left her and did so alone, ultimately ejaculating onto the stone of Mount Dindymon, which was also called Agdus. The stone "drank up [the] foul incontinence...in the very heart of the rock, a child was formed."[20]

Sexual interactions involving deities are always complicated to assess by human standards. Arnobius points out that taboos against incest are a human business, while incest among the gods is no less natural than the rain impregnating the soil. Nevertheless, it is clear that this interaction was unambiguously sexual violence and was certainly traumatizing.

Obviously any assertions about the effects of trauma on a goddess are primarily conjecture. Lacking a human body to somatically process or transmute the trauma of the rape, it can be extrapolated that she would need to consciously or unconsciously find other strategies for healing.

A common effect of sexual assault is a lasting bewilderment about the difference between love and terror, and difficulty distinguishing between acts of love and acts of violence.[21] As a Mother Goddess whose attributes include unconditional divine love, Cybele would be severely impaired by unprocessed trauma resulting in damage to that capacity. In order to prevent such harm, she would have had to find some other way to completely excise the traumatic experience from herself.

20   McCracken, George. (1949). *Arnobius of Sicca: The Case Against the Pagans*. New York, NY: Paulist Press.
21   Van Der Kolk, *supra*.

From the constellation of information provided by Arnobius, gnosis, and modern trauma theory, a hypothesis may be formed that instead of being able to process the trauma through her own body, Cybele instead quarantined and dissociated it into a separate entity entirely. This dissociated, traumatized shard of her self, then, became embedded in the stone of Agdus, gestated there, and grew into Agdistis.

This interpretation of Agdistis' origin gives new context to their actions. If they are a being created from and in reaction to an experience of violation and violent control, and if they are by nature incapable of processing that trauma, then their demeanor as sexually voracious and violently resistant to control can be understood as an attempt to protect themself from further violation.

It was under these circumstances, then, that they drew the attention of Olympus. Still trapped and reverberating in the sexual violence perpetrated upon Cybele as she slept, they were then subjected to further violence perpetrated upon them as they slept. They were retraumatized as the memory of their mutilation at the hands of Dionysos became inextricably entangled with their memory of Cybele's rape, and neither could be processed. Already a mad daemon primarily composed of traumatic memory, they exploded outwards in time and descended into noncorporeal madness, fractal trigger states, and furious catatonia. Their pain and fury became a generational trauma infecting and echoing through the timelines of their descendants.

> "When something is damaged, for a long time, the damage becomes part of what you see when you picture yourself. And after a long time you stop noticing, whether it's really still there or whether it's just what you see when you picture yourself. Maybe it healed a long time ago and you never even noticed. Maybe the pain is something you don't need anymore but you've had it for so long ...it just doesn't occur to you. I spent so long damaged. I was so angry at him for breaking me, and that anger and that damage and that tangle, all that red string... it grew itself into a shell that was so hard I didn't even notice there was nothing underneath anymore. That was just the shape of me."[22]

Little information survives on Agdistis' nature. Arnobius describes them as ferocious, lustful, and violent, a monster consumed by rage and hatred. This is consistent with the idea of them as a trauma shard; their rage and hurt renders them incapable of experiencing any distinction between safety and danger, or between contact and violence. In divinatory and devotional contact, the daemon is insatiable, vengeful, and mad. This antagonism is directed generally, but also specifically towards Dionysos, seeking revenge and punishment for their suffering at his hands.

22   Agdistis. (2016, Dec 5). Channeling through Rocket as transcribed by Alder Knight.

"I wanted Dionysos to give me his pain. I wanted to eat it out of him. I wanted it to go through him and into me. I've hurt people, you know. But not like he hurt me. Not like a coward. I didn't make him cut his own balls off, you know, he did that to himself. I didn't want his cock, I wanted mine back. I didn't want him to suffer at anyone's hand but mine. And if it had been me, I'll tell you. He would have opened his eyes and seen me, and he would have seen his own blood reflected in my eyes and known what a real god looks like."[23]

It is clear from Agdistis' own words that they are motivated, at least in part, by revenge, and thereby closure. Their fury is not the anger of a person wronged, but a sadistic, insatiable bloodlust unmediated by reason or any understanding of compassion. This lack of compassion is in stark contrast to the vast divine compassion that characterizes Cybele. The rage that she felt in response to her rape could not coexist with her ability to provide infinite divine kindness and empathy; to preserve that ability, she had to quarantine those feelings and desires into Agdistis, a being who knows only the pain that conceived them. To work with Agdistis as a hybrid ancestor-divinity, then, consists of directing the two trauma processing tools outlined above to offer them the healing that may be effectuated through the living human body.

As previously stated, the first tool is to allow the traumatized person to process painful memories by connecting and being present with others. Practically, this can involve sharing one's pain, working to remain grounded in linear time, and being extended compassion and empathy. In working with Agdistis, this involves allowing them to connect with members of their line to process the memory of their story. The arc of that story, from brutal creation to brutal destruction, comprises the mythological foundation for the Mysteries of Agdistis. Many mystery cults, such as the Cult of Cybele and the Eleusinian Mysteries, have such a mythological foundation. Referred to as their *hieros logos*, the foundational story plays an integral part in the initiatory rites of the cult. The *hieros logos* is recited by hierophants as one of the three primary parts of initiatory rites, called *legomena*. The recitation of the story of Agdistis, in connection with living members of their line, allows the daemon to experience the painful memory without being flooded by it or forced into involuntary trauma-based time travel.

The second tool is offering Agdistis new experiences to contradict and heal the effects of their violation. These experiences can include somatic *katharsis* through physical embodiment as well as ancestor veneration. For any entity that has experienced

23   Agdistis. (2016, Dec 5). Channeling through Rocket as transcribed by Alder Knight.

helplessness and hurt, slowly learning and rebuilding the capacity to protect oneself, be held, and experience non-violent interactions is a great tool for healing.

This work is mutually beneficial. Offering compassion, *katharsis*, and healing to Agdistis allows practitioners to experience the same. Not only is the generational trauma emanating from Agdistis' hurt slowly alleviated by their healing, but also, a devotional relationship with them eases certain types of distress specific to members of their line. The couplet included as an epigraph in this piece petitions Agdistis for relief and strengthens a reciprocal relationship, which the daemon understands as consuming the pain, fear, and madness of their kin.

> *"If I am your ancestor, will you feed me? Have you ever tasted fear? If you let me drink it out of you I will tell you what it tastes like. Do you think it's too much for me? Sweet child. It is a great pain. How great would a hunger have to be to hold it? I know it's scary. And I don't want you to not be scared. I want you to be scared and then I want you to give it to me."[24]*

This prayer makes the pain and madness into an offering to Agdistis and abates the suffering and overwhelm associated with them, while simultaneously strengthening the connection between the devotee and the daemon, and nourishing both with that connection.

The couplet is a prayer for the "small madness" as distinct from the "great madness," a distinction that appears in sources both academic and spiritual. The great madness is involuntary and destructive; it overwhelms its victims, irreversibly diminishing or removing their ability to function in the world. It can manifest as severe episodes of mental illness, suicidality, emotional breakdown, and other types of significant psychic suffering. The great madness threatens many, particularly those whose movement through the world is shaped by violence and oppression, and a variety of tools exist to manage its weight. While individual practitioners must craft their own toolboxes of therapeutic, chemical, magical, and other modalities to resist the great madness, one such tool is the ritualized and *kathartic* application of the small madness.

> *"If you do not find the small madness, the great madness will take you."[25]*

The small madness can be understood as certain types of *katharsis*, frenzy, or voluntary surrender. It can be accessed through a variety of conduits, including entheogens, dance, sex, pain, and channeling. When directed devotionally through a relationship

---

24   Agdistis. (2016, Dec 5). Channeling through Rocket as transcribed by Alder Knight.
25   Cybele. (2014, Feb 2). Channelling through Rocket as transcribed by Alder Knight.

with Agdistis, through these conduits, and through the couplet, the small madness acts as a pressure valve, inoculating practitioners against the great madness.

In general Hellenic and Anatolian cosmologies, the practice of the small madness falls primarily under the domains of Cybele and Dionysos. Each deity had mystery cults involving ecstatic dancing, booming drums and crashing cymbals, frenzied bloodletting, orgies, gender transgression, and other ecstatic and socially deviant practices. Dionysos' maenad followers were recruited from respectable village women, who, under his influences, defied the rules of acceptable feminine behavior. They would run through the woods, dancing and singing, hunting wild animals as prey and then tearing them apart bare-handed and eating them raw in a ritual known as *sparagmos*.[26] The cult of Dionysos took its lead from the cult of Cybele, where his own youthful madness after his interaction with Agdistis was healed. The transgender priestesses of the cult of Cybele in Anatolia and Greece, the Gallae, used the small madness extensively in their practice. Many of the practices of the Gallae were lost as Mysteries, and what remains was mostly recorded by Roman scholars outraged by their public deviance and gender non-conformity. During the festivals and rituals associated with the cult, the priestesses would drum and dance ecstatically, rub their hair in the dirt, whip themselves into a frenzy, and, as part of their initiations, mutilate their genitals and paint the streets with their makeup and blood.[27] Agdistis, bridging these two mystery cults and holding within them the madness of both, holds a unique ability to guide their followers in walking the delicate line between the great madness and the small.

The cosmology of this practice requires the merging of Hellenic (and other traditional) polytheist mythos, somatic trauma theory, various traditions of ancestor practice, radical politics, harm reduction, nonbinary gender praxis, and magic for the creation of practical tools for survival in a hostile world. The *hieros logos* begins with Cybele's experience of sexual violation and moves through the exclusion and hazing of Dionysos, the attempts to contain and ultimately destroy the threat posed by Agdistis' gender and sexual behavior, and the resultant trauma, madness, and search for healing with which all three dance as time passes. These mythic underpinnings of the cultus contain reflections of many experiences that resonate with the line of TGNC descendants.

For that reason, this practice of working to provide *katharsis* and healing to the line of ancestors, including Agdistis, echoes *katharsis* and healing back to the

---

26   Meyer, *supra.*
27   Roller, *supra.*

practitioners. The veneration of TGNC ancestors allows them to become a resource and a source of healing for their living and recently dead descendants. Working with these traumatized, mad, time-struck deities and spirits is a resourcing practice. To address their pain directly is to remove the source of infection and allow the line to begin to heal itself. Further, the use of ritualized frenzy, or the small madness, and the same tools of compassion, trauma processing, and safety building are valuable for individual practitioners in the day-to-day work of surviving and healing in a violent world. Finally, contextualizing oneself as a TGNC person, as traumatized, as subject to violence and full of fear and rage, in the legacy of that line and connected with the ancestors and divinities that populate it, provides strength to fight and endure. Particularly as people often separated from biological family, present-day TGNC people benefit from these connections with ancestors and divinities. These connections and this work provide the opportunity for healing shared between practitioners and with Agdistis and other ancestors. They are a bridge to an intergenerational and ancestral legacy of mutual aid that not only stretches through time, but queers it.

Between Starshine and Clay:
DIY Black Queer Divination

---

by Almah LaVon Rice

i had no model.
born in babylon
both nonwhite and woman
what did i see to be except myself?
i made it up
here on this bridge between
starshine and clay...
— Lucille Clifton, from *"won't you celebrate with me"*

Noctuary.

Leaf belly up, means yes. Leaf back green and still, means no. A black queer girlchild at night–who writes poems and incantations everywhere, who calls the moon *the sun in her nightgown*, who is afraid of fairies and the Sandman, who hears the steps of lumbering monsters in the thumping of the furnace–this star-riddled child divines by moonlight. Alone, staring out of the window at the tree she calls Lucy: if one of Lucy's leaves blows upward, revealing its pale underside when she presses a question to the sky, well, that is God's way of answering to the affirmative. If a Lucyleaf remains inert, that is God shaking her head. No. During the day she may be alone in a world that is silent when she needs a word, and noise where she needs the ineffable; but at night, the world speaks in all the right places: wind, leaf, moon.

Oraculum.

Black queer girlchild stumbles forward through the years. Falls into Ifá, a West African system of divination and sign, and in particular, becomes a daily devotee of the oracle of Dilóggun. Every morning and every night I would throw the cowrie shells on the mat to get answers to questions I posed to my ancestors and the orisha, the deities innumerable that constitute the pantheon of the Ifá. The syntax of shells directed many of my core life decisions, from where to move to potential partnerships to pursue. The world was alive, and was achatter. Spirits crowded at my mat to say their piece, and often, they rattled my peace.

Palimpsest.

In the end, I wanted a looser relationship with divine dictation. This anti-authoritarian began chafing at feeling like I was lashed to the mat, and to ancestral directives that started to feel too much like the arid, punitive Judeo-Christian tradition I was raised in. I decided I was a free-range mystic, allergic to organized religion of any kind. That being said, I still love the orisha, and am still grateful that Ifá provided entrée into ancestor veneration for me—but now I have more elliptical, more diffuse, and less heavy-handed relationship to ancestral guidance.

Hypnagogic Hotel.

Before I left my more formal relationship with Ifá, I met with a Babalawo who told me that I had "a gift for dreaming." To strengthen my dream divination practice, I started setting up one-night pop-up altars (with offerings to the Givers of Dreams like a sprig of wildflowers, a packet of tea, herbs), complete with a handwritten note asking for answers to specific questions, as well as longer-term altars to honor my dream guides and signal my receptivity to more visitations. I even created a live dreaming installation at the Transmodern Festival, an annual showcase of radical live art in Baltimore. I called it…

…a slumber party for artists

…a studio for sleepers

…a playboratory for dreamers

…a soporific salon, a night mystery school, a somnolent summit, lullaby theatre

Witness the tableau: a darkened room full of figures in repose, sharing dreams and dream-recall hacks with each other. There's a tea station to get participants in a reverie-ripe mood—a Muse-um of Mugwort. A copy of The Girl Who Dreamed Only Geese is open on the table, inviting sleepwalkers to wander from dream to dream, story to story.

Afro-approfondement.

Tom Robbins says that "approfondement" is a French word that means "playing easily in the deep." Feeling too feral and too fanciful for more rigid, institutionalized faith systems, I claim myself as a practitioner of sacred whimsy. As a Black queer person who has not found an easy home in any faith tradition but who is still ensorcelled by spirit and divining, I have realized that I needed, to paraphrase the opening lines from Lucille Clifton, to invoke and invent here between sky and earth, starshine and clay, transcendence and immanence. Divination is the ultimate interPlay of dimensions; I see my prayer/divination mat and altar as an earthly address for what has no location, a playground for divine conversation.

Dark Delicious Divination.

Imagineered by Alexis Pauline Gumbs, Indigo Days was a gathering of Black women and genderqueer healers inspired by Indigo, the Black girl healer folklorist in Ntozake Shange's novel, *Sassafrass, Cypress, and Indigo*. At Indigo Days, I shared my "Afro-Surrealist Dark Delicious Divinatory Writing Workshop" in a living room full of Black women and genderqueers, with a particular focus of the art on bibliomancy. Bibliomancers-to-be packed the room, everyone in chairs or sitting on the floor–and poetry books from Alexis' library were prophets among us, arrayed around the room and ready. I asked attendees to let a question bloom inside them, and then open the books to an auspicious, answering page. Folks expressed awe at the resonance they found in verses that knowingly spoke back to them. Later in the workshop, participants riffed on the found lines, writing affirming letters to their future selves, to Black queer youth, or some other imagined audience.

Dark Sciences.

With Alexis Pauline Gumbs, I dreamed up Dark Sciences: A People of Color Dream Retreat. The retreat center had a slot for our event in April and in August of 2015–which date to choose? Alexis recommended that we wait upon dream missives to make a decision. Not too long after she voiced that idea, I dreamed I was sweltering a some gathering; Alexis was also there, and she was eight months pregnant. The retreat center is in Austin—which is scorching in August—so Alexis said the dream said *the 8th month*. August it was! Divination: the deepest, darkest science.

Through guided meditation, we dove to the ocean floor to sit cross-legged with Olókun, radiant in her/his pearls. We woke up early and, still wet with dreams, pulled oracle cards for each other. We paired up for an automatic art exercise: while Partner A daydreamed out loud, the Partner B drew Partner A's visions in oil pastel (and with eyes closed and heart open). We composed and then dropped haiku in a fishbowl, later pulling them out "at random" as oracles. We built a collective altar to anchor us over the course of the retreat. Over lunch, we held a troubleshooting dream clinic—what if you don't remember your dreams? *Remember that it's all a dream, we never wake.* What if you remember them all too well, and are hounded by nightmares? *Try extracting wisdom if you can, like draining venom from a snake.*

Some of us slept more soundly than we had in years, meeting grandmothers who have been waiting for us all this time down by the riverside.

Love S(cry).

I worked on summoning a life partner for ages. I paid for spell casted honey. I bathed with rose soap. In accordance with what I know of Feng shui, I erected a love altar adorned with pink, red, and white candles in the love bagua of my bedroom. A love attraction coach gave me special oils to use. But I also improvised using my longing and imagination: I filled a heart-shaped change purse with slips of paper on which I had written affirmations from my partner-yet-to-arrive. When I felt demoralized and hopeless, I would pull a slip of paper from the purse for a reassuring message from my incipient beloved. Call it quantum entanglement love divination.

Envoi.

> Joan: "I hear voices telling me what to do. They come from God."
> Robert: "They come from your imagination."
> Joan: "Of course. This is how the messages of God come to us."
> – *Saint Joan*, by George Bernard Shaw

My next big adventure will involve using divination to drive a book-length project. Despite identifying as a play evangelist, writing is often a place where I get stuck and stricken with what I jokingly call "adult poisoning." Bringing Divine Chance into the process helps me shake off rigidity, and instead welcome in an untamed beauty that is beyond my inner critic's wildest dreams. What might this look like? Collected words and phrases jotted on scraps of paper and tossed in an alchemical shoebox; these words will mingle and transmute, to later be drawn from for provocative juxtapositions. It might look like using Random.org to play with word order. My approach would be heresy to some, but my ancestors and guides are my mentors in play—over and over again, I find irreverent reverence is rewarded. After all, in the physical realm, I had no model so I had to make it up, one Black queer outrageous step at a time.

Manx poderosx: queer abundance
by Inés Ixierda

Finding the Unnamed Path

by Michael Greywolf

When I started my journey on the pagan path and found the Unnamed Path, I had been searching for a couple of years for a tradition that reflected who I was as a gay man. I came into paganism after a falling-out with the Christian religion in college. I was coming to terms with my sexuality after years of repression and self-loathing. The Church wanted me to change who I was, they wanted me to fit a preconceived notion of what they thought it meant to be religious, spiritual, and a man. When I found the pagans on campus, they were much more welcoming and didn't demand I change who I was to belong.

Like most baby pagans I started as a solitary witch, practicing a Wiccan-inspired set of beliefs, and that worked for me for a while. I worshipped the Goddess (not a particular one, just the general idea of Goddess) and shunned the God, or sacred masculine, for a few years. I find many gay or queer men who come to paganism or witchcraft are drawn to the feminine aspects of being a goddess worshipper. For most queer men we are often told we aren't masculine enough to be 'men.' Thus many just completely embrace goddess worship and deny any bits of the sacred masculine within them. Coming from a patriarchal religious background, I find this to be very common among converts. This practice threw me out of balance. I was turning my back on energy and power that belonged to me as someone who identifies as male.

When I tried to reconnect with those masculine aspects of myself, I felt push-back by the hyper-masculinist energy that was coming from a heteronormative mindset. It still didn't feel completely right and my spiritual growth floundered after a few years. A heterocentric view of religion just didn't fit me. I regularly felt like I was stuck in the middle when I attended group rituals. Over the years I had heard about all-female covens and circles, and some that were Lesbian-identified, and I started to wonder if such a thing could exist for men, especially Gay men.

Research into the variety of pagan paths for queer men had led me to sites for several groups, but none had any circles or groups in my current area. It wasn't until the 2013 Beltane celebration, with the Council of Magickal Arts in Texas, that I met an Initiated Brother of the Unnamed Path (UP), Cliff Camacho. This brother was a regular attendee of CMA's Beltane celebrations and that year he happened to be advertising Stone and Stang, the Unnamed Path's biannual public gathering. I had not previously heard of the Unnamed Path, but as Brother Cliff was explaining his experiences in the brotherhood, and his deep personal interactions with the Dark Goddess of the Unnamed Path, I became intrigued. My head nearly exploded when he said the Gods of the Path were actually consorts to each other and not the Goddesses. I decided at that moment that this tradition might be something to look into.

After the gathering had ended, I reached out to Cliff and he put me in touch with the brother who would become my teacher, Chase Powers. Brother Chase suggested that I listen to the Unnamed Path Podcast, to get a feel for what the UP was, and to get back to him if I decided to do the Apprenticeship course. Initially I wanted to jump right into classes because the idea of a new Path specifically for Men Who Love Men excited me beyond belief. But after receiving advice from several close friends about getting a better grasp on the tradition before jumping head first, I spent a couple of weeks listening to Hyperion weave the history and practices of the UP online.

At that point, the UP was only about six years old – in February 2017 the Unnamed Path celebrated our ten-year anniversary. I learned how Eddy 'Hyperion' Gutierrez Sanctus, the founder of the path, had decided to seek out the Ancestors of Men Who Love Men during a journey into the Spirit World for healing, and about the joy and mission they had for him. They wanted him to bring their teachings back to the Men Who Love Men in the middle world, to retake our place as teachers, historians, medicine men, and servants of our communities. These recorded teachings of Hyperion's relayed information about the four branches of the tradition: Shamanism, Magic and Prophecy, Death Walking and Energy Healing, as well as the two Goddesses and two Gods of the tradition. The relationship between the Gods as lovers and the Goddesses as confidantes and companions fit with how I lived my life. All this knowledge cemented my belief that the Unnamed Path was something I desperately needed in my life.

Though the Apprenticeship classes are generally a year-long course, mine actually lasted a bit longer because my work schedule was inconvenient at times. With the UP being my first, and thus far only tradition, I had a lot of learning to do. Learning to meditate was definitely a challenge; my mind is very hard to quiet at times and when I started learning to clear my mind, my thoughts and subconscious got louder. *LOOK! They are listening finally!* With Brother Chase's help I was able to work with those distractions and eventually get to a place where I could quiet my mind.

I cannot provide many details about what we covered and learned, but I can say that the first part of the course is about learning to listen to one's Shadow Self, your emotions, thoughts and past experiences and healing your past wounds. There is an exercise that requires you to sit and 'review' your day, which is especially helpful if you've been having a bad one. As you review your day bit by bit, when you come across something that sparks a fearful, sad, or upsetting response, you start to peel back the emotional layers that caused you to respond that way. This was difficult for me, because I found I was projecting my own fears and insecurities onto others around me and not taking responsibility for my own shortcomings. It led me to isolate myself, which is not useful when doing intense Shadow Work. This is part of the process the UP teaches so that we may heal and build better relationships with our Shadows. I feel like this was the part of the training that I enjoyed the most. I was able to come out of this with a better understanding of who I was, and why I would sometimes choose to follow self-destructive patterns, and how to either avoid or heal these traumas when they occur. I would like to add that Shadow Work is never done. It is only over once we have passed on from this life. Much of what we were taught in the classes was covered briefly in the Unnamed Path podcasts, but in the classes we went deeper into the work and expanded on the ideas and teachings.

It was during my training, and right before my first in-person class, that the founder of the Unnamed Path, Eddy 'Hyperion' Gutierrez Sanctus, passed away from a sudden heart attack. Being someone who was half-way between being Student and an Initiated Brother, it was an interesting experience to see the effect Hyperion's death had on the brotherhood. I have always had an interest in how people process and deal with the death of a loved one. Being of Mexican descent, I am used to big wakes - or viewings- and funerals, where people will sit and commiserate over the dearly departed. It shocked me when I learned that some people did not do this too. The few funerals I have witnessed for those who are of other ethnicities have fascinated me with how different cultures approach the act of sending off or honoring loved ones. With these men, I saw men who lived miles apart from each other collectively grieving. I witnessed all these men with whom I had started to build relationships withdraw into themselves to mourn in various ways. I would also see brothers reaching out to those who were withdrawing and help guide them back or help them process their loss in a constructive way. One would think that after losing their leader that the Brotherhood would fall apart, but they didn't. They mourned and continued Hyperion's workings, as well as their own.

During my training it was my privilege to help the brothers host the first Circle of Sight, one of the Unnamed Path's holy days, at the Council of Magickal Arts annual Beltane celebration. As a student, it tested all I had learned up to that point, but it was a thrill to serve my community in such a way. In the Circle of Sight, one or more Brothers takes on the role of an Oracle, an individual who enters a half-trance and takes questions from members of the community. After questioning the Oracle journeys to the Spirit World for the answer. Another brother serves as an energy anchor, this brother channels energy from the Ancestors into the Oracle to keep them from becoming exhausted.

After the ritual had come to a close, the feedback we received from the community was overwhelming and full of love and excitement. My brothers were flushed with joy, hearing praise about the ritual. I feel it was also because we were living up to something Hyperion would always say, "We are shamans for our community, not shamans for ourselves." It was a few months later, with Brother Chase's help and guidance, that I completed the apprenticeship course and was his first student to become an initiate of the Unnamed Path in August of 2015.

In the time following my initiation into the brotherhood, we have continued to grow and expand on the legacy Hyperion left us. We continue to have Stone and Stang on a biannual rotation, and we have started a new podcast. When Hyperion passed, none of the current brothers felt like they could or should take over the reins of producing episodes for the show. But in September 2016, Brother Mathew Sydney and myself, with the blessings from our brothers, started the new podcast *Walking the Unnamed Path* on the Pagans Tonight Radio Network. We try to continue Hyperion's work by expanding on the teachings given to him by the Ancestors of Men Who Love Men, and also covering general topics that pertain to queer pagan men. Mathew and I knew from interacting with other queer men online that there was a desire, a hunger, for more information on the Unnamed Path. Some individuals even believed we had died out since the last of the original podcasts was dated February 2012 and our online presence was very small. This is obviously not the case, but our brotherhood had gone through a period of trials and it seemed like we were constantly dealing with personal issues and even another death. Our brother, John Ravenmoon, joined Hyperion and the Ancestors in 2016. Brother Ravenmoon's passing was a bit of a kick in the ass. We knew we had work to do and we can only hope we are doing our community, our Brothers, the Ancestors, and Gods proud. We continue to train new teachers and brothers each year. We number over thirty initiated brothers as to date. We work to continue to plan and host Stone and Stang, and in addition various brothers host workshops at numerous other pagan gatherings. Our work continues and we do it with pride and love in our hearts.

Anba Dlo/Under The Water

by Alex Batagi (Bonkira Bon Oungan)

It is a Saturday night in late November, and I am on my knees in the middle of a packed temple while a Vodou ceremony goes on full tilt around me. It is not my first experience in ceremony, but it is the first time that the attention of a lwa (spirit) who has come down in possession is fully focused on me. He is seated in a ti chèz (small chair) turned backwards, and his body cannot stay still. While he washes my head, hands, and arms with strong smelling cologne, he vibrates in his seat; body shivering and bouncing to an internal rhythm. His motions ask a question that I don't understand until the priestess keeping a careful eye on our interaction leans down and whispers to him in a language I am unfamiliar with. He nods vigorously, and she details for me what it is that he wants from me. This spirit asks me for maryaj lwa, a marriage between a person and their spirits.

I tell him that I need to think about his offer, and he nods in understanding before motioning for the priestess to come closer. She steps in and he lifts both my hands in his, carefully placing them between her hands. More cologne is poured over our combined hands, and I do not need a translation to understand what he is putting in place with the priestess who would become my spiritual mother.

Vodou is the indigenous religion of Haiti and the Haitian people. With deep ties to the concepts of revolution and balance framed within Haitian culture, Vodou addresses life with a three-pronged approach: magic, which seeks to rebalance an unjust world according to the needs of the people, healing, which addresses sickness of the body and the spirit, and service to the lwa, who bring the will and the word of the supreme divinity into our lives. None of these areas can exist without the others, and the heart of each aspect of the religion operates with the same core principle: magic is cultivated in the many relationships—with people and spirits alike—that each *Vodouizan* (Vodou practitioner) nurtures and holds close.

Vodouizan who may be familiar with other minority religions outside of Haiti are fond of saying that there are no solitary practitioners in Vodou, and this is true. No one can exist in a singular vacuum in the religion; we cannot learn, serve our spirits, rise to expectations that the spirits have in mind for us, or evolve as individuals in the religion without the community. Our communities are our families, headed by priests and priestesses who offer direction for our spiritual development. And should our spirits direct us into the *djevò* (initiatory chamber), these priests or priestesses lift us from *anba dlò* (below the waters) to take up the responsibilities that our spirits direct us to. In this way, our relationships become re-shaped. The priest/ess becomes our spiritual parent, we become their child, and their other children become our siblings. The *djevò* solidifies our relationships with our spiritual parent, with our spirits, and with our community-at-large, made up of other *Vodouizan* who see us, know us, and recognize the bonds we have forged and formalized through our initiatory sacrifices and spiritual devotion.

We are reborn through these relationships and, for those of us who have not found welcome in other religions--who exist in liminal spaces, who embody a gender that falls outside of social expectations, who have a sexuality that exists beyond the label of 'straight'--Vodou offers a reprieve from outside attitudes and confirms the identities we live in every day, either through explicit ritual activity or a simple open welcome. Notably absent in Vodou are any proscriptions around sexual orientation or gender identity, as these things are largely beyond the concern of community or spirit.

When we enter the *djevò*, we are simple seeds that are ready to be planted. We are hull and flesh, skin and potential, and the *djevò* is where we go to become more than that and find what we can grow into. In the same way that seeds have a sole purpose--to be nurtured into a root that grows deep and a plant that grows tall--we exist as singular identities when we go to *kouche* (lie down). We become a reflexive being that is defined by who we are to our spirits, who we are to our spiritual parent, and, as a look to the future, who we will become in our community. It doesn't matter what genitalia I was born with or what words I use to describe how I relate to the world, as I am only a seed. My religious identity will wait for me at my *baptem* (baptism), and I will float in the waters of *Ginen* (the realm of the spirits) until my mother's labor pushes me back out into the world.

It is a cool Sunday afternoon, and I am sitting in the kitchen of the priestess whose hands were placed around mine many months ago. I watch her cook, and everything she does is precise and practiced, with nothing left to fate or happy accident. She cooks like food is a story that has been told for years until it is known by heart and by smell, and by relationships recalled over a steaming plate of diri ak pwa (rice and beans), with chunks of tender pwason (fish) placed carefully on top. No spiritual skills are needed to discern that something magnificent shimmers around her, and it reaches back to her own spiritual mother, and her mother's mother, and on into the roots of the tree that holds us all up.

It has been almost a year since my spirits proposed maryaj (spirit marriage) and then asked for my kanzo (initiation) as well, and it is past time to have the conversation that I have been avoiding since the beginning. My stomach has been tied into knots for days, and I have rehearsed what I need to say over and over and also prepared myself to be dismissed out of hand. I feared learning that Vodou was another place that people like me, a visibly queer and transgender person, do not belong. I am terrified to discuss the topic with anyone even remotely involved in Vodou, because I am afraid of the answer. Though I don't really know the weight of what has been presented to me, I know what these spirits have told me and I am not sure what I will do if the door closes here.

I fidget with my hands and the paper in front of me as I tell the priestess that I cannot be made as a manbo (female priest)because for me being made that way would feel like a death sentence. My heart pounds in my ears and I swallow my stomach while she is quiet. I cannot look at her, but in that forever long moment of silence, I know she is looking at me.

"Then I'll make you an houngan." She says it simply and with finality that my ears struggle to process. It feels as if there is air in my lungs again. In the future, I ask her two more times if this is what she will do and she answers me with the same finality, each and every time. My spirits ask me to trust, and so I do by putting myself into the hands of this powerhouse of a Haitian woman.

When I am in the *djevò*, time and place cease to exist. I am elsewhere and I am not who I was when I was brought in, with all things being stripped away so that I may be rebuilt anew. When I dream of things my spirits tell me I must do, my spiritual mother is with me doing those things, too. When my dream-self balks at instructions, her hand is on my shoulder and she reassures me that it's time and she is with me through it. I am not scared because, as she told me before, she will fly with me until I can fly on my own.

In the waking world, my spiritual mother quietly explains that I am being made an *houngan* and not a *manbo*. In Haiti, 'transgender' is something new (though there is a local queer community) and it is an adjustment for those who are learning how things are outside the country, just as I am learning things inside the religion and inside the culture. She picks her words carefully and times her explanations to make them rest easy with those members of the community who listen to her. My unaltered, pre-transition body sends one message and my mother delivers another, and her words are heeded without resistance as we all respect our mother and her wishes.

All ritual work is done with the idea of who I will be when I emerge from the cocoon of the *djevò*. I am built by the vision and hands of my mother, upheld by all her children and the community that has come to see this transformation. I am because she is and because they are, and her shoulders are strong enough to hold us all. As the community grows, Vodou grows with the community. A transgender person may not have entered her *djevò* before, but my mother knows that the spirits welcome all their children and so she brings all of us to them with the same deep love and exacting care. In that, my gender and sexuality is both irrelevant because the ritual work does not change based on gender, history, or love, and intrinsic because all of me is welcomed to the table. Vodou is a process of constant balance, of 'yes, and…', and of embracing all possibilities in one vessel.

My mother's voice calls me and her hands lift me from Ginen. I have rested and worked for these nine days and learned who I am and who my spirits want me to be, and she has labored as a mother labors to birth a child. Born from water, lifted from water, and with new breath in my lungs, I am born as I am meant to be.

I can feel the press of bodies around me while I wait to be given a new name that marks who I am and what I will be. The priest who intones the prayers of baptism first does so over one of my sisters, and my mother carefully writes her new name down in the book that holds the history of her love for her children and, through them, her love for the spirits. I cannot yet see her clearly, but I know she stands before me.

It is my turn and my heart pounds like it has at every step of this new becoming. My godparents are behind me, and the candle that lights the way for this new name and new self rests on top of my head, held strong by the hands that have plucked my name from the lips of the spirits. The priest prays and my mother is poised with pen and book.

It was my *parenn* (godfather) who pointed out how significant *baptem* could be for me, and he was not wrong. A new name and a publicly-recognized, community-supported, spiritually-backed male identity is a powerful piece of magic to place upon someone and, for a transgender person, it's a new start. Prior to my journey into the *djevò*, I had largely socially transitioned to a public male identity but had held off on a medical transition due to a multitude of fears and worries regarding what hormones would do to me and the ripple effects it would have in my life. After *kanzo*, I found that I could no longer wait and the drive to begin altering my body to match how I felt was impossible to squish down. The settling of magic on my head and in my hands that spoke directly to who I was at my core created an environment where I was no longer able to deny what would, in many ways, save my life. Within a few months of returning to the United States, I began hormone therapy.

My parenn relays my new name to our mother and she directs the priest to announce my birth as a new houngan. I roll the syllables over my tongue as the priest and my mother continue down the row of my brothers and sisters. My name holds secrets that I can't fully understand yet.

Bonkira. What is good is rare.

In Vodou, names are their own magic. They inform us of our life's path, of our work in the religion, and who we are at a deeply personal level, embodying gifts and lessons, blessings and burdens all in one. At the same time, they are also a reflection of that which shapes us and, when I consider my name, I think of my mother and her hands. She insists in her quiet, self-contained way that what she has made is both good and rare, and that what I am to become can be both, if only I learn the lessons that she and the spirits teach through our collective interactions. I am a reflection of my spirits, but, perhaps more importantly, I am also a reflection of her. If I am good, it is because she has nurtured that and placed important pieces of herself and her understanding of the spirits and the world in me. Our relationship supports me as I grow as a man and as a priest and, combining both of those identities, as her child. The *lwa* wove us together, the *djevò* solidified our relationship, and my name indicates how our hands can make magic together.

I sit beside my mother in the same temple I knelt in when the lwa decided we could create something powerful together. On her knee sits a small pile of raw cotton, filled with seeds and bits of husk, and she pulls off a small chunk for me. "Here," she says. "Now watch."

Her delicate fingers make quick work of the rough, uncombed cotton. She tugs it carefully into shape, applying just the right amount of pressure to keep it from tearing apart while shaping it into the form she needs it to hold to make ti mèch, a small wick for an oil lamp. As she molds it into usefulness, she carefully plucks away the imperfections that would render the wick unable to burn properly. Not the smallest piece of debris escapes her view, and she works quietly, bringing into being the memories of hundreds of years of sèvis lwa (service to the spirits).

When she begins another ti mèch, I take up the cotton she handed to me and begin to work it as she did, only with fingers that move much slower and that need more practice and discipline.

She watches me out of the corner of her eye and, when I need guidance, she directs my attention to her hands and uses slow, deliberate motions to illustrate what I am missing.

I make the movements of my fingers match hers as best I can, and soon we have enough ti mèch for the lamp. They are placed carefully in the small basin, and oil is added to provide the fuel. She lights a wick that she made first, and then lights the rest from that one; transferring her light to the wicks I have made. As the lamp begins to burn, she shapes the ti mèch for the best possible burn, lifting and placing them in the most useful positions to achieve the brightest flame. Years of practice and a ritualized knowledge of how they will burn leave her unafraid of the bite of the fire, as if the flame would dare not burn her when there is work to be done. I memorize how this confidence looks and feels.

After a moment, she begins the prayers that speak to God and call the lwa and the ancestors in French and then Kreyòl. She sings quietly into the lamp and I feel the air around us contract as those who are unseen draw close to listen. This presence is like a heartbeat that encompasses us both, weaving and tugging magic into place between us, for us, and through us. She sings for me as her mother sang for her and how I will perhaps sing for my own children's needs, with love and hope and the knowledge that what has been worked between us cannot be undone.

Watch Out Tree

by Inés Ixierda

A Drag Queen Possessed And Other Queer Club Magic

by Aaron Oberon

Magic in America has been presented in a very particular package. This package has often included certain elements that market it as socially acceptable while still being outside the norm. The most glaring of these elements for a queer witch is the constant reminder of how heterosexuality is not only the norm but the supposed source of witchcraft. In recent years however queer witches and folk magicians have decided that working within the heteronormative lens of fertility based witchcraft doesn't work for them. New avenues have been explored and entirely new streams of witchcraft have surfaced that emphasize practice within the immediacy of the witch's environment rather than a set of core beliefs that the witch must adhere to. Animism, the belief that everything is imbued with spirit, is one of these streams that has changed how many contemporary witches are viewing their craft.

Animism allows an individual to look at the entire world around them and see magic and potential. In an animistic worldview, the entire landscape has power. This allows a queer person to look at a place like a club or a bar as something powerful. Instead of trapping oneself within the confines of a circle, every aspect of a building or landscape can become a place to practice magic. This also means that certain kinds of magic—such as glamour, protection, lust, and even possession—might be more potent in a queer night club than in other places throughout your landscape."

Liminality

Witches are creatures of liminal spaces. Witches keep one foot planted here in the everyday world, and the other foot planted in the world of spirits. This liminality, being between states, is one of the things that gives witches power. Many, but not all, queer people can identify with this as well due to our very existence. Queer people live a half-legal existence, a place where some of the community remains protected while the other is always at risk. Employment becomes a balancing act of private and public images, as does presenting the 'socially acceptable queer' that may or may not fit the individual.

My own personal experience in the pagan community has put me in a liminal place when attending most gatherings, even ones that are led by other queer people. Many times I have seen, or even been the target of, the idea that all gay men are "good witches" because they "have more feminine energy" than their heterosexual counterparts. Supposedly queer friendly rituals still include the Wiccan Great Rite ritual in which the officiates reiterate the importance of heterosexual intercourse for the creation of magic.

Magic is often polarized as "male" and "female" and any kind of other view of magic is discredited. Involvement of gender fluid, gender nonconforming, or transgender individuals is often minimized and still packaged into a binary. Spiritual possession is often limited to "same-sex possession" meaning that only a male identifying individual has permission to become the vessel for a God, and the same with female identifying individuals and Goddesses.

Some queer people may find empowerment through these lenses, while many others are reminded that even within paganism, there is a heavy stream of heteronormativity that is difficult to escape. When taking these issues outside of a social lens and into a magical lens, this in-between state can be another aspect of queer empowerment. By embracing this inherent social liminality, we can use that to inform our witchcraft. Not all queer people will feel as if they are liminal, but for those that do this can be yet another tool for our craft.

Club Craft

With animism and liminality in the back of our minds, we can look at a club as a place where magic is at every corner. The medieval-themed roleplaying of some pagan events is not required to be the setting of meaningful magic. Clubs are inherently liminal, often acting as a stopping point on a night of ecstasy whether through drinking, dancing, or grinding. The concept of the club as a queer safe place imbues it with protective agency. The spirit of a club is one that not only encourages interaction but also actively works to protect those within it. Flirting in a queer club is an act of celebration in one of the few places where queer people can flirt with no reservation. This freedom and celebration exists within this space for a few hours between sunset and sunrise, making it a kind of queer witches Sabbath.

Two of the defining aspects of going to a club are drinking and dancing. In my experience, these two things can be incredibly powerful if put to use in a magical way. Alcohol can become both a libation and an entheogen. Toasts can be given to the queer ancestors to open a night and be shot back to open ourselves up to ecstatic aspects of clubbing. For me, this becomes a moment of honoring the queer people who opened the way for the younger generations as well as an opportunity to acknowledge the spirits attached to queer life and ecstatic experience. I identify one of these spirits as "Intoxication" and always acknowledge it when walking into a club, at every toast, and with every dance. It only takes a few seconds to pay homage to these spirits and bring them into your world with some small act of acknowledgement.

After these first offerings and entheogens the dancing takes off. This dancing becomes the crux of ecstatic experience and the most crucial part of spirit possession. Spirit possession plays a massive role in many religious traditions around the world. Growing up as a Christian in the American south, I saw many folks become "filled with the Spirit" or who had "The Holy Ghost pass through them." These experiences had several hallmarks of ecstatic spirit possession, including ecstatic movements, speaking in tongues, and on rare occasion delivering messages from The Holy Ghost. Modern paganism has its own context for possession, such as in the Wiccan ritual of Drawing Down the Moon. While some pagans utilize spirit possession in freeform ways, most rituals that include possession follow a script and are strongly bound by gender norms.

With Club Crafting, possession can be performed by whatever it is the dancer is seeking. I often dance for Intoxication and lose myself to that spirit in order to deepen our bonds and celebrate the land, my queerness, and the space that we share during this time. Queer cultures have certain aspects that blend into these ecstatic approaches. The dance style of voguing, which began in Harlem and was primarily done by African-American and Latino queer folks, has become synonymous with queerness since the early 1990's when it was introduced to the mainstream world through Madonna's hit song "Vogue" and the iconic 1990 documentary "Paris is Burning." Although vogue originated as something learned through the House system (self made families of queer people performing and sometimes living together) and featured ball competitions, it has in time become a worldwide art form that is uniquely queer. Many queer people who may not be proper voguers will use elements of vogue in the way they dance and express themselves. The free form nature of some styles of vogue lend themselves to ecstatic dance, queerness in motion.

Modern witchcraft traditions that utilize possession often stress the importance of costuming, which can be effective if done correctly, or result in "play acting" instead of possession if done poorly. Those who act as vessels for deities in these witchcraft traditions may wear grand head pieces, intricately crafted garments, and makeup that is evocative of the nature of the deity being called down into the vessel. The act of costuming for spirits is incredibly similar to the rituals drag queens go through to build their drag persona. Everyone does their makeup a little differently, including the rituals involved with prep work. Some queens may put on the same movie every time they start painting. Others light candles, or put on Barry Manilow to set the mood. Regardless of the method, there is a process of dragging up that puts the queen in a headspace to become their persona.

For witches, the process of drag can become a ritual of achieving headspace and devotion to a spirit by mimicking their form. Empowerment of the witch's queerness is also an effect of this process. A queen could seamlessly bring together each of these elements to possession: alcohol as entheogen, dance as ecstatic, and drag as a vehicle. This kind of drag as possession would be uniquely personal, queer, and magical.

Possession traditions around the world oftentimes emphasize the importance of possession as a vehicle for public service. Possession is not only done because it's inherently magical or enjoyable, but because there is a profound role it fulfills in service to the community. These traditions are also often accompanied by social structures that give them a place to conduct possession and long-held traditions for care and upkeep of a vessel. For many queer witches, this is not inherently true. Many traditional witches and animists conduct a solitary practice, and the queer community as a whole is often completely secular, creating a lack of public spaces to conduct possession or to show respect for spiritual traditions.

To circumvent this kind of challenge, queer witches would either have to create their own infrastructure and places to have this kind of ecstatic and queer experience or develop a personal practice of their own. This is also limited by location and resources. Where I live in Southwest Florida, there is a deficit of both an active queer community and witchcraft communities. This has, out of necessity, forced me to create a personal approach to possession. Possession for me becomes wholly connected to the devotion of my spirits and imbibing my life with their influence. Possession is not about serving a community, but drawing spirits closer to my life and giving them an outlet through my body and the space that I have set aside for them. This stresses the importance of how liminal and unique every witch's experience is.

There are even more ways that the queer landscape is alive, and ways that queer people can express their relationship to spirits. These lines are not firm or to be held tightly in the seemingly straightforward concepts above. Makeup is a powerful transformational tool, but it is not needed for very feminine spirits to inhabit my body. I can wear the most masculine clothing and still share this space with goddesses. My experience with spirit possession for small groups includes both full regalia with shifts in consciousness and just slathering on flying ointment in a tank top sitting in the kitchen. Your experience will be determined by your approach, your spirits, and your location.

Doing The Deed: A Ritual of Possession

Start by determining the spirit you want to call into yourself. Don't merely flip through a mythology dictionary and draw a god at random; this should be a spirit you have a long-standing relationship with. Next, determine why you want to work with this spirit in this way. Use your judgement to determine if this is the best way to conduct the process. If you're looking for answers to a given question, could divination be a better option? If the spirit itself has told you They want you to host them, make sure it's something you actually want to do. If you're working in a group or for a public ritual, determine the atmosphere. What we've been talking about isn't intended for a highly scripted or stuffy environment.

Be ready for the possibility that you may not become possessed during the ritual. This is ecstatic and wild work, and there is no guarantee of success. Be ready to dance and perform for a long time, and make sure that everyone in participation knows what to expect. Ecstatic possession has more in common with a feast or dance party than it does with most modern pagan rituals. Participants should be comfortable being ecstatic as well; if you're at a drag show EVERYONE wants to lip sync to the song the queen is performing. That kind of group involvement is part of the devotion; it attracts the spirits.

Turn Pre-Gaming into Head-Spacing. If you will be consuming alcohol, use it as a chance to make those offerings. Try to find that liminal space between fun and spiritual work. Be receptive and be fluid. Use makeup as part of your ritual, a tool to shift. Visualize every brush stroke wiping away your features and replacing them with the features of the spirit. You don't have to be a talented makeup artist to transform your face, although a little practice can help you feel more confident in the work. By the time you're putting on outfits and a wig, you should feel dreamy and otherworldly.

Get ready to dance for the long haul. Possession in this context may not be what you expect it to be. The first few times tend to be more akin to channeling, where you are in control of your motion but are guided by the movement of a spirit. You may be aware that you are talking but you don't know where the words are coming from. You may feel sudden urges to go somewhere but have the full choice of whether or not to do the action. As you progress in this work, your relationship with the spirit may change. Over time, you may find yourself giving over entirely to the spirit and having no recollection of the experience at all. This is one reason why possession is best suited for at least a small group.

Small group settings allow the vessel to have a safety net and a spotter. A spotter's job is to keep the vessel safe. Think of your spotter as a spiritual designated driver. Possession comes with risks, and can sometimes be very intense for those involved. Unfamiliar spirits may try and take advantage of the possession state. Your entheogen may affect your judgement, and dancing may lead to dehydration if you are not careful. Having a spotter on hand is one way to ensure a higher degree of safety for the vessel and other precautions should be exercised.

Precautions can be as simple as planning how much of an entheogen should be used, having easily accessible clean water, and putting spiritual guards (as determined by your personal practice) in place before possession work. A spotter should have training in basic first aid, know which spirit is being drawn, know how to spot/sense unfamiliar spirits, and have the ability to anticipate when a vessel may be engaging in potentially unsafe behavior. I've heard horror stories of spirits possessing someone and attempting to drink several bottles of whiskey single-handedly.

The most important factor of a good spotter is being able to pull someone back from a possession. How a spotter brings the vessel back will be determined by personal practice; but some commonly used approaches include basic grounding techniques, physical touch, addressing the spirit directly, or even splashing the vessel with cold water. My go-to is an incense blend created specifically to bring me back from possession (I use a mix of rosemary, lavender, and sage). My spotter burns the blend and politely addresses the spirit after a set amount of time. This allows the spirit to get its business done and have a respectful exit from my body. In extreme cases, the spirit may need to be forcibly removed, in which case I have a banishing powder (rosemary, stinging nettle, a pinch of sulfur, and agrimony) on hand just in case. I have never had to resort to this, and I attribute that to my preparations for possession every single time. The spotter and the vessel should determine whatever methods they are going to use well in advance.

In my experience, most possessions are somewhere down the middle in terms of intensity and they feel very dream-like. I can remember snippets of important information, but nothing specific. I can remember my body being close to someone and my lips moving, but I have no recollection of what was said to the other person. The work is hard, exhausting, frustrating, and exhilarating. I've danced many nights with the intention of undergoing possession but had nothing but a good night of dancing to show for it. Adjust your expectations, and make sure your group or crowd also has realistic expectations of at most a powerful moving experience and at least a night of ecstatic dancing. When you dance in honor of the ancestors, especially the queer ancestors, nothing is a waste.

Castro Madonna
by Adare

From the San Francisco Sisters of Perpetual Indulgence, Sister Eve Voluion is magic incarnate! Providing the sanctity of a confessional with the acceptance of a pride parade, the Sisters of Perpetual indulgence are an open exploration of spirituality, sexuality, gender, and unadulterated sass, all while raising funds for charity through the wonders of drag.

Embodying the Phoenix: The Transformation of Queer Erotic Alchemy

by Tai Fenix Kulystin

The Phoenix exists in all worlds. It is earthly, cosmic, and divine, made up of flesh, fire, and ash simultaneously. It is the bird that rises, whole and vibrant in its majesty. It is the bird that flames, sacrificed in the cleansing fire. It is the bird that reduces to ash, soon to be reborn. It is also a verb: phoenixing, or to phoenix, which is the process of transformation itself. As witches, as magicians, as beings currently experiencing the manifestation of soul and spirit into matter, we stand as the reconcilers between the worlds, walking within and belonging to all. We can harness this power of the Phoenix and of phoenixing as we traverse the worlds to enrich our magic and inhabit our whole selves.

There are two kinds of alchemy generally recognized: *chrysopoeia*, or gold-making, and *apotheosis*, or god-making. These are often discussed as the difference between practical alchemy, or alchemy that works with matter, and psychospiritual alchemy, or the alchemy that works on human manifestations of divinity. The purpose of alchemy is to transmute the base material we are working on to its purest and most perfected state. When I say "purest and most perfected," I mean being made up of nothing but its own self, or as free of impurities and outside influence as possible.

The Phoenix is often utilized in alchemical symbology as an emblem for the final phase of the work, sometimes called the Philosopher's Stone. It is both representative of the completion of the work—the transmutation of the lead of base matter into the perfected gold—as well as the entirety of the work itself, which is the process of phoenixing. It is *solve et coagula*, literally meaning to dissolve and coagulate, or to separate and recombine. This is the fundamental process of alchemy: separation, purification, and recombination. This is transmutation, transformation, and change.

To embody the Phoenix is to embrace the ever-changing nature of reality and the beauty of destruction and creation. The more comfortable we are with change and death, the more fully and deeply we can experience life. By feeling and experiencing deeply, we embody life, death, rebirth, and all the pleasures and pains that result from these experiences. We get the opportunity to engage in and be present with the flow of life and existence, which is change and growth. We have been sold the lie of a consistent self and consistent body, but we are not static; we are verbs. We are ever-changing amalgamations of selves, of cells, of emotions, of desires, and of atoms, made up of vastly more empty space than matter. We are constantly in motion. We are change.

The Gift of the Queer Other

We each exist as discrete individuals who are also part of the whole, able to affect the whole just as the whole affects us. We are individual reflections of the wholeness of all that is, able to affect change in the universe simply by being, by existing, and by living our truths. Each one of us is creating the universe with every breath.

Each one of us has a place in this world and something to give to this world. This is not necessarily something we have to produce, but something we do or something we are. This is what we give the world simply by existing and filling it with our presence. Phoenixing allows us to become more wholly ourselves so we can more fully do our work and be in right relationship with ourselves, others, and the world around us. We are all the recipients of generations of trauma and joy, pleasure and grief, and we get to determine how to move forward and how to heal our lineages.

As queer and trans folks, part of our gift—and sometimes our greatest challenge— is simply being alive. We challenge the status quo by existing and reminding this heterocisnormative capitalist kyriarchy that gender and sexuality are meaningful and diverse, not inherent or predetermined based on the shape of our genitals. As a culture and as a people, we are on the precipice of transformation, with people of all genders and sexualities having a role to play. I believe that we queer and trans folks have a particularly useful perspective in this transformation. As we shift into a new paradigm, new mythology, and new consciousness, we assist the shift simply by being in this world and working to bust open restrictive notions of gender and sexuality, no matter where on or off the binary we fit.

For much of recent history, society as a whole has been fearing and reviling the Other, the unknown, and Mystery in the name of false safety and comfort. Safety is not something that we can feel from external sources; we can experience support and protection from the outside, but the only safety we can experience is internal. Most of us are so disconnected from our own selves, our own life force, and our own beings that we routinely allow others' ideas, concepts, messages, and moralities to guide us and stand in for our own. Each of us needs to find our own genuine and authentic beliefs or ways of being. As a people, we need to be self-full: to get in touch with who we are on the most basic of levels and to live from that place. We are unable to embrace our own whole selves if we push away the unknown and the darkness that the Other so often represents. We need to learn to embrace and celebrate difference, otherness, and diversity rather than run away from it. This is part of the gift of queerness. This is part of the gift of phoenixing: we can burn and thereby cast off the ideas and restraints that others have imposed upon us.

The magic we need right now is *phoenixing*, the verb and action. The more we can release the notions of others, the more we can inhabit our entire Selves. The more we can inhabit our entire Selves, the more we can truly live from a place of our own power with—rather than over or under—others. Here we become our most divine selves, doing the work of god-making, or clearing the way for more of our divine nature to come through in every breath.

The Phoenixing of Queerness & Transness

My personal connection to the Phoenix and phoenixing is greatly influenced by my queerness and transness. To illustrate the perspective I am coming from, here are some labels as indicators of my various levels of privilege and oppression. I walk in the world as a queer, fat, fem, genderqueer trans guy who is educated, middle class, polyamorous, kinky, abled, neurodivergent, and of Northern and Eastern European ancestry. I have a magical background primarily centered in Feri witchcraft, hermeticism, and various types of ceremonial magic.

We queer people have been placed into a phoenixing role in contemporary society due to the work required to claim our queer selves. Queerness, as I use it, is a rejection of labels; it is an anti-label. It is about our sexuality of course, but it is also a rejection of heteronormativity and traditional essentialist identity politics. Queerness is constantly reinventing itself and questioning the status quo, not simply in a reactionary way as could be inferred, but to create new ways of being. To be queer, to live in queerness, is to phoenix. It is finding that which is not working, finding the inequalities and injustices in our lived experiences, and working toward change. It is also finding the places when we are the Phoenix that soars, when we are self-full enough to be in our own power and rise.

The process of claiming queerness in a heteronormative society requires us to be the Phoenix: to find the heteronormativity, homophobia, and transphobia (and other cultural power dynamics) that have been placed in us by this culture and allow them to burn. This is not a one-and-done process. For as long as this culture exists and we are in it, we must confront the messages we are inundated with that attempt to reinforce the heteronormative power structure.

The same process is true, possibly on an even more obvious level, for trans folks and cisnormativity. Though not all of us have the desire to transition socially or physically, I believe this is still universal on an internal level. I have often thought of my own process of transitioning as transmutation, as alchemy, and as phoenixing. I am intentionally refining myself and my experience so I can become more wholly myself on all levels. It is allowing me to be seen for who I am and who I declare myself to be. Transition is one of the only things in my life I have done just for me, not for anyone else, and I have had to fight for it every step along the way—often fighting myself in the process, or at least some part of myself that was holding on to internalized transphobia, cisnormativity, or femmephobia.

The deeper I dig into myself and the more I do the work of phoenixing with my own ingrained cultural prejudices and oppressions, the easier it is to see the structure that underlies and supports them. The more work I do in this way, also, the kinder, gentler, and more patient I am. I am better able to hold complexity and nuance, both for myself and those around me. I move toward deeper ways of knowing myself, others, and the world. I am less interested in control or violence and more interested in pleasure and power sharing.

Erotic Alchemy and the Sacred Whore

One of the methods through which I engage with the Phoenix and phoenixing is through what I call Erotic Alchemy. In my definition, Erotic Alchemy is alchemy that acknowledges and centers the erotic nature of all that is. Erotic Alchemy utilizes alchemical processes and methods to understand and encourage the unification of matter (the body), consciousness (spirit), and mystery/shadow (soul) within an explicit and intentional erotic context. The goal of Erotic Alchemy is to bring about the perfection of the Self while recognizing the inherent nature of the erotic within the wholeness of existence.

When engaging in erotic alchemy, I take the approach that we are doing physical and psychospiritual alchemy, as we are still working on the physical nature of our own embodiment. This is not the same as the perfection of physical substances in a laboratory setting, of course, and I am an ardent practitioner of both physical and spiritual alchemies. It is similar to the processes applied to all materials, and our psychological and spiritual experiences are, in the end, written within our own flesh and therefore manifest in matter.

When I use the term "erotic" I don't simply mean sexuality, though certainly that is one important aspect of the erotic. I use erotic synonymously with life force, creativity, soul's desire, and personal power. It is the desire that moves us toward becoming who we truly are and connecting with our purpose. It is the aspect of the Self that desires. It is desire in all of its meanings, from the most basic to the highest aspirations of our souls, that leads us toward connection with ourselves, others, the world, and the rest of the cosmos. It is bringing ourselves present to the current moment as much as possible by bringing our intention, attention, and awareness forward in service to integration. This is also embodiment.

I often find that embodiment is approached as simply focusing on the sensations arising in our bodies, but this is missing the important aspect of integration and the multifaceted nature of being. The body is important, yes; sensations are important, yes, but they are only aspects of our embodied existence and experience. Integration requires engaging all of our selves or aspects. A model I like to employ for this corresponds to the seven directions (simplistically defined here): air as intellect/mental capacity, fire as inspiration/drive, water as emotions/connection, earth as sensations/touch, above as spirit/transcendent self, below as soul/shadow self, and center as body/egoic self. All directions converge in the center, in the physical body, as the focus of our manifestation. When embodying anything or anyone, we can work to engage one, many, or all of our directions, integrating and empowering as much of our whole self as possible in the process.

The erotic is a natural force that both creates and shapes us. In this culture, we find eroticism through sexuality and often not anywhere else, but we can open up to experiencing the erotic in all things and in all kinds of desire. We can also engage with sexuality as a gateway to understanding our own erotic natures because it is where we have relegated the erotic to in American culture.

Engaging with the erotic has an aspect of moving us toward wholeness and liberation. It is rooted in the body and in feeling and doing. It is allowing ourselves to feel deeply, to listen to and trust our own experience of the world, to live centered in our own desires and our own Selves before anyone else's, and to live connected to our own power. When we are living from our truth within right relationship with ourselves and those around us, and when we recognize those around us as whole beings in their own right, then we are much more challenging to control.

When we are living in connection with our erotic natures we are connected to feeling and our wholeness in a way completely counter to what capitalist kyriarchy tries to demand from us. We are connected to our wildness and the nature of our beings in a way that is fundamentally in opposition to the power structures that exist. This is a particular type of queerness we can live from. We are no longer interested in engaging with others except as equals and encouraging others to experience their own powerful whole Selves in the way that is right for them. The erotic is the transformative pull of desire, leading us in the direction of wholeness. When we are in right relationship with the erotic and our own selves, we are able to stand in our own power with others.

As such, I work with alchemy as a sacred whore, or sacred whoredom as an alchemist. The sacred whore is an erotic priestex of any gender who embodies sexual sovereignty, knows all parts of the body to be sacred, and celebrates the erotic in all of its forms. The work of sacred whoredom begins with the body: recognizing all bodies as holy and working to embrace and inhabit all parts of the body. Alchemy fundamentally begins with the body, with the *prima materia* of the Self that is the body. True knowledge rests in the body, is embodied. So the sacred whore works to be wholly and purely themself through engaging with the sacred erotic nature of the body. As a lover of all and an erotic priestex, the sacred whore is queer and works to see the sacred erotic nature of every being they encounter. This does not mean they have to have sex with everyone—we still get to have boundaries around our own bodies—but we can recognize the erotic spark in all things.

The sacred whore, as a healer, also assists to bring others to phoenixing. We lead another or others to that *petite mort*—that little death and exquisite experience of orgasm—which is a moment of surrender and release. It is a time when great magic can be worked, with the release of life force and intention. We can encourage them to hold off from orgasm for as long as they can stand, so they may be in the fire of their need for just a little longer, letting their body be the *athanor*—the alchemical furnace of transformation—that burns up that which is no longer serving them.

We can assist with their release and encourage the surrender necessary to turn to ash and create room for something new. We can strengthen their intention to bring in that which they desire so they may rise again through intimacy and aftercare.

The sacred whore and the Phoenix are both doing the work of the erotic, which is phoenixing. It is utilizing our own erotic life force as the fire of transformation to perfect our own beings and those of our beloveds. It is harnessing our own erotic life force, recognizing it as the source of our power, and living from that place as much as possible. Too often, I see healer-type folks forgetting that we are just as deserving of receiving our own healing power as those that we love. It is easy to focus on our beloveds before ourselves. So many of us were taught that focusing on ourselves is selfish and therefore bad, but here I want to flip the script and remind us all to be self-full. Living from this place of power is where we find our gift to the world, and is what phoenixing is all about. We find our whole selves and discover the complexity and paradox of all that is and all we are, and recognize that those are one and the same.

Phoenix and Phoenixing Praxis

There are many ways to work with the Phoenix and phoenixing. You may already have ideas for exercises or practices you can engage in. The following are three exercises I have developed to tap into this work, but are certainly not the only ones available.

The Mantle of the Phoenix

The simplest exercise is to visualize yourself experiencing the phoenixing process. You can do this by visualizing a Phoenix in front of you that you can connect to, or shifting the image of your body into a Phoenix. To visualize your own self changing into the Phoenix, you can imagine your arms becoming wings, nose and mouth becoming a beak, growing tail feathers, and so on. Or, should you work with an external Phoenix first, you can visualize the Phoenix in front of you with as much detail as you desire, and ask to merge with them, stepping into its form, either with physical movement or in your mind's eye.

Once merged, breathe into the experience. Engage as many of your senses as possible: what can you smell, touch, taste, hear, and see as the Phoenix? Once you have taken on the form of the Phoenix, you can then move through its cycle: burn up, dissolve to ash, recombine anew, grow, and take flight. You can do this without anything in mind aside from connecting with the Phoenix at first. Once you become comfortable with it, you can include intentions that you may declare aloud or simply speak within your mind. I particularly like to do this when I am feeling stuck and I know something needs to change but I am not sure what. I can gain quick clarity from this exercise, or simply trust it to assist in the necessary shift.

Embodying Transformation

For this exercise, you begin by placing yourself as the Phoenix in the center of a directional sphere that is representative of your psyche. For this practice, you connect to each of the seven directions of the psyche as mentioned earlier and feel into your connection to each of them, working toward integration. You can do this within a cast circle or not and with intention or not. Similarly, with the previous practice, I encourage you to get comfortable with the practice before including intention. This is not calling the quarters or the watchtowers, if you are familiar with those practices, this is finding aspects of yourself reflected in each of the directions.

To begin, center yourself within your own space, body, mind, and soul in whatever way that means to you. Come into the present moment as much as you can, and be gentle with yourself if any resistance comes up or if there are any parts of you that do not want to be present. That's okay, you can let them be. Recognizing that resistance is part of the purpose of this exercise.

Connect with the directions around you and the aspects of yourself that they each represent. The horizontal axis is all body-related and aspects of your manifestation in this earthly world. The vertical axis is connecting to the parts of yourself that inhabit the other worlds beyond this one. The divine, chthonic world below and the celestial, universal world above are reconciled in this world: the terrestrial, mundane world here and now.

If it is useful, you can imagine cords or beams of light extending in each direction, one at a time, finding the aspect of yourself in that direction. Notice each direction with as many of your senses as you can. Be curious and open to each one. Notice what your connection is like to each direction. You can work with them in any order that you like, in any way that you like.

I sometimes like to do this exercise seated, visualizing engaging with each direction. Other times I like to stand or move around the room I'm in, setting my body/egoic self in the center and moving toward each direction in the ways that I am able (it becomes trickiest with above, below, and center). Do whatever is most interesting to you, and try both ways eventually, or something else entirely.

Once you have connected with each of these directions, you can work to strengthen or balance your connection to each. Engage with those that feel lacking and see what might be necessary to strengthen or explore there. Notice how each of the directions interact and intersect with each other and how life force flows between them (or doesn't). Are there blockages or challenges in any direction or any flow? You can bring the Phoenix or phoenixing to these blockages or these directions and work to strengthen the connections. Play with these however you would like. When finished, simply let the visualization fade from your awareness, move your body, lightly pat or move your hands along your body to feel where you begin and end, and come back into usual conscious awareness.

Owning Your Erotic Power

The next exercise is one I've developed through my erotic alchemy praxis, specifically engaging with the three principles of alchemy: salt, sulfur, and mercury, which relate to the body, soul, and spirit of all things, respectively. I like to work with these as they can be mapped to different areas of the body. The purpose of this exercise is to engage with three important aspects of your Self: your mind as it relates to your intellect and mental capacity, your heart as it relates to your capacity for feeling and connection, and your pelvis or genitals as they relate to your capacity for creativity and desire. The goal, similar to the previous exercise, is to connect with each piece, strengthen them, and then work to strengthen their connections. This assists with integration and wholeness.

Begin by noticing your breath and your body, either sitting, standing, or laying comfortably. Notice what sensations you are feeling, what it feels like to breathe, and where in your body your breath is filling. Take deep breaths if you desire, and feel free to stretch or wiggle or move your body in any way that might feel good in order to bring attention to your physical experience. Focus first on bringing air in through your nose and exhaling through your mouth. Breathe. Then, see if you can notice your lungs expand and relax. Breathe. Then, see if you can notice your belly expand and relax. Breathe.

Shift attention from your belly to your pelvis, your genitals, your pelvic bowl, or your perineum, wherever you feel is the center of the base of your body. Imagine a sphere nestled here, the size of a marble, growing larger with each breath, made up of your erotic lifeforce. This is one of your power centers, related to creativity, to soul, to shadow, to sexuality, and to all else that you associate with this part of the body. From this sphere extends, in all directions, cords stretching out to all those who have influenced you in this area, and all those you have ongoing connections with. Pull these back in or cut them off, whichever feels appropriate, until this sphere is connecting to nothing except itself. You can always extend these out again after this exercise if you wish. Feel that all of your power in this area is contained and held for only you. Take your time here. Breathe here. Notice what it feels like, what sensations, thoughts, desires, or feelings arise.

Once you feel ready, keep that sphere bright and full, but let your attention, intention, and awareness travel up from your pelvic bowl to your head, the bowl of your skull. Here, focus your attention at the midpoint of your skull, where another sphere is nestled, growing larger with each breath. This power center is related to intellect, to imagination, to spirit, to transcendence, and all else that you associate with this part of the body. Find the cords this sphere has extending out of it. As before, retract or cut off those cords until the sphere is solid within itself. All your power is held and contained for you only, for the moment. Take your time here as well. Breathe, feel, and notice what arises.

When you are ready to move on, do the same to your heart center, the bowl of your chest. Again finding the midpoint and expanding this new sphere of erotic lifeforce. This power center is related to connection, to feeling, to the body, to love, and all else that you associate with this part of the body. Notice the cords, pull them back or cut them off as before. Breathe, feel, and notice as before.

Now that you have engaged each of these spheres, see if you can be aware of them all at once. How does it feel to hold your power just for yourself? What is arising in your body? How do you want to move (if at all) from this place? Notice the connections between the spheres. Is there flow here, or discomfort? Blockages or ease? See if you can flow between the spheres, up and down the central column of your body, or up and around in a figure-eight/infinity loop, or in any other pattern you might like. Do this for as long as you like. You can employ phoenixing on the blockages, or engage with the mantle of the phoenix while connected to these spheres of power. When finished, simply let the visualization fade from your awareness, move your body, lightly pat or move your hands along your body to feel where you begin and end, and come back into usual conscious awareness.

The destructive and painful process of phoenixing is worth the challenge it takes to become the Phoenix that rises majestic and strong. The entire process is done in service to that bird, no matter how many times we need to burst into flames so that we may rise again. May all your transformations clear away that which is not true for you or does not serve you, and bring you to greater wholeness and harmony within yourself so you may be your best, queerest, most fabulous you.

thaMind-Sol Lady's Revenge

by M.C. MoHagani Magnetek

Misgendered. Hot, bothered, and mad with so much to say that I sprinkled Black Girl Magic Dust over a blank page in my notebook, and jumped in. On the other side of the sheet, I walked out of a closet and set foot in the aftermath of destruction on Spenard Road. Passengers on the Route 3 bus were suspended upside down as they clung to the handrails. The less-fortunate lay on the inside roof contorted. I heard their agony and pleas for help while the horror of pedestrians and drivers of stalled cars ruined a damn good day. I inhaled a deep breath until my internal cellular network imploded with electric currents to be directed by my hands to a parked excavator crane left by construction workers that had abandoned it in the madness. I whispered a few magic words to operate the crane and turn the bus right-side up. My eyes scanned the crowd for the culprit and all hands pointed right. Speechless, I crossed over sunken permafrost holes and felt the tightness of dry air constricting my esophagus. On the trail before me, chaos wrecked buildings, destroyed cars, and tossed over baby strollers.

From the shadows leaning against a wall, I heard their voice, "It's about time you get here."

"What did I miss, Mind-Sol Lady?"

"For starters, your bigoted bus driver is a page ahead. You must reach him before he gets to the end to tell the story his way."

"What's so bad about that?" I asked.

"Your world and mine will forever be sealed in ignorance."

"Well that's cool with me. I like ignorant muthafuckas, they are fucking funny."

"I don't know why I bother with you. You can't win in this shadow dimension without me."

My bifurcated spirit walked a vengeful path in silence, no longer separated by a fourth dimension. thaMind Sol-Lady lead the way with a blazing machete thirsty for blood and I was right behind her, pissed off at another hater who got away. But not this time. Not after this crime. I played by the rules. Presented myself to be cordial and kind, but the bus driver's venom fractured my mind.

Under normal circumstances, thaMind Sol-Lady wouldn't give a fuck about people but she reconstructed their habitats with her shadow manipulation abilities as we followed tracks. Oversized and heavy boot prints marked the travels of our greatest foe to date. The bus driver's hatred for me drastically increased the heat, shrinking the lakes and ponds of my city, Anchorage. My hair became more brittle the closer we reached him at the Coastal Trail, a bike path that runs along the water's edge. My shadow raised her blade high after we heard the rustle of desiccated leaves. The Public Transportation Representative blocked our path with a hoisted Glock on his hip and his feet shoulder length apart, eager for a gunfight.

"Magnetek. Stop. There's no going any further. I read your complaint."

"Then you know what I must do."

"As the lawman, I can't let you do that. An eye for an eye…"

"Yeah… I know. It leads to a gang of blind muthafuckas."

"You leave me no choice," the manager said, lowering his hand over his pistol in a position to quick-draw his weapon. Magnetek stepped aside and allowed thaMind Sol-Lady to lock eyes with the bureaucratic junkie-turned-sheriff. In her fighting cat-stance, my darker side deflected his barrage of bullets with the graceful strokes of her raging machete. Ricochet bullets caught blaze in the dehydrated forest, sparking wildfires all around them. She advanced on the government lackey like a figure skater, dicing him into a half dozen pieces with only three moves. Head, arm, arm, torso, and leg slid off in chunks before the other leg tipped over. thaMind Sol-Lady stepped over the remains, but I walked around and followed her onto the second page, my pencil madly catching every word my heart poured out.

Standing on the frozen Cook Inlet, my enemy, the bus driver had grown to become a gigantuous extremist blocking out the sun for all the good people and animals of the city. Over five-stories tall, flaming red eyes, volcanic erupting muscles, and a too-small bus operator uniform. We didn't care who he was or what he became, we gave him three chances nonetheless. Side by side, thaMind Sol-Lady and I braced for the battle with the uncanny but got nothing but hot breath in our faces.

"Sir. Show me your I.D."

"Oh. I see you still got jokes. I already told you I am a woman."

"You look like a man. You sound like a man. So you must be a man."

"Your vile disdain for me has destroyed the city and murdered the environment."

"Yes, the dark side has made me quite powerful. There's no way you can defeat me. Take your faggot ass back to the closet of filth you came from."

"Just for that, I am going to beat you like scrambled eggs before my doppelgänger obliterates you for good," said thaMind Sol-Lady, relinquishing herself from the gravitational pull off the earth and levitating to meet the monster eye-to-eye. The Bus Driver launched at her but failed to connect. I amplified her speed with my magnetek propulsion blasts. Before he could exhale his last breath, she riddled him with her Five-Point-Palm Exploding-Heart-Technique. I refused to let the legend of five steps stand alone without help. I merged with my shadow to become Ultramagnetek. We used our electromagnetokinesis to yank an asteroid out of orbit and smashed the bus driver, crushing all 206 his bones just before his heart stopped on the fifth step. We summoned an elevator out of nowhere with sheer imagination and a slight bit of pleasure to imprison his soul. We left his foot trapped in the door before pressing the little green button that sends his ass straight to hell.

With all my rage left behind on the last page, I separated from my shadow and walked back through the closet from whence I came. Looking back over the page, I couldn't possibly submit this complaint, so I rewrote the entire letter which resulted in the following official submission:

> **Date:**   February 24, 2014
>
> **To:**   People's Motivation Transportation
>
> **From:**   Magnetek
>
> **RE:**   Sexist Transgender Discriminating Bus Driver!!!

I just got off the Number 3N Northern Lights Inbound Bus heading to the downtown transit center at 6:45 pm this evening February 24, 2014.

I am submitting this formal Complaint because this is the 2nd time this has happened to me by the same bus driver who is a large Caucasian Middle-

Aged looking Man.

I don't know his name or his badge number to give you, all I know is that he has a very funky nasty attitude filled with prejudice and disrespect toward other people.

For the 2nd Time!!! This man, AFTER I have already scanned and paid with my UAA ID asked to see the Picture on my ID. He has seen me before and knows that I am a Transgender African American Woman!!! He is aware and it is very obvious what my gender identity is.

When it happened this time today I told him that he ALWAYS does this to me. And each time has DISRESPECTFULLY called me SIR in his responses as a malicious way to demean me.

I sat down momentarily but got up and went back to the front, standing behind the line, to let him know that his ACTIONS are SEXIST and DISCRIMINATORY against Me and other Transgender People!!! (Using much more Colorful Language)

And to show just how SEXIST and DISCRIMINATORY his attitudes are, he tells me that "You are not Special Sir!" and that he cards everyone; which is a Damn Lie!! Because I sat there and watched other passengers get on without request from him to see their ID cards the first and the second time. The first time this happened was one day last summer.

What truly makes this event SEXIST and DISCRIMINATORY is that UAA Student ID/Bus Cards do not state a person's Sex or Gender on the cards, only a picture and name. So he knows damn well that his intentions are hateful and dead wrong!

He has no REASON to ask an already PAID customer/passenger to see their ID Card.

He does not work for the Transportation Security Administration nor is he a Law Enforcement Officer; he is a Bus Driver and has No Authority to question anyone's Sex or Gender just to ride public transportation. He was not going to put me off the bus either time, but I guess he is just extraordinarily sexually curious to know more about me.

This man is a HORRIBLE person and deserves reprimanding and Cultural Gender Sensitivity Training.

It is a DAMN Shame that Myself or any other Transgender passengers have to endure such SEXIST and DISCRIMINATORY Practices from one of your Municipality Employed Bus Drivers!!!

According to The Anchorage Public Transportation

Department's Commitment to Civil Rights - Title VI located on your website:

"The MOA Public Transportation Department (PTD) assures that NO PERSON shall, on the grounds of race, color, or national origin, as provided by the Title VI of the Civil Rights Act of 1964 and the Civil Rights Restoration Act of 1987, be excluded from participation in, be denied the benefits of, or be otherwise subjected to DISCRIMINATION under any program or activity."

HIS ACTIONS ARE IN FACT DISCRIMINATORY AGAINST A TRANSGENDER AFRICAN AMERICAN PERSON!!!

Please have someone contact me immediately via email or phone.. I will follow up in the morning doing regular business hours to discuss this matter with competent and qualified People Mover administrators.

My name is Ms. Magnetek and I am Appalled that Tax dollars are spent employing this Simple Minded Sexist Transgender Discriminating Bus Driver!!!

It should have been easily resolved. I put my prettiest dress on, a flower in my hair, and talked to management the following morning. That very evening, on my way to my Feminist Theory class, I waited for the bus, only to discover the same bigoted driver at helm of the wheel. Once again, he demanded to see my student I.D. and I was like, "Aw Nawl, Hell Nawl!!!"

I lost all kinds of cool and composure before I told him that I was going to ride the bus to the ends of the earth, until transportation management arrived to sort out this mess. With other fine citizens as witnesses on the bus, he called me out by name and constantly called me a man. I said, "I've already filed a complaint on you. You should know the deal. How many times do I have to tell you I'm a woman? Can't you see I'm wearing a pretty dress?" His beady eyes pierced through the reflection of the rearview mirror at me along with his nasty and oh-so-hurtful words. Just before I called my attorney, I asked him, "How would you like for me to call you out by your name? I don't think you would like being called asshole very much." With my lawyer now on the phone, she suggested I take his picture. I waited for the bus to come to a stop, stood behind the yellow line, and used the rearview mirror to capture a picture of his face before he turned around and knocked the phone from my hand.

I was hotter than the surface of the sun, and called 911 to report the harassment and the fact that he put his hands on me. We argued for five miles before the bus stopped at the University library. The police were there, but the bus transportation management wasn't there, so I decided to stand my ground. An older black woman who had been there for half of the ride, sitting across from me said, "I understand if you gotta take a stance. Do what you gotta do." I was like Rosa Parks on that muthafucka, with people at the back of the bus yelling at me to just get off. However, I wasn't going anywhere when police came onboard and told me to get off. I noticed they were gearing up to drag me off the bus, so I complied because I was just too cute that day to be manhandled by the police. I got off and a few notes where taken, but they wouldn't do anything about him verbally and physically harassing me. I left hurt, heartbroken, and dismayed. By the time I made it to class, I could only put my head on my desk and cry. My classmates were upset, angry, and there to support me during such a heavy moment.

Weeks later, I got an apology letter from the public transportation people which I accepted, but my problem was still there. I wrote mad poetry and popped Xanax for anxiety every time I got on the bus for the next few months, never knowing when I was going to have him as my driver again. After a while, I began to see him driving the route again. The anxiety encapsulated my spirit every time he looked at me with disdain. I got on with a classmate one day after school and my friend asked me if the bus driver was eyeballing her and I told her no, he was looking at me. I then told her the story. I was at my wits end. The bus is my only mode of transportation and there was no getting away from this ugly man.

I determined that extreme over-the-top kindness was called for in this situation. From then on, every time I got on the bus and saw him, I greeted him with kindness and forced smiles. After months of this tactic of popping Xanax for anxiety, and ever increasing rehearsed smiles, the bus driver began to crack open smiles in return to me. Soon he was waving me on, telling me to have a good day as if we were chummy old friends. I don't know if it was cultural and gender sensitivity training or a change of heart that made him turn around. I like to believe that what made this negative into a positive was my Black Girl Magic Dust. Resorting to my alter-ego thaMind-Sol Lady tactics could have delivered vengeance but not peace, which is all I wanted in the first place when I stepped on to the bus that evening.

QUEERMAGIC

YOU

ARE AWESOME,
BRILLIANT, AMAZING, INCREDIBLE,
AND TOTALLY WORTHY OF HAVING A SACRIFICIAL ALTAR BUILT IN YOUR HONOR AT THE NEAREST AVAILABLE VOLCANO

Gentle Affirmation
by Dmitri Arbacauskas

The Magic of the Eight Queer Deities

by Adrian Moran

The first step is to prepare to walk the labyrinth. This journey back and forth, moving toward the goal but never in a straightforward path, is a central part of our worldview. The journey prepares us, separates us from the mundane. The center holds a sacred encounter. We will meet a Deity. We will meet our selves. We will be challenged to burn away what is not needed, what is holding us back.

I follow an emergent neopagan tradition called Fellowship of the Phoenix, formerly known as the Brotherhood of the Phoenix. Founded in 2004 by experienced magical practitioners from a variety of traditions, the goal was to create a spiritual tradition free from the heteronormative structures such as a dualistic Goddess and God worship and the gendered roles for the divine that are central to many neopagan traditions. Until July 2017 our membership and most of our rituals were for men who love men, but now we welcome LGBTQ+ (Lesbian, Gay, Bisexual, Trans, and Queer) people of all gender identities, ages 18 and over. Centered in Chicago, The Fellowship has a presence in other places such as Seattle, but we are trying to figure out ways for these teachings to be available to people everywhere who can benefit.

Many of the members have their own spiritual practices, but when we come together, we celebrate the Gods who have revealed themselves to us. They are the eight Queer Deities or the eight-fold Queer God. Like many other neopagan traditions, we have eight holidays, but ours have been refined into a series of encounters with these eight Deities.

Some of us see our Deities as archetypes, or embodiments of ideals for a Queer life. Being a polytheist and an aspiring ecstatic, I can tell you that I have a personal relationship with these eight. To me, they are real and distinct personalities. The Fellowship has no dogma on this point, and I would never claim to have any definitive knowledge of the Deities' true nature. I suspect their nature is far beyond simple human understanding, and I would expect each person's experience of them to differ somewhat. I can only share the experiences of myself and of others in my group.

In our public rituals, we cycle through celebrating each of these Deities in turn through the year and the Fellowship provides instruction in methods for personal devotion. At the same time, as our relationship with them has grown, it has become clear that we are not the exclusive conduits of their gifts. These Deities want the World to know them, and want to expand their reach.

The Divine Youth teaches Wonder. When we give ourselves over to everyday stresses and mindless routines, we lose sight of what is special and sacred in our world. We must see the world through fresh eyes, and greet the world as beautiful and full of possibility. The fog brought about by our mundane routine clears as we embody this sense of wonder, and we once again see things as they are, not as tools to achieve an end or simply a part of the background. We are filled with a desire to play and appreciate what the world offers us.

The Explorer teaches Courage. Growth and change will be stifled if we never go beyond the familiar and the safe. We must be willing to step beyond the comfortable and protected spaces. It is vital that we try new things, see new places, and meet people who are different from ourselves. We will truly listen to new ideas and try on different identities. A lust for travel and adventure fills us, along with a desire to learn and push past boundaries.

The Lover teaches Love. Every human seeks connection, support, and affection. Love means a thousand things to a thousand people. It is both necessary and hard to define. We open our heart to another person. We allow them to help us and feel compelled to help them. We want to give and receive pleasure, in so many ways. It can come naturally, without thinking, but it can also be a choice – a choice to refrain from judgement, to be generous, and to be open. We recognize the beauty of relationship and support, of affection and gratitude.

The Healer teaches Healing. Sometimes the world grinds us down and throws us out of balance. Infections take hold and bones break. Obsessions take hold and hearts break. People will tell us that we are worthless. Pain can be physical, emotional, or spiritual. We must help one another to heal. Eating well, sleeping well, getting fresh air, and seeking help from professionals – this is all a part of the solution and we can help one another to achieve these ends. We can also present the hard truths that can be the first step to healing – a damaging habit must cease or a toxic person must be cut off. We can also truly listen to one another, give emotional and spiritual support.

The Warrior teaches Strength. Threats come in many forms. We must protect those who are vulnerable and stand up for what is right for ourselves and for our community. We must stay vigilant against those who would disrupt what we know is good and spoil the common good for their own selfish aims. Conflict can build resilience and challenge character, but we must also keep in mind what we are defending. Our battleground may be activism or politics, a battle for hearts and minds. It may be physical protection for those in harm's way, or it could be a willingness to sacrifice our own safety to protect something greater.

The Androgyne teaches Balance. To be transformed, we sometimes need to let go of limitations we place on our own identity. Categories can be helpful, but they can also stifle freedom. Sticking to rigid forms will only make us brittle and ready to break. Balance requires a constant juggling in the changing world, and the more skillful we are, the more agile we become when dealing with everything that comes our way. We must push back against the boundaries of who we were told we must be to find our own true path. We can flow into roles and positions outside of what we have learned. We can create a new sense of self – one that is whole and complete.

The Shaman teaches Gnosis. Sometimes knowledge imparts itself in unexpected ways. Not all knowledge comes from school, or even from the experiences of the mundane world. We must be open to paths that take us beyond regular experience in order to unlock something greater. Divination, ancestor work, speaking with spirits, using esoteric arts – all these can lead to knowledge of ourselves and of our world that will guide us further on our path. Unseen presences may guide us, but we must recognize that this path can bring dark revelations. Each step leads toward a deeper understanding.

The Elder teaches Wisdom. Knowing who we have been is essential to knowing who we are and what we can become. Memory, experience, contemplation – we must know the lessons of the past and recognize the value of what we lost and gained through the passage of time, through the ups and downs of history. We must take the time to listen to the stories of those who came before us as we seek to write our own story. Contemplation will make sense of past actions and give us sympathy for those who followed a different path.

Our tradition uses a variety of magical tools, but most of the work that we do is aimed at Transformation. That is our primary magic: transformation of self, transformation of community, and transformation of the world. This is what the center of the labyrinth contains – the ability to forge ourselves anew. The Eight Deities will help this process. We embody both the Youth and the Elder. We Love and Fight. We explore this world and the next. We heal ourselves and find our balance.

The path of these Deities is not about who can be the most physically attractive or who can make the most money. It is not about being a "consumer" or getting the most hits on social media. It is not about following an expectation of a gendered relationship, and a version of fertility based on gender duality. They do not lead us to embody stereotypes or shallow versions of what others expect, whether those are the stereotypes associated with queer people or the expected roles of the larger society.

Our work with these Divine Beings helps us to create our own true selves and to become part of a community. They teach us to respect ourselves, other people, and the world around us. This is the magic that the Queer Deities can help us to create. By connecting with these Deities and embodying them, and by learning their lessons and making them a part of our lives, we are deepening our own selves and sense of purpose.

As it turns out, the Deities have challenged us within our own Order, and as it has become clear that their gifts are not only for men who love men per the founders' vision. We are now in a process of redefining who we are and what community we serve. The process is not yet completed, but what was once the Brotherhood is being reborn into a Fellowship, a form that is less tied to gender. As we left behind the confinement heteronormativity, we will also be open to a wider spectrum of gender and sexual identities.

Talk Story
by Adare

Joshua Lanakila Mangauil is a Mahū Hawaiian, which is a word term that refers to a third-gendered person. Lanakila is the storyteller seen here in "Talk Story." He advocates for his people, and is also a hula dancer and keeper of the indigenous old traditions of Hawai'i.

Redefining and Repurposing Polarity

by Ivo Dominguez Jr.

When I first became involved in Paganism and Wicca in the 1970s, one of the impediments to acceptance into some systems of magick was a heteronormative perspective on the nature of polarity. I was very open about my sexual orientation, about my beliefs that gender is not binary, about being polyamorous before the word existed, and that I was as kinky as a cheap garden hose. As such, some of the groups and teachers that I approached sometimes gently, or not so gently, tried to steer me away as not fitting well with their group or teachings. I was not persuaded nor was I dissuaded and chose to dig in and learn all I could with the goal of adapting and evolving the teachings that I received. It was common in that era to arrange ritual circles boy-girl-boy-girl for the supposed sake of promoting better energy flow, and I knew in my core that these, and other teachings, limited the possibilities that magick held.

From their perspective, I was a bit of a question mark. From my perspective there were several layers of dismay and reaction. Despite the circumstances, I experienced the numinous power of the mysteries in some of their rituals. Something that they were doing was real and effective although the reality of my experience and my internal guidance told me that their theory of how and why the numinous power worked was woefully incomplete. In one of those early ritual groups, I suggested polarity was at play whenever people held hands in a circle because of chirality, because of the polarity of left hands linking to right hands. There were enough energy healers in the group that this made immediate sense to them from their understanding of energy circulation in the body and encouraged me to dig deeper. Over the years, many of my colleagues and coveners that followed the old perspectives expanded their viewpoints through strong metaphors and direct experience.

Much of the traditional theory, related to the mechanism of action in the raising and the shaping of energy, was locked into some very limiting paradigms. Concepts related to polarity seemed to suffer the most strongly from an overlay of the prevailing cultural norms. The astrological influences of the Age of Pisces also tended to emphasize dualities such as dark and light; female and male; hot and cold; and so on. My personal experience was very different from what I was being taught. I took this as a challenge to develop my own theories of polarity that would include what I had observed in myself and in others. The word *polarity* suggests an inherent problem as it implies having two and only two opposites or aspects. That said, polarity also implies a full continuum of gradations whereby *the two* become *the many*. There is also the common metaphysical principle that states that all that exists, that is manifest, is a mixture of things. This leads to the conclusion that the polarities we can experience are relative rather than absolute. Relative polarities are non-binary as a direct consequence of the mixed nature of the world in which we live. Absolute polarities would only be possible in a world where pure essences exist, and that is not the world we inhabit. Imagine three buckets filled with water each of which varies in temperature. If you place your hands in two of the buckets you might find that one can be called warm and the other cold. Then if you place your hand that had been in the warm bucket in the remaining bucket, you may discover that the warm bucket is cold relative to the third one. If a small amount salt had been added to the water in varying levels, then whether the water is salty or sweet would depend upon the order that the water is tasted. Any given thing can have multiple attributes, and the assigned values of those attributes is given relative to its context.

The study of the Tree of Life also began early in my introduction to Paganism and to the Western Mysteries. One of the standard teachings in Hermetic Qabala is that each Sphere is negative/receptive to Sphere before it and positive/projective to the next in the sequence. It is also said that the first and the last Spheres of the Tree are within each other. There are also complex polarities that abound in the analysis of the structure of the Tree. The left and right pillars of the Tree are capped by the Spheres that represent primal female and male energy. As you descend within each pillar the lower Spheres are increasingly a mixture of qualities assigned to genders. There are also interesting polarized relationships between each of the Spheres that are connected by horizontal and diagonal paths. It seems clear to me, in the lore, that polarity was much more multiplex than it was generally presented.

As a general principle, when reexamining magical or spiritual teachings, it is more productive to determine which parts are not necessarily wrong, as they are incomplete. Einstein's physics extends and expands Newton's understanding of physics rather than replacing and erasing the older teachings. If the goal is to evolve our metaphysics, then it is advisable to preserve older understandings and adaptations, even if you have no use for them. The metaphor of evolution is applicable. Your genetic code remembers earlier patterns even when they are inactive, archived, because some future generation may need them to build a new pattern. It is also productive to view teachings that seem flawed in the same way you can sort through brainstorming and prototypes as you refine your insights. These perspectives are useful because they remove some emotional from the process of separating the wheat from the chaff.

It may be that we need a better word, a more expansive word than polarity. I have played around with replacing it with the word *valency*. I am not sure that word is quite right, so until someone comes up with a more fitting replacement, I continue to use the word *polarity*. A part of this process is the expansion of the existing definitions which also result in a rethinking of the practices that involve the use of polarity. These are some of my expanded definitions for polarity in the context of magick and ritual:

> *Polarity can be thought of as any difference in position, alignment, state of being, or attribute that causes, directs, catalyzes, or encourages the flow, production, or expression of energy.*

> *Polarity can also be an entangled state, of mutual interaction, of relationship, between forces and/or forms that share essential natures, thematic resonance, or primal attraction.*

Please be aware that these definitions are an *and*, not an *or*, to other definitions of polarity you may have. They are also incomplete and only my working definitions. They are not presented as more than that.

Let me give an example of polarity at work in a ritual that does not rely upon gender or declared opposites. When someone engages in a divine embodiment, drawing down, or trance possession of a God/dess, they are also activating the polarity between the microcosm and the macrocosm. The Hermetic Axiom of "as above, so below" and "as within, so without" or any of its extended formulations speak to the idea that we are whole beings that are both informed by and make up a greater whole that is the universe. When a person engages in a divine embodiment, that which is similar within themselves calls to that which is similar outside themselves, and the frisson of the difference in magnitudes of order of spirit provide the attraction.

The north and south pole of the Earth or of a magnet are examples of polarity that follow the textbook pattern of dyadic polarity. This is also a classic example of a polarity that is not a linkage between opposites. Magnetism has no charge and no inherent direction. The characterization of north and south or positive and negative as applied to magnetism may be useful, but they are assigned and not inherent. In physics, particles that have no charge can still be polarized when their intrinsic spin is parallel and anti-parallel to their direction of motion. A polarized pair need not also be a dichotomous pair, although in certain circumstances it can be such as in matter and anti-matter pairs.

Polarities, when viewed from a broader metaphysical and mundane perspective, can and do function as a pair of linked states but are not limited to only two poles of interaction. There can be multiple centers of power, and many axes of orientation. As an astrologer, when I begin to make sense of a birth chart I often start by studying the aspects, energetic interactions, formed between pairs of planets. Often planets form aspects with multiple planets who may, in turn, share interactions with other planets as well. Understanding the pulse and the variability of energy moving in sets of two, three, four, or more is essential to understanding what is actually going on in a birth chart. The patterns of energy interaction and reciprocal flow in a birth chart are a good analogy for multi-pole polarity. I often conceptualize in shapes and each polarity is like an axis in a graph depicting a multidimensional surface. The dynamics of a group of people doing ritual together is also an example of polyvalent polarity.

These explorations lead me to a variety of conclusions. In most cases, if something can be named as belonging to a set, then there are potential polarities to be activated. If there is a non-trivial relationship that can be described between two or more things, then an exchange of energy or influences that can be described as a polarity exists between them as well. These interrelations and linkages can be internal within a being or any system or phenomenon that behaves as a microcosm. These interrelations and linkages can also occur between beings, systems, and phenomena with differing sizes, scales, and orders of wholeness.

When we hear that right combination of notes sung together, the sounds can bring about a sense of yearning, satiation, straining, or relaxation. The addition or subtraction of notes at the right intervals shapes the qualities of the energy.

Notes that are an octave apart sound both identical and disparate, which is a clear expression of the enigma of polarities. Different combinations of frequencies and phases, whether of sound, of light, or of etheric vibrations can result in polarities that can generate and shape power. We are changed when our senses, both physical and psychic, respond to these vibrations. We become a part of the music of polarity. The subtle play of neurotransmitters such as dopamine and serotonin, or of hormones, or the many messenger chemicals in biology also represent polarity of a different nature that is a sort of music in the flesh.

Polarity is woven into all of the manifest universe. Union and separation; the dense and the subtle, evolution and involution; and much more form the rhythm, melody, and harmony that are the eternal powers of creation at work. As a manifest being, these powers exist within you, and as such you are whole within yourself. You are not alone. In fact, you are connecting to the multitude that makes up the universe. This is the paradox of the *many* being also *one*, which is the web of polarity that holds the manifest universe together.

To call the powers of creation and transformation that arise from polarity, first become aware of the qualities and properties that live and move within you. Then become aware of the relationship they have to the qualities and properties that exist outside of you. In a sense, this is a recapitulation of the beginning of creation when the universe became aware of itself and the naming began. This is *like* calling to *like* across time and space. It is the resonance that you summon, stir, and spark into being, which creates the conduits for the polarities that empower whatever spiritual or magickal work that you choose to do.

The first models for polarity that I encountered were clues, prototypes, and a foreshadowing of more to come. When I looked closer and deeper I found that polarity reveals a universe filled with co-creation, and a myriad of potential poles of agency and passion that join in an innumerable array of combinations. Becoming aware of more ways in which it is possible to raise, move, affect, and transform energy and essence through an expanded understanding of polarity is a valid pursuit in and of itself. This pursuit also provides an opportunity to examine what is inherent, what is culturally created, and what is aspirational so as to parse the dialogues, the polarities between these, with greater precision. It is a great windfall that the work of expanding the definitions of polarity also provides opportunities to educate ourselves, and sometimes others, on how the vast possibilities of the universe express themselves within us.

Power Sigils for Our Times
by Laura Tempest Zakroff

Power Sigils for Our Times

by Laura Tempest Zakroff

chapter 23: the plague years

by wolfie

1989 - the first one

the song came soaring out of my mouth, pouring itself into the sky, words riding waves of tears. i was standing on the back deck of my friend's house in redwood valley, northern california. i had spent the day at my friend devin's funeral.

devin had been my best friend for as long as i lived in the town of willits. we were the only two queers our age that we knew of. i was fully out, he was not due to his large and largely southern baptist family. we would hang out late at night when he was working graveyard at the all-night deli/gas station.

devin was the pretty one with long red-gold hair, huge dark blue eyes, 'stache, and a penchant for hippie boys and burly biker daddies.

i was the weird one with my then-purple hair and penchant for mixing punk and hippie fashion. i was still a baby witchling with my copies of "drawing down the moon," "another mother tongue," and "das energi" always at hand.

when he tested positive, it was devastating. this was before "aids services" and agencies. hell, it was only a few years past the "grid" stage, when they called it "gay related immune disorder" he decided to tell his family that he got it from sharing needles, asking me to never tell them what had really happened.

willits being a small town, word spread pretty quickly. he got fired from his restaurant job right away, on the basis of "well, you can't handle food anymore, people wouldn't be comfortable with that."

then the local restaurants started to refuse him service. one day, we were walking down main street, and someone driving by spat at him.

he declined pretty quickly, even though he was on azt, the first drug on the maket for treating aids. It was horribly toxic, and while people did live longer, that extra time was often miserable.

i was there almost daily. his mom and i grew close. his immediate family loved me for not bailing on him, for helping them, and for staying and not being afraid. i would crawl into his bed and hold him, singing him lullabies. he made me promise to sing his favorite one at his funeral.

the rest of the family, good southern baptists all, were certain that since i was obviously queer, i must have given it to him.

on his last birthday he could still sit up, but just barely. his family gathered and i tried to be as innocuous as i could, failing miserably at it. only a few of the extended family showed up. his grandmother gave him a hardback copy of a billy graham book about who will and who won't get into heaven.

i wasn't there when he died. i got that dreaded phone call that begins with "are you sitting down?" fuck.

the day of the funeral was bright and sunny. his entire family, the whole clan, showed up, all in black and gray. i was wearing black and rainbow tie-dye. the evil glares i kept getting from the crowd unnerved me and i told his mom i didn't think i could sing after all. she hugged me and said she understood.

about 20 minutes later, while everyone was milling about, i overheard the pastor's wife reading the list of hymns she'd picked out for the service. every single one was about how suffering on earth was necessary in order to get to heaven.

no fucking way i was letting devin get sent out with that.

i had never sung solo in front of a group before.

i went back to devin's mom and said that i had to sing after all, whether i was up for it or not. she hugged me and whispered in my ear that she was so grateful for my being there for devin.

i asked the lady for strength. it was the first time i ever really called on her. i'd sung the songs in circles and chanted the incantations, but this was the first time i full on reached down to the earth and asked for help.

and then, there i was. i was in front of 250 people, 246 of whom hated me, singing for the love of my friend, singing him on in a way that their baptist stuff could never touch.

i had my eyes closed, seeing devin's face, his smile, the colour of his hair, pouring my voice into his ear as i had done for months. his favorite was janis ian's "lover's lullaby," and with a slight shift in the words, it could almost be taken for a christian song. i held it together through the last word, the last note, and stepped down from the stage. i made it all of two steps before i fell sobbing into his mother's lap. she held me as we cried together, and whispered her gratitude in my ear.

i didn't stay after the service. his folks knew and I knew they understood.

i went to my friend's place in redwood valley since i knew i wasn't up for the drive home. the house was full of my friends and teachers, witches all. we sat and made small talk. everyone knew what my day had been like. after dinner, people were lounging, smoking, and just hanging out.

i needed air, so i went out onto the deck. the tears returned. as they welled up, i looked up and saw her. the lady was bright and waning, slightly veiled by a patch of mist. i nodded and said thank you to her for the strength. a breeze blew by whispering 'sing to me,' and the song came pouring out.

by the time i was into the second verse, several of my friends had appeared and gathered behind me. as the last note echoed in the trees, they enfolded me in a group hug and i finally lost it completely. i was held in a circle of strong witches who were not afraid of my grief, my rage, or my tears. i howled and screamed, sobbing incoherently. when there was nothing left to scream and the sobbing began to subside, my clan-sister eldri turned my face back to the moon, reminding me that the lady was always there for me, that now i had a direct relationship to her, and that she loved me.

eldri lifted my tear streaked face, looked me in the eye, and said "hail the new made priest of the lady!" and other voices echoed her. she then gave me a lopsided grin and said "of course you'd pick something like this for your initiation."

i had discovered magick at 14, learning what i could from the first gay man i ever met. chuck was a thelemite. i met him in a psych ward where my parents put me after a suicide attempt. after i'd been in there a month, one day there was a guy sitting in the corner, wearing all black including heavy eyeliner, and playing with a deck of cards unlike any i had ever seen. i asked him about them, and he showed me the whole deck. it was the thoth tarot deck. he tried to explain who aleister crowley was and i was enthralled. i was raised in a very strict fundamentalist church so all of it was fascinating to me and made sense in ways the church never did. shortly after meeting chuck, my first ever gay person, they placed cindy, a big rollicking butch dyke in as my roommate. she was the first woman i kissed, the first woman i had sex with, and after we both got out, my first girlfriend.

i have long said that they put me in the madhouse, and i found my people.

ten months later, when they discharged me from the hospital, i went looking for books on magick, hiding them from my mother and reading under blankets late at night. i managed to get disfellowshipped from the church, much to my personal glee.

my parent's threw me out not long after i was released from the hospital for the last time. after many other adventures, i moved to northern california. i found my way into the hippie pagan world and the deadhead culture. i started learning about crystals, goddesses, psychedelics, meditation, herbs, and ritual. i was circling with straight hippies and was always the odd dyke out. the rituals were fun, but something was missing. i'd be standing there in circle, looking around and wondering when i would feel the "energy" that they all kept talking about.

after a year or so with that crowd, i finally found some pagan dykes, and went to one of their circles. it was lovely, and far more real to me than most of the heteronormative stuff i had experienced thus far. the more i went to those rituals though, the more i kept feeling something was missing, some lacunae i couldn't identify.

then, in the summer of 1990, i met the radical faeries. with them, specifically with the black leather wings faeries, the fae who were also leather queens, it finally all clicked. Ritual, energy, magick, all became vastly more real to me. i soon found myself living in oakland.

living in the bay area, i soon found myself immersed in the plague. faeries and queens were still dying from aids too fast, too soon, and way too frequently. not as bad as in the mid to late 80's, from what everyone told me. the plague dynamics shifted drastically with the introduction of azt, in horrible and fabulous ways.

when i entered the plague zone, i had little idea of what it was like. i jumped into groups like act up and queer nation, and started to educate myself more. i'd spent the last few years working with earth first! and doing clinic defense, so activism wasn't new to me, but i learned that activism in the big city is a vastly different creature.

the first time i ever brought magick directly into an action in san francisco was at the international aids conference in 1990. multiple groups had come together in the streets and it was intense, chaotic, and brilliant. the crowd was huge, die-ins were happening everywhere, streets were blocked, and the cops were swarming. they had converted the parking garage at 850 bryant street into a giant holding pen, separating people by gender, with metal barricades to keep us apart.

i was arrested around midday and thrown into a police van. they put me in the smaller compartment, and put a bunch of my friends, all male, into the larger back of the van, leaving us to sit there in the sun. after about half an hour, they opened the door to my compartment, and shoved in another protester. he was an elderly queen, dressed in fabulous drag, a long dress with quilted panels. we smiled at each other.

as the heat grew intense inside the van, some of my friends in the other compartment began to freak out. rich started throwing up and screaming for his meds. that triggered a panic amongst the others.

the only thing i could think of was to sing. i started with one of the goddess chants, singing softly, and glancing at the elderly queen next to me. he had the biggest smile on his face and had begun singing along with me. we lifted our voices together, and he reached out and held my hand as we sang songs of calm and quiet power. everyone's panic subsided, rich curled up in someone's lap for comfort, and we waited for them to drive us to the holding pens.

front line activism was incredible to me. what i learned about humans sitting in those endless consensus meetings has been invaluable in my life as a witch, as a magick practitioner, as an educator, and as a human. learning how to truly listen, to be patient, to actively look for the larger and broader vision is a lifetime journey. ghawdz know i'm still struggling with it.

i will forever be profoundly grateful to the people who have been a part of my learning process, 'cause queen, when i fuck up, i fuck up big, and my choices and actions have sometimes hurt people. there are no apologies vast enough to reach them all, and yet, i will loudly say "i'm sorry. i was an ass." and hope they read this someday.

i started doing hospital support for friends, mostly faeries. we were co-conspirators. many of us had been kicked out of our families, so we formed our own.

1994

in the early midst of everything, i met kalyn tranquil'sson.

from that first day we met, the first hour really, we knew we were soulmates. this was odd as fuck, him being a kinsey-7 radical feminist faggot, and me at the time an opportunisexual butch leatherdyke. it was a match made in some very twisted version of a heaven. people described us as an old married couple, joined by our hands around each other's throats. we lived together, wrote together, did ritual together, published a pagan newsletter together, fought mightily, and loved each other fiercely for almost four years.

"now that's worship!"

that was the last full sentence kalyn spoke. he died moments later, in my arms. he had chosen to go off the respirator because his pneumocystis had eaten most of his lungs and they weren't going to come back from it. he'd been fading in and out of consciousness, and i was sitting beside him holding his hand, singing bhajans which are devotional songs to kali. he had introduced me to her 4 years earlier, shortly after we first met and began our relationship.

a month before he passed, kalyn had been in the hospital for a week, and nothing looked good. his birthday was the next day. at the time, he didn't have any tubes attached. he looked at me from his hospital bed and said, "you know what i want? i want sushi! i gave up sushi six years ago, because they said don't eat raw fish, you could 'cmv' or some other 3 letter acronym. well fuck it, i've already got them all!"

being the kind of friend i am, i rustled up two of our mutual friends and a van. we got his wheelchair and snuck him out of the hospital to the best sushi place we knew. he gorged. he was smiling in a wasabi haze. we all knew it was his last birthday with us, and we all celebrated that for the gift that it was.

at a certain point things began to get weird with my body. i was having some serious pain issues, and i began to have this really odd set of sensations in my legs, losing touch with my feet, and occasionally motor control. i started walking with a cane. i felt exhausted, had trouble sleeping, and everything hurt.

i went from doctor to healer to specialist after specialist. they ran every test, called upon every ghawd, poked and prodded everywhere. it got so bad that i couldn't walk more than a block or two before i was in tremendous pain and falling down. i ended up in a wheelchair, which i stayed in for several years.

i realized that front line activism was not really possible for me anymore. i couldn't run, couldn't be out for hours, and was being more of a draw on resources than a contributor.

the combination of that realization and the occasions where i'd been told to leave my friends' bedsides as "visiting hours are over" inspired me to go to seminary. pagan seminary, to be specific. once in seminary, i was in possession of a clergy card. they couldn't kick me out anymore once i was a priest.

i was still living in oakland, which was fortunate, because the only pagan seminary in the country was in berkeley at the time.

queens were dying. anything that i did was punctuated by death and dire illness. in some ways, azt just made it longer and more drawn out.

as a community we learned not only to grieve, but also to stack grief. the faeries would gather at wolf creek sanctuary and howl our rage into the earth and sky, sobbing and fucking and dancing in both light and shadow.

1995

diet popstitute was our hero. he was one of the guys who started the homocore movement within the bay area punk scene. diet was the lead singer of the popstitutes, one of the first ever blatantly queer punk bands. later he founded klubstitute, a monument in sf club history, and playstitute, a radical queer theatre troupe.

when diet was dying, faeries and klub kids swarmed his hospital room. we showed up in drag, we decorated, and someone was always with him. until one morning. suddenly, out of nowhere, his family showed up. the family from boston. the ones he hadn't spoken to in 20 years.

when they showed up at the hospital, everything changed. suddenly we were not allowed to see him outside of strict visiting hours. we were only allowed in 2 at a time, if at all. all of the decorations were torn down in his room. his family looked at all of us like we were lower than dogshit. his brother, a screaming closet-case if ever there was one, yelled at us that his brother was dying because freaks like us gave him aids.

like so many queens at that point, diet didn't have any paperwork filed. no medical power of attorney, no will, no nothing. with none of that on file, his family, the next of kin, had all the legal rights. they were bound and determined to wipe out the last 20 years and leave no evidence that he had ever been the amazing queer socialist freak that he was. thank the ghawdz that his two best friends had keys to his apartment and were able to get his photo albums and recordings out before his family got to them.

i was in the hospital room with him, chanting to him softly, when his mother walked in with a catholic priest. she was telling the padre that "michael" had always been a good catholic boy. i, not being one who holds my tongue well, or someone who lets lies slide, popped up with, "yes, and a champion of queer rights, and a great magick user as well!"

shortly after that i was banned from his room entirely because my chanting "disturbed" his family. i offered to only be there when they were not there, but no, i was flat out banned. i waited until the shift change, and snuck into his room. he had been on ventilators and a host of other machines, and had mostly been unconscious. i knew he could hear and understand what was going on though.

i got into the room, and he was under an oxygen tent, rather than the ventilator tube they had him on the two weeks previous. i held his hand and told him that his mom had banned me from the room. i told him that i was going to wolf creek where i would pray and do ritual for him daily. he opened his eyes, turned his head to me, and hoarsely said "thank you" and squeezed my hand. i made it to the parking lot before i began to sob.

i spent a week at wolf creek. on the fifth day i woke up knowing that something about the day was… different. i walked into the kitchen and was met by a faerie named frail who was holding a coffee cup. he said, "i knew i made this for a reason," and handed it to me. i asked him what it was, and he told me "mushroom tea" with a big smile. i drank the whole thing and asked how strong it was. he smiled even bigger, his eyes shining, and i knew i was in for a wild ride.

that trip changed my life and my work. after a series of fascinating vignettes, i ended up underneath the tree we call grandmother maple. she is well over 200 years old and absolutely amazing. i was peaking as i got to her. fritz, my sweetie at the time, was trip-sitting me, holding my hand as i lay down at grandma maple's altar. i gazed up through her branches, scrying and listening.

suddenly, i knew i had to be face down and snorting dirt. i rolled over and i breathed deeply. everything slowed. as i inhaled the scents of the earth and grandmother's root system, my consciousness completely shifted. all that i had learned intellectually suddenly activated in my synapses. i could see the energetic connections and felt them intensely. time dilated. for the first time, i fully experienced the web of life and truly grokked it. It was the first time that grok, to understand something deeply, as on a cellular level, made perfect sense. it was a synesthesia unlike anything i had ever experienced, my senses combining like never before, and this was certainly not my first time at the 'shroom rodeo. the roots, the grass, the insects all buzzing, the breeze a droning tone, were all punctuated by the staccato of fritz's breathing. all of it was one glorious symphony of energetic connection.

my breathing slowed, and as i exhaled, i experienced another profound, yet subtle shift in consciousness. whatever it was, i wanted to go deeper into it, so i began breathing a fourfold breath. i could feel my heart slow as my breathing slowed. the energetic connections i was experiencing became blurred at the point of contact. i breathed the syllable 'ah,' the syllable in tibetan that dissolves the lines that keep things separate. there was no difference between my self and all existence in that moment.

as i kept exhaling, exquisitely slow, i felt my own edges begin to dissolve. this was more than fully connecting, this was dissolving and disintegrating. this was what going in to the mother truly was. it was warm, fuzzy, and was a sense of joyous release of self. i knew, i grokked, that i could just let go of the last few particles of my discrete self and be done, no longer separated from the earth. something informed me that i would keep dissolving as long as i exhaled.

i was thrilled, to say the least. my logic brain, my internal geek observer, was pondering the ramifications of dissolving, and it started a debate in my mind of whether or not i should inhale at some point. would i re-aggregate? did i want to? the debate was drawn out and thorough. having spent a sizeable percentage of my life wading through the bog of suicidal ideation, i was leaning strongly towards breathing myself out. no more stress, no more grief, no more fear, no more pain, and no more not knowing.

suddenly my earthsign mind kicked in. my few remaining focused brain cells collided, producing a spark of pragmatic intelligence, which reminded me that i had a ten-year-old spawn at home waiting for me. it would be horribly selfish and unfair of me to check out right then.

so, i inhaled. just as slowly. it was like someone had flipped a reverse switch in the meta-reality, and my cellular structure began to reform. i had to go through the process of re-collecting my self, and it was just as fascinating.

when i felt completely contained within my skin again, i lifted my head, saying "fuck that was amazing!" i slowly turned my head to look at fritz, and they were pale and trembling. "what happened?" i asked. they looked at me wide-eyed, and said "you just stopped breathing for like, a looong time. i was getting scared."

i sighed. then the realization hit me and i wondered if i could do that again? i immediately planted my face back in the dirt, and lo, was able to go right back into the synesthetic cloud of everythingness on a fourfold breath. as i floated and reveled, i felt an energetic tug. it was faint yet clear. i was reminded of the description of 'enfolding' from sally gearheart's "the wanderground," the form of psychic communication used in the book.

my breathing slowed more, as this new frequency and i became more familiar. time dilated again as my meld with the multiverse was rippling throughout me, and then i hit a point where the energy of the tug made sense to me. i lifted my head, and told fritz i need to finish re-aggregating, and that we needed to go to the peace pendulum.

the peace pendulum had been put up in 1991 by moonglow as part of a global network of pendulums built all around the world. over the years, it had become a place for ancestor ashes and had been at the heart of many faeries' experiences. we would spin it one direction to broadcast energies, and another for receiving energies.

fritz helped me up, and over to the pendulum. we got there, and i gave it a good spin. i spun it out, and quietly said "beacon" to fritz. once it slowed down to a stop, i spun it the other way with the word "here."

we watched it spin to a slow swirl. all of a sudden i was instantly completely back in my body and felt very cold. we headed towards the main cabin. as we got into the house and sat down, one of the faeries walked in with the phone in his hand. he was talking in that tone, experienced and resigned, slightly somber, mostly relieved tone of a caregiver. he finished his conversation, and walked back in to hang up the phone.

"diet's gone," he said. our eyes collectively asked, when?

that was the moment all the parts of my brain fit back into place, and i knew what happened. i looked at fritz, who carried a watch. my relationship with linear time has only ever been tenuous at best, so i rarely tracked time.

"around 4." i kept watching fritz, who did the time/math and they looked at me and said, "probably around an hour before you got to grandmother maple." frail looked at us and wanted to know what had happened. fritz shared their experience, i shared mine.

we all looked at each other, in the recognition that faerie magick worked perfectly. simultaneously, all of us said, "welcome home, diet."

as i thought back through the day, i realized that not only had i chosen life, i knew now that leaving life was joyous dissolution. i knew what my work was. i knew magick worked. i was no longer afraid of anything.

that night, i sat under the dark moon and sang. i sang for diet, and for all the faeries and friends i'd held as they crossed. many more than i've named here. i sang to the great mother, tears streaming. i sang of joy pain lust grief love and connection.

i thanked the lady for my voice, for the strength she gave me, For all the grief, the stress, the pain, and for the terrible beauty of death.

all of this has made me what i am. a priest. a witch. a psychopomp. a magician. a radical binary-averse genderqueer.

so much has brought me to now.

none of this is what i thought i'd be when i grew up. clearly, if i ever grow up, i'll have other choices to make.

Blood, Body, Birth, and Emptiness

Queer Magic in My Life and Work

---

by Yin Q

Magic is inherently queer as a kinetic and ever-changing force. When I address magic, I speak of the innate powers that reside in all of us, that each of us may hone when they are listening to their inner selves. We cultivate magic through ritual, the performance of mindful actions. Rituals allow us to celebrate life/the moment by recognizing the passing of it, the closing of the circle, the acknowledgement of death.

It is through our systematic categorizing of binary structures that magic is relegated to feminine/masculine spaces. Even within pagan rituals, the more indefinable and therefore threatening powers were cast as feminine and thus, condemned as witchcraft and appropriated by political, patriarchal religions. Magic that strives for an audience or commercial gain, such as the trickery of magicians and illusionary showmen, seems especially laden with patriarchal symbols: the wand, the top hat, the showgirl victim/assistant who is dismembered or vanishes and then reappears unscathed. New Age magicality sways to the opposite side of the binary-- relying heavily on feminine powers and iconography. I am not, at the moment, arguing against the powers in these forms of magic.

The powers of intuition that arise when a person grounds themselves and calls upon greater forces are unexplainable. It is slippery stuff to write on, which is why it is doubted and undervalued, though we all wish to believe in it. Whether we believe in the powers of magic or not, we undeniably feel them. Magic and Queerness are similar in the way of being elusive to name, to specify. What we need to welcome in our lives of queerness and magic is the unsettling restlessness of the potentialities of those identifications.

Magic, spirituality, soulfulness, mindfulness, conscious living, and queerness are everywhere, even (perhaps especially) in the mundane. There are those with plant magic whose potted flowers seem to be supernatural in growth and beauty. Computer hackers have a keen sense of technological spell casting. Musicians, artists, and dancers, midwives and doctors, the technical magician who can fix anything, and writers, of course. Magic may flow through every craft.

The magic I practice is of blood magic and the rituals I guide stem from an animist and Taoist ideology. However, I do not use the Yin/Yang symbol when I meditate on the balance of forces. For my practice, the well-known symbol is too binary, too neat. I call upon the wildness of a tidal wave crashing, as forces grow and meld and split violently. I reflect upon the tree, its many leaves, its deep roots, its quiet, slow, yet sublime reach towards the sun. I whisper to the stars to remember the vastness of light and dark, of matter and space and time, of black holes and nebulae. I heed the blood inside me that is the DNA message from every living organism in history to the future blood of the last living thing. I listen to the stories of blood and let them flow.

> *Cutting is an erotic act. With a slice, the skin is split and a rip of electricity shoots up the spine, firing through open eyes and gasping breath. A euphoric wave floods through the stomach to tailbone, pumping sensation into every pulsing hole. Red fluid trickles and smears. The blood shot, (synonymous with the cum shot in pornography), is proof that the pain is real. Not all participants are seeking the erotic, but it is undeniably about opening the body for meaning, be it grief or joy. It is relief, a masturbation of one's emotions.*

I began blood magic as a teen age cutter. Through years of formal leather training in BDSM, I learned how to wield it with meaning and intention. However, I cannot begin to speak about blood magic without first bowing to my ancestors—to my Chinese heritage—their blood and their magic.

My mother, a Chinese immigrant from Beijing, was a genetic engineer. In her laboratories, she morphed mono-clonal antibodies and transformed them. She played god. She was one of the scientists who helped create the first reliable AIDS test in the 90's; she is one of the many heroines of the blood war. In addition, she was an artist with a deep reverence and fixation on Chinese spiritualism and superstition. Feng Shui and Chi energy were just as important to my fate as eating my spinach and studying algebra.

My father, from the Southern province of Hunan, was a chemical physicist. His particular genius was concentrated on the calculation of measurements between electrons. However brilliant he was in atomic science, my father was oblivious of social proprieties. His intellect was entwined with madness-- undiagnosed depression, violence, and schizophrenic delusions.

My childhood home was filled with magic and madness. Northern and Southern China mixed under my American-born skin. Tales of cursed blood and birthmark prophesies marked my body, my old-soul hands, and my dark-tea colored skin.

I first explored self-cutting as a form of leeching the blood of my ancestors from my body and of tapping into madness. Driving both sides of the sadomasochism, I claimed both my mother and my father's roles in their relationship: victim and abuser. My rituals were death driven, but filled with sex lust. I licked the blood, offered it to the moon, rubbed myself with it to frenzy. During the days, I wrapped my wrists with leather strips to hide the scars, and to exalt in the sensation of wounds rubbing against hide.

In my early twenties, when I finally began the path of formal leather training, I learned rituals of flesh that spoke to rage and sorrow, with grace, mercy, compassion, and agency. I began to crave cuttings as rituals that affirmed life, whereas in prior years, I had focused on the thrill of annihilation. With the education of the leather ways, I learned to honor myself, and the ancestor-blood that pulses under the skin I wear. As a Shamanatrix, their ghosts and madness would be my muse and my magic. My rituals now are life affirming and death acknowledging. Queer with ambiguity and transcendence.

During my early years of BDSM explorations, I underwent piercing and flesh hook ceremonies, stemming from a mix of Native American O-Kee-Pa and South East Asian Kavadi rituals, guided by Cleo Dubois, founder of the Academy of SM Arts, and Fakir Musafar, grandfather of the Modern Primitive movement. Throughout my journey, I've sought out their guidance for private ordeal rituals as well as communal leather ceremonies. The circles they conducted were emphatically queer spaces, drawing from a San Francisco Bay community of leather queers and trans folk.

From Cleo and Fakir, I learned how to utilize surgical needles as temporary piercings, tied with lines of string, ribbon, or weights to create and release psychic energy. The pulling of the pierced, yet intact, flesh induces an altered state of consciousness and can also be sustained for an hour, sometimes more, unlike the slice (however slow) of the blade. The piercing action is invasive, pushing in, forging new openings. Queer openings. We too need to push into our language of magic and of BDSM to create these new openings.

In my earlier years of practicing BDSM and rituals of flesh and spirit, the icon I called upon was the Bodhisattva Kwan Yin, the East Asian Goddess of Mercy. Her tale evolved from a Hindu history, originally born as the merciful lord of utter enlightenment, Avalokiteshvara. The male deity was overwhelmed by the cries of human suffering and, in his despair, shattered into a thousand pieces. From the pieces, they were reshaped as a goddess endowed with a thousand arms, each hand embedded with an eye to see the distress of every soul, so that they may encircle the suffering. Kwan Yin, whose name means "the hearer of sounds/the listener of prayers," chose to remain on earth to aid human suffering.

When I first learned Kwan Yin's tale of gender transgression, the idea struck me as a significant key to why I was attracted to the icon, as I have never felt wholly attuned with the ideas of the pure feminine. Even in the arena of the professional female dominatrix, I shied away from Goddess and Priestess terminology, and completely rejected female supremacy, a mere mirror to patriarchy but with its misogyny even more shrewdly hidden. The idea, too, that Kwan Yin does not fight against nor annihilate the suffering—she listens and holds space for it to happen—is also a powerful and queer magic. One of my first moments of feeling the power of this kind of magic was as a bisexual (as I identified then) teenager.

I was sixteen and Jay Lee was a boy from a few towns away. He had silky, black hair that angled sharply along his thin face to his chin and cool, heavy-lidded eyes. He was taller than me, but our waists were approximately the same width. Our Chinese skin was similar in pallor. He was not really a boyfriend, but we went out to museums and dance clubs together. He said he loved looking at my face, that he loved the lipstick I wore, the black pencil liner around my eyes.

One late night, as we were hanging out in my room, he stared at me with such longing, that I mistook it for lust and leaned forward to kiss him. He kissed back reluctantly. Frustrated, I pulled back feeling rejected, and saw that my dark red lipstick had transferred onto his mouth. I watched him press his lips together, the way women do. I was wearing a sheer, silken shirt and intuitively, I undid the buttons and took it off. Holding the blouse open, I encouraged, "Do you want to wear this?"

"oh yes," he whispered and slipped it on over his slender shoulders.

"You're beautiful," I told him. And he/they were. I learned at that moment the power of allowing another person to be seen, how that act of seeing is transformative, how acceptance can be revolutionary.

When I began to pursue a career of professional BDSM work, an area of dominatrix work that puzzled and repelled me was that of "forced feminization"—when a cis male, usually straight, would wish to be degraded for dressing in lingerie and other feminine garb. It seemed anti-feminist to me and I didn't find the idea of verbal humiliation and slut shaming to be erotic or interesting. I enjoyed aiding the transformation of the masculine to degrees of femininity, to praise and marvel at the "slave girl," to commend the "good slut." Shame has been laden on sexuality in heaps already and it has been my personal battle to contend with it. I am not adept enough to use it gracefully as paradox. I am also not at ease with racist jokes, no matter who is telling them. Transformation magic is something I enjoy as a sacred act, erotic and vulnerable yes, but not humiliating.

My work now in the BDSM/kink community is to offer rites of passage, rituals of ordeal, and transformational rituals. Of the former two, much of my work is in re-contextualizing the sensations of past trauma or of consciousness hacking. In the latter arena, the work is with a wide variant of gender transgressors. Some sessions are a temporary shedding and redress of gender, allowing the participant to express another self. Other rituals are of letting go of the former body, to allow grieving if necessary, and acting as the doula to the birthing of the individual's self-actualized body. Each ritual is personal and planned with the individual's story in mind. There is often no sadomasochistic element involved—sometimes a simple piercing at the third eye to symbolize birth. Bondage is often incorporated as metaphor for the shed body. There have been self-birthday ceremonies with witnesses and active participants, partners and friends, but most are private.

My personal practices of queer magic are in constant cultivation and bloom. I have passed into another stage of the witch as a mother and elder in the leather and sex work community. Motherpotence (rather than "motherhood") is what I call queer mother magic. Motherpotence is fierce protection and advocacy for the future of the creatures that are born from us. Listening to their magic and wildness, bestowing rituals of animism, art, music, laughter and rituals of sorrow and acknowledgment for that which death unfolds. Motherpotence is about taking a moment of prayer before dinner to express gratitude to the earth and elements for the food we eat, prompting my child to think about where their food is grown and how it is prepared, what nourishes our bodies. Motherpotence is about leading the children under the full moon and howling with them into the city streets. It is changing storybooks as I read them aloud to mix up gender roles. It is sowing faith in the powers we cannot see or name—intuition, dreams, and emotions.

The altar in our main room includes two sculptures of Kwan Yin: On the left side is the white porcelain God/dess, riding her familiar, a dragon, with lotus flowers and a vase holding the waters of creation; the Other sculpture is of the figure emerging from the wood with no gender-norm indicators. My home is aligned with crystal prisms in every direction, splashing rainbows across the walls throughout different times of the day. Feng Shui mirrors and vessels of water are placed strategically, as are altars of dried flowers, precious stones, snips of my children's hair, homage to ancestors, poetry, spells, sacred geometry, divination cards, bones, sea shells, candles and other burns, and bells. And empty space. Emptiness is essential to magic and Queerness.

* Italicized excerpts are from working memoir.

Power from the Edges: An exploration of magic to support justice workers.

by Charlie Stang

Queerness is how I found magic. Lying in the lower bunkbed of my classmate in kindergarten, I remember wanting to be in the bed with her if only to be close to her. I also remember feeling like something about this desire was wrong and that I shouldn't tell anyone that I wanted to be close with her. I buried my feelings in books and the little spot of forest that grew next to the freeway and the train station just down the street from my house. I remember staring at the ripe berries on the poke plants growing near the sewer that spilled out into the creek. Their brilliant deep purplish blue drew me into a place of mystery and imagination when I stared at them. The brilliant berries seemed so out of place, yet right at home at the same time. When I sat and listened, this plant always seemed to be saying something about letting go and loving myself.

Our magic comes from deep within. Magic is a process of crossing the boundary between this realm into the unknown. Magic is found in the places where we stand at the edges, where we cross borders. As a young queer bisexual, I felt like I never fit in anywhere. In both gay and straight spaces, I found myself passing—always being read by the perceived gender of my partner (if I had one with me) or whatever projections others shot in my direction. In the 1990s, bisexual was a bad word. We were still fighting our way onto the radar of mainstream gay rights organizations. In 1994, someone from Human Rights Campaign told me that the half of me that was gay would be covered by any legislation that the organization pushed forward. "Really, and which half of my body would that be?" I spat back.

As a bisexual queer, I've been pushed to the margins from multiple communities. It's from these margins that I've learned the power of my queerness. From a threshold, a place of crossing between, there's often a unique ability to see both sides. Walking back and forth between gay and straight worlds has taught me about wielding the power of edge walking and how to draw upon that power in my magic. Learning to code-switch and passing without choice in this world has taught me about divine connection and walking through this realm and beyond.

I came out in middle school to a small group of friends. They were supportive and held the nuances of a semi-closeted identity with me as well as any 11 or 12-year-old can. Within the first few months of high school, suddenly I was out of the closet to everyone. I didn't understand how this happened so quickly until I learned that I had been placed on a list of kids to pray for by a prominent Christian youth group at my public high school. The adults asked the kids to pray for me because I was a "lesbian Satanist." I tried to laugh it off— "just a few errors there—I'm a bisexual pagan but you know—what's the difference, right?" My first year in high school was hell, filled with some classic bullying tactics—I endured name calling, the yelling of scripture at me, personalized graffiti, and sometimes students spitting on me.

During my second year in high school, I was pretty fed up. A close friend of mine had come out of the closet and we started talking with a counselor at the school about starting a gay/straight alliance. By the end of the year, we had the club up and running. Through the meetings, we queer kids found each other and learned ways to offer support and solidarity in the halls. After we began this endeavor, things slowly started to improve—suddenly teachers stopped looking the other way and started interrupting the bullying. It was through this alliance that I began to understand the power of working with others to effect change. By senior year, we were mentoring freshmen queers, watching out for each other and educating staff. It was my first organizing effort and I felt the impact that collective action can have. I was bit by the organizing bug.

Since then, I've been involved with many different social justice efforts from actions against the second Iraq War to Black Lives Matter, from solidarity with local indigenous efforts protecting sacred sites to health care reform. One thing we do a lot of in organizing is telling our stories. It's an important part of the work; Where are you coming from? How does that story connect with the stories of others you're working with? How can the sharing of these stories foster solidarity and enable us to envision and experience the places where our struggles intersect? Whenever I'm in these conversations, my mind often wanders back to my organizing experience in high school. It was then that I began to connect with the power we have as edgewalkers to bring about change.

The work of justice is not easy. Surviving as a member of a marginalized group is a victory. Those of us who experience multiple oppressions and yet still survive is a *powerful act of resistance*. In the words of black lesbian change agent, organizer, and ancestor Audre Lorde, "I've come to believe that caring for myself is not self-indulgent. Caring for myself is an act of survival." As witches, we can use our magic to support organizing for change. Magic is a tool that can ground our justice work and nourish our tired spirits when the weight of the world is overwhelming. Below are three different magical and ritual suggestions to support you in the work of justice-making. May they bring you nourishment in your work to bring forth justice. Blessed be.

Working with Queer Ancestors and Allies

In the early 2000s I had the privilege of organizing alongside Howard Wallace who was doing labor organizing. Howard was one of the first openly gay men in the labor movement. He was the key organizer of the famous Coors boycott after he was approached by the teamsters who realized that Coors was discriminating against anyone connected with the union and against anyone who was gay. It was through working with Howard and other older queers in the movement that I began learning the stories of queer activists who had come before me. Many of the stories were of men who died in the AIDS epidemic, of old lovers, and of other activists. When Howard would tell these stories, his eyes would light up and I could feel the ancestors with us in the room. It was through organizing with older queers that I began to work with our queer ancestors as divine beings to guide me personally, and to guide our collective struggles for liberation.

One of the key ways that we can begin to develop a relationship with the queer ancestors is thorough our elders. You can begin the journey of connecting with the ancestors by connecting with queer elders and olders in your community. If you're not in relationship or community with older queers, seek them out. There might be an LGBT seniors group in your area, a local pagan community with some older folks, or volunteer opportunities with LGBT senior organizations. If not, consider posting on craigslist or a social media site to reach out and make new friends. My experience has been that older folks love to share memories and wisdom from their lives. Unfortunately, in the current political climate, the need for understanding historic survival and resistance tactics is even more critical.

Ask the elders in your world to share stories with you about folks in their lives who have died. What memories do they have of friends and lovers on the other side? What do they know of the queers who came before them? Open your heart and listen to the stories they share. Open your senses and see if you feel the queer ancestors come sit beside you as their lives are remembered.

A Ritual to Connect with the Queer Ancestors and Allies

This ritual is an invitation to begin a relationship with these ancestors, creating an herbal bag or sachet to magically align yourself in connection. Plants, our green-blooded relatives, can be a powerful support in calling the ancestors. Some plant-magic that you can work with is laid out in this ritual. The creation of a magical tool is a way to continually draw you back into connection with these ancestors after the ritual ends. This is key to the intention of this magic. This ritual is the opening of a doorway. The real magic begins when you keep returning and developing relationships with the ancestors.

Create sacred space in whatever way resonates with you. This may be casting a sacred circle and calling in the elements and deities; it may be sitting in quiet meditation holding an intention in your heart to create sacred space; or it may be something else entirely. Do what you know and what speaks to your heart. After you have created sacred space, invoke the queer ancestors into your circle. You might begin this invocation by reading quotes or poetry by a queer ancestor. Call them out by name—James Baldwin, Leslie Feinberg, Billie Holiday, Harvey Milk, to name a few—first the ones you may know and then ones who may be new to you.

After you have invoked the ancestors, place before you the materials you have. A piece of cloth, a needle and thread to make the bag, and the herbs, stones, and whatever else you want to place in the bag. Perhaps this could be a piece of a beloved article of clothing, a fabulously glittery sparkly pink cloth, or maybe just a piece of plain fabric. Then consider the plant allies that you would like to have with you in this work. There are several herbs that I experience as "queer herbs." These are plants that have special magic moving between worlds and dancing on the edge. Mugwort, Blue Vervain, and Bay Laurel are wonderful allies in calling in the queer ancestors.

With a prayer, and with intention, begin to sew this bag. As you are sewing I invite you to sing or chant. You might take poetry or writings by the queer ancestors and make it into a chant for this part of the ritual. As you are sewing, take some deep breaths and imagine the queer ancestors there with you as you sew. Stay connected with your breath as you insert each stich. Allow the rhythm of sewing to open your spirit to feeling the ancestors there with you. As you sense their presence, ask them to be present with you through this magical sachet that you are creating. Listen for any whispers that they may be offering. Keep your intuitive heart open for any messages that may come.

When the bag is almost finished, add the contents slowly and with intention. Then close the bag up with the final stiches. Once the bag is complete, take it in your left hand and charge it with the energy of the circle. Imagine that the energy that is present in the room is pouring into your body through your head, running down your neck and your arm, and then coming out of your hand into the bag. When you have a sense that this is complete, place the bag on your altar.

Take a moment to offer a prayer of gratitude for the queer ancestors, the plants, and all the energies that are there with you in this ritual. Then bid farewell to the ancestors and open the circle. You can use this magical bag to reconnect with the queer ancestors whenever you need to. You might place the bag under your pillow and ask the queer ancestors to dream with you. Or you might take the bag with you to an important event, social justice action, or hot date—whenever you feel you want the queer ancestors at your back. As you complete this ritual and begin to work with the queer ancestors, be sure to write or draw in your journal or book of shadows any wisdom that comes through.

Shielding

Because most of us live submerged in a dominant culture that emphasizes rational thinking rather than intuitive knowledge, for most people new to magic, the first number of years of work involves unlearning. Because of this, most magical teachings emphasize the shifting of consciousness towards being more open, developing intuitive knowledge, and sensing and reading energy. The practice of shielding is unfortunately often omitted or skimmed in many basics of magic classes. What happens to many students is that they learn to open and shift their perception at will without learning how to close their perception and get their "shields up." A lack of ease with shielding can create significant challenges for magic workers and I encourage you to develop your comfort with this magical tool.

As queers, magic workers, and change agents, this skillset is even more important as there are times when having our senses wide open can be a dangerous vulnerability. Shielding is a tool that I have used as a defense tactic in many different contexts. From threats of violence and gay bashing as I'm walking down the streets to a survival strategy in a hostile work environment, this tool enables us to have more choice in how we will respond to what the world throws at us. I have used shielding in a tough community meeting with a politician who was trying to intimidate us, to tear-gas filled streets doing medic work during protests. Once you develop comfort with this tool, it's one that you can use in a myriad of contexts.

I also want to be clear here. I'm not suggesting that shielding will protect you from assault or will in and of itself bring forth justice. Oppression and injustice are powerful forces in the dominant culture and we cannot overcome these forces with magic alone. I am encouraging you to develop this tool so that you have more options in ways of defending yourself in situations wherein intense energy is coming at you.

There are many plants that can be supportive allies in developing skills around shielding and energetic protection. Some wonderfully protective plants that you probably have in your kitchen are Rosemary and Basil. Both are clearing and protective. Another plant that is well-known for its support in shielding is Yarrow. Part of the medicine of this magical being is supporting you in breathing into your divine connection and your power. Yarrow works with your divine connection to amplify protection.

Shielding Exercise

Find yourself in a comfortable position. Take some moments to ground and center. As you are centering, do a quick personal check-in and notice how you are feeling in your body, mind, and spirit. Notice the energy in your body. How does it feel? Do you notice any sensations or textures in your energetic body? Just take notice of your being. You don't need to do anything to shift them right now. Connect with your breath, the earth below, and the sky above.

When you are ready, imagine that there is a shiny, shimmery reflective ball of energy above you. You may want to call upon a deity or ally to support you in calling forth this energy, or you may simply use your imagination to call your own power. When you have a clear picture of it in your mind's eye, imagine that this ball of reflective energy cracks open like a raw egg and begins to slowly run down your head. Feel the energy as it runs down your head, neck, shoulders, arms, chest, torso, stomach, pelvis, sex, thighs, knees, calves, feet, toes. Allow this energy to encircle your whole body. Notice sensations that arise and feel your energetic body as this reflection moves across your physical being. As the energy encircles your body, take some deep breaths and connect with your center. After a few more breaths, notice how you feel encircled by this light reflective energy. Do you feel anything that is different in your energetic being? Do you notice any sensations in your body, mind, and spirit? There are no correct answers here. Just notice. When you are ready to drop the shield, strongly exhale three breaths and with these breaths, envision the shimmery shield dissolve, burst open, or disappear. Again, notice how you are feeling.

This magical tool is one that you will develop and strengthen as you practice with it. Becoming proficient in magic is a lot like a physical endeavor. We develop our "magical muscles" as we practice magic. The more you work with shielding, the more you will develop the skill to call up your shields at will without the visualization practice. So how do you practice shielding? Begin with practicing this exercise regularly. You might incorporate it into your daily practice, if you have one, or just set an intention to do this visualization three times a week over the next three weeks. Try out different ways of working with the shield. Instead of dropping the shield with the three breaths immediately after forming it, keep the shield up and notice how it feels to spend an hour or a day in a more shielded place. Pro tip: Don't forget to take the shield down at the end of the day. My experience is that it can be a bit draining if you forget, though the shield will usually naturally dissolve in 24-72 hours.

You can also try working with the plants listed above as you develop this practice. You might take a drop of tincture or a sip of tea before sitting down to practice shielding. Or you might place some of these plants on your altar, carry them in your pocket, or take a bath with them.

Another suggestion is to envision different kinds of shields around you. I suggest exploring different elemental shields. Many people experience the one listed above as watery. Try envisioning leaves, branches, fire, wind, sunlight, moonlight, or any natural spirit around you as you work with shielding. Notice the subtle differences as you work with different kinds of shields. The more you practice shielding, the more ease you will develop in calling forth shields when you need them. Regularly practicing with shields leads to ease in bringing them up in tense situations such as direct actions, protests, crises, and other times of emotional or energetic intensity.

Working with Grief and Rage

To live in this world is to experience loss. Grief is another side of the love that animates the universe. For without love, we do not know the pain of loss. Grief over the loss of a beloved partner is a journey that unfolds throughout a lifetime. Fundamental to our identity as witches is a deep-rooted love for the earth. This earth is filled with so much beauty and wonder. The sun that rises each morning gives nourishment to ecosystems filled with blessings that cannot begin to be comprehended in one lifetime. There is a particular pain of living in a time when so much of our beloved earth is at stake. There is a unique rage that we feel when our communities are under attack because of homophobia, transphobia, racism, xenophobia, and oppression.

A key part of being able to sustain ourselves in resistance to collective attacks is allowing ourselves to feel the painful emotions that are a part of this journey. These emotions can be fuel for flames of resistance or they can be flames that consume us from within when we bury them. Working with our powerful emotions ritually can be a key way to give these emotions space, voice, and breath so that we may allow them to move, transform, and heal us.

Building an Altar for Strong Emotions

There are a lot of different ways to work with strong emotions such as grief and rage. One way that I suggest is to create an altar to honor these feelings. By giving our strong emotions a place to be felt, honored, and tended to, we give them permission to have movement. In the face of great suffering, it's often easier to slam these emotions down deep within. The ability to suppress pain is an important survival skill that marginalized people have depended on across generations. If you feel you are in survival mode and this is your only option, I encourage you to stay with that. Come back to this practice at a time when things feel different, and instead, focus on shielding and working with the queer ancestors for support in survival mode.

If you have the spaciousness and centeredness of mind and spirit to try this work, please do so. Grief and rage can be powerful offerings and expressions of love for our ancestors and allies. There are beings that are nourished when we express these emotions and our offerings help to maintain the balance in the universe. When we create an altar for grief (or rage, or any of your strong emotions), we acknowledge the sacredness of this pain and the healing that is possible through feeling and through allowing our feelings to move.

But what is an altar? An altar is a doorway that we create that opens a connection into other realms. It's a physical manifestation of our communication with the gods. It's a portal for divine communication to come through to us. An altar is also a way that we can communicate with other parts of our being that are less accessible through cognitive thought. An *emotions altar* is a way of telling the parts of ourselves that reside deep within that we honor our emotions and that we make room for these emotions to be felt.

To begin your preparations, take some days or weeks to collect items that signify the emotion or emotions you're working with. There may be elemental representations—for example a piece of burnt wood to represent fire, a bowl of salt water representing tears, etc. You also may add pictures of loved ones, newspaper clippings, or other physical items. Use your intuition in uncovering what will go on the altar. If you have a sense that something should be there, but are unclear as to why, bring it into the process nonetheless. It is likely that the significance of the item will be revealed as you sit with the altar.

Decide a space that you will use for this altar. Ideally this should be a space that you can sit and move in front of. Take some time to ground and center. Physically and energetically clear the space. This may mean cleaning around the room the altar is in, clearing energetically with smoke from a plant you burn, sprinkling with salt water, and/or clearing with sound such as a bell.

To create and charge the altar, gather your items together and begin with connection with your breath and with the earth. Create sacred space in whatever way is in alignment with your practice. Take some breaths and connect with any ancestors, allies, or deities that you would like to be present with you in this work. You may call in the spirit of these powerful emotions to be present with you as you build this altar to honor them. After your invocations are finished, take some time to be with the space where you are creating your altar. Take some deep breaths and connect deeply with the spirit of the emotion(s) that you are working with. Slowly and with intention begin to build your altar. You may want to chant or sing as you are doing so.

As you are placing the magical items on the altar, allow yourself to feel whatever emotions come up. You may find tears begin to fall as you do this, or you may find yourself laughing, or you may experience nothing at all. Welcome them all. Just as there is no right or wrong way to feel, there is no right or wrong way to create this altar. Listen to your inner knowing and allow that which is needed to come to you through this work. Take the time that you need. When you feel the altar is "complete," light candles, sit, and listen. You may want to write in your journal or book of shadows, draw, paint, or sing. Do whatever feels right. Take the time you need. When you feel complete, thank the energies that have been present with you in this work and extinguish the candles.

I invite you to keep the altar built for as long as you would like to continue working with these intense emotions. After the ritual is concluded, you may find that a daily practice of sitting with the altar allows for energies to move, deepen, and grow. You may want to consider making offerings at this altar. These offerings could be your songs or tears or they could be things like food, flowers, or incense. I invite you to consider setting an intention to sit with the altar for a brief period of time every morning for a length of two or three weeks. This will give you some time to continue intentionally working with the intense emotions.

Joanna Macy, earth-based Buddhist teacher and elder, speaks of the time we are living in as the time of "the great turning." While theologians and activists alike argue about the particular significance of the obstacles we are facing, one thing is for sure: we are living in a time of great challenge and in a time of great change. Life-threatening challenges mount due to deforestation, global capitalism, climate change, and increasingly unstable systems of governance. These times are increasingly calling us into action to protect the earth, to protect our fellow humans, and to protect the future of life on this planet. As you are called to the work of justice for the earth and fellow humans, I invite you to listen to your guides, and connect with your ancestors. There are other realms that are reaching out to support us during these times of great challenge.

Candlespell
by Inés Ixierda

The Maypole and the Labyrinth: Reimagining the Great Rite

by Sam 'Eyrie' Ward

The ritual will begin soon. I have been chosen to carry the voice of the ancestors, and as the fire tenders coax the embers to flame, I am painted by my tribe: half skeleton, half bird, white runes and black spirals. A broken limb bound to my side, ashes of my beloved and my own past held in a precious box soon to be offered to the flames. I hear the drums, distant down the hill, and the whoops and cheers as the dancers provoke the crowd to movement. Later, I will dance with them, fuck with them, love and heal and howl with them. For now, however, I am alone. It is solstice night, and I am the only one to brave the labyrinth that honors the beloved dead of our community.

Perhaps it is the strange shadows caused by moonlight, or the liminality of the shifting of the seasons, but as I kneel at the entrance to the labyrinth, it seems to spiral down as if the land has sunk into itself. The old grandfather tree that guards the clearing seems superimposed upon the cyclic path from my prostrate view. I have hung from that tree, as have others who made offerings to the spirits that sing to their souls. I know there is risk in entering, but the labyrinth called me here for a private offering before the public spectacle, and the greater risk seems to be in refusal. I trace where the roots of the storm-weathered grandfather tree entwine with the boundaries of the spiral path, and laugh at my first revelation of many that evening. The tree, the labyrinth, the fire far down the hill: they exist in one great circle, bounded by river, rock, and road. This is not a somber letting go. This is the exquisitely passionate act of choosing life over the cold certainty of death, while honoring both.

Paradox. Duality. Tension. Separation. Union. Some of the most powerful insights and soul-searing rituals are born in the dissonance of two irreconcilably opposite yet simultaneous truths. This essay will attempt to examine a dissonance at the heart of much of modern pagan practice, and offer just one of many possible paths forward. Those truths are such: that the Great Rite is a powerful ritual tool core to many modern traditions, and that the core symbols of that Rite are problematic and exclusionary to many initiates and seekers within those traditions.

The Great Rite is a sex and fertility rite in which a person with a penis copulates with a person with a vulva/uterus to represent both the union of opposites and with intent for great energetic workings. The blatantly sexual nature of this ritual carries certain discomfort both within and without pagan communities. Thus, the Great Rite occurs far more often in its symbolic form, with a knife blade replacing the masculine energy, and a cup, bowl, or chalice of some sort representing the feminine.

In this symbolic form, it is weighted with perhaps as much climactic mystery as the holy communion of Christian believers, and holds a similar place in the arc of a typical Wiccan ritual. Embraced by many Wiccans and found in variations across other pagan groups, the symbolic Great Rite is a virtual catechism to the tenets of modern pagan religious traditions. As such it can be difficult to challenge its role and impact on diversity in these subcultures.

The precise meaning of the objects used for the symbolic Great Rite for each participant are indiscernible. Personal engagement with symbols entwine with transmitted knowledge, and the public source material of modern magical traditions are limited, as oral traditions and private written texts shape an initiates journey toward that mystery.

Stepping back and examining the Rite from a cross-cultural and historical perspective, both the symbols and the transmutation of energy it facilitates are rooted deeply across faiths and histories. Classic western examples include the marriage ritual of placing rings on a partner's hand and the myths of the holy grail. Perhaps this is why the energy of such a ritual is so compelling: it taps into the faceted gestalt of energy and experiences that occur when dualities collide.

Rituals are rooted in our hearts by engaging with deeply common experiences, and we arrive at the roots through engaging the mind in ways that allow the heart to see. For this to happen, effective ritual evolves to meet the language of the mind, yet paradoxically remains unchanged, speaking truths to hearts across time.

The core symbols of the Great Rite are the blade, the chalice, and the union of the two. The obvious sexual symbolism in the performance of the Rite is part of what makes them such abiding choices. Spiritual food and spiritual fucking speak directly to the basic needs of our biology. As above, so below. Both blade/knife and chalice/cup are ubiquitous items in Western cultures. This accessibility is yet another reason they make such excellent symbolic choices. A knife as a penis and a cup as a uterus. The very simplicity of these symbols that allows them to be accessible objects to so many seekers can also serve to deeply alienate others.

The simplest representation of the Great Rite is in the joining of masculine and feminine energies, and the macrocosmic blending of all dualities. As above, so below. The blade and the chalice are used as ubiquitous symbols for this concept within Western magical cultures, each with heavily stereotyped gender associations. The knife is not just "masculine," but represents the penis, and one that is weaponized at that, as it is uniquely designed to injure, penetrate, and draw blood. The cup is the womb, the uterus, and the vulva, and in the traditional rite it is passive, held lower than the knife.

The same simple beauty of union found in this ritual by many who have a frame of reference for consensual heterosexual sex can become a disturbing symbolic reminder of identity oppression, cultural dominance, or coercive or violent sexual encounters for others. In this way, participants who identify outside the gender binary, whose gender and sex organs don't align, or for whom masculine sexual aggression has caused injury struggle to participate fully. At worst, the Rite is experienced not as a celebration but as a cultural tool for othering, alienating, and silencing.

So where do queer, gender-nonconforming, asexual-spectrum, and/or people who've experienced trauma find a place in this communion? Some pagan groups have started to allow members of any gender identity to stand in either role during the symbolic Rite, which is a thoughtful and necessary step toward progress. However, holding on to the symbols of this "traditional" ritual denies the very existence of the many divergent representations seeking to find an identity outside of the pressures of oppressive mainstream religion. Particularly since this ritual was perhaps invented barely a century ago by Gerald Gardener, a respected practitioner who nonetheless had problematic perspectives on sexual power. To find an alternate expression in the beauty of earth or goddess-based spiritual traditions, and then to be asked to accept core symbols that still reflect the oppression inherent in the dominant culture does not seem in keeping with the espoused values of such communities.

Once something is deemed "tradition," it can be very difficult to challenge or change. Yet, modern magical traditions seem capable of adopting new ideas incredibly fast. This makes the resistance to examine and rewrite existing traditions frustrating but understandable. The safety of anchors of meaning in rapidly shifting times is attractive.

It is time to consider alternative symbols to weave into the powerful dualities expressed in the Great Rite, or replace them altogether. As our communities shift in their understanding of harmful institutional structures, the Rite stands to lose its potency if it cannot likewise shift to embrace the diversity of its participants.

Fortunately, the wonder of sacred symbols is that each is a faceted representation of an object or an idea that contains multiple meanings; some simple in the subtle nuances, others in ways that can seem irreconcilably opposed at first examination. It thus becomes possible to explore alternative symbols just as (or perhaps even more) potently associated with the duality and union of energies the Great Rite embodies, while expanding to be more inclusive of alternative narratives of sexuality.

Symbols are flexible, and those who use them for magic could become just as flexible. Depending on the nature and purpose of a group or individual working, there may be a place for almost any of these symbols in pagan high ritual. The intent of the symbol and how it is understood by viewers is far more important than the choice of symbolic representation. Yes, Carl Jung, Joseph Campbell, and other psychologists, anthropologists, and social scientists have posited a certain universal unconscious map of core symbols, but there is still a clear understanding that symbols are most powerfully engaged in personal meaning. This is the beauty and sensibility present in both dream divination and the many versions of modern tarot, and this pliancy is useful in considering the evolution of symbolic uses within modern magical traditions.

Many books on modern paganism have glossaries of deities, symbols, and magical associations. The gendered association of a particular symbol is often tied to the gender of the corresponding deity. Thus, a symbol typically associated with femininity in one place and time, such as the moon's dominant association with goddesses in the west, can have masculine associations elsewhere, or even be distributed across deities of either gender (such as in Egyptian mythology). There are also powerful non-gendered fertility symbols, such as bees and honey, that are genderless and thus accessible outside the binary.

However, the duality of the symbols is core to the powerful tension of the symbolic Great Rite. In *Vs.: Duality and Conflict in Magic, Mythology, and Paganism*, a dynamic range of practitioners take on this concept and explore the tension and interaction of numerous dualities including twins, enemies, and the union of divine and mortal energies.[1] Duality is not unique to sexuality. With an expanded perspective, the duality, conflict, and union motifs can be found in the pairing of almost any perceived opposites, and sometimes in things so close they seem, at first glance, undifferentiated.

While any powerful pairing of symbols could fit as an alternative to the blade and cup of the Great Rite, two symbols stand out in particular: the maypole (as a type of fertility rod) and the labyrinth. Each contain potent cultural and religious symbolism, and each contain both essential dualities and paradoxical contradictions and ambiguities within.

The Maypole:

He pins me to the maypole. "Hold still." A slight breeze tickling through the overcast spring sky draws goosebumps to my flesh, hardening my nipples. I hold and hold, and the dancers circle round. Each grasping a ribbon, they weave in and around. I watch the web weave itself above, and as the dancers weave closer, so do the ribbons, and soon I am bound. The dancers have sheathed me to the maypole, tied off just at my navel, my face and chest free but the rest bound in the dancers' web.

Each dancer smiles before stepping back to seek the hand of their beloveds. As bodies languidly tangle on the grass around me, a lover's playful smirk captures my attention. He comes toward me, teasing my nipple, reminding me that I am bound. Two friends come close, attending to my legs with touch and kisses, lifting and spreading me open.

Rather than a somber and aggressive weapon, like the blade, a maypole is a type of fertility pole that traces its roots to some Northern Hemisphere holiday practices. Traditionally made from the wood of a young tree, the maypole represent sexuality that grows, sprouts, and spreads its seed. While still an obviously phallic symbol, a maypole's highest purpose each year involves being adorned in flowers and ribbons by the feminine energy it couples with: a giant penis in drag. It's a cock that waits patiently while wanting to be sheathed by a pretty, tight hole, and by and large it is the biggest strap-on of anyone at the party. It's like a double-ended dildo, thrust firmly in the earth while still straining at the sky. It's nearly impossible to take its

1   Huggins, Kim (2012). In *Vs.: Duality and Conflict in Magic, Mythology, and Paganism.* London, England: Avalonia Books.

full length, so to couple with it requires creative lubrication. Hold it between your thighs and it easily wants to both take you and give itself to you to take.

A maypole suggests active desire and the willingness to pursue it. While the phallic shape suggests masculinity, in a liberated model of sexual expression it simply represents the lead in the dance. The romp, the flirt, the initiator. The Top, Dom, Mommy, Rigger. While it stands so rigid, its promise is one of movement at any pace. Wildness and playfulness and want; a scientist's centrifuge; a chef's pestle.

Maypoles are such potent fertility symbols that even centuries of Christian influence have not been able to eradicate them. They remain part of community spring festivals in England and elsewhere. One of my earliest memories growing up in rural England was of the local church vicar blessing the maypole before the spring May Day festivals.

The Labyrinth:

I stand at the gate. Through the woods, into the clearing, the moonlight and some instinct within led me here. The mouth of the labyrinth opens and offers two paths: a sacred circle and a cosmic spiral encompassing each other. The container is important – it holds. As time and space curve back and out again, so do I; the path inward is as easy or as long as it needs to be.

The path is a line moving within a circle. The circle becomes a sphere, the sphere a cave. The labyrinth is a doorway and also a map. I spiral inwards, and in so doing, find myself also coiling and uncoiling up and down to some other place, while remaining present as well. This circle is always cast yet never closed.

In a society driven by productivity, busyness, and forceful direction, aimless wandering and indirect paths to goals seem like a fool's journey. Meander. Let your head follow your heart, let your heart follow your feet.

The rational brain can see the destination, just a few steps away. It insists that you cross the lines, straight toward the center to claim the prize. The labyrinth tells us something different. Take the lines out of a labyrinth, and you have an ancient pattern called the meander. A winding course, a flowing river, the coils of a snake. Be swept up in the flow. The center cannot be reached directly. You must have patience.

There is a cultural draw to the weight of deep places: burial mounds, great Egyptian tombs under pyramids, massive creatures of dirt carved into landscapes across the globe. It is impractical to build tunnels into hillsides or to seek lost and forgotten caves of initiation. Modern labyrinths are often simply marked paths of rock, grass, or other natural materials. Labyrinths can also be spiraling patterns laid flat on surfaces, engraved medallions, inked flesh, or painted canvas. Yet you can feel the dimensions of the labyrinth as your feet trace the path. Sink with it into the earth. Feel the roof of the chamber above, even if that chamber is the expanse of sky, or a circle of trees. Reach out further again, feeling the shape of its presence in time: now, then, what will or might be. The labyrinth offers more than the gift of procreation. All transformations become possible in this space. The path will welcome any traveler. The entrance and the exit are one and the same. Yet in the turns of the path through the inward and outward journey, it is impossible to return to the place you started. This is the mystery of all passages, gateways, and initiations. They are liminal spaces, thresholds between what is and what might be.

Feel the earth beneath you, the land's heartbeat. Feel the cock between your thighs. Feel it throb to a melody. It is well past midnight, and I'm offering myself yet again. Wrapped around the Maypole, my cunt throbs too, wanting. Staring up, my vision is filled by a silhouette of darkness thrust high into shrouded heavens. I'm fucking this barkskin pole, and it fills me in ways I've never experienced before. Tendrils of ribbons from an ancient dance tease my flesh, reminding me of a May Day dance from months before. The next time I open my eyes, the sky is no longer shrouded. Something shifts within me and without, and the dark silhouette is no longer the 30-foot cock I'm grinding against, but has become my own cock. The land's heartbeat, the cock, and my cunt find synchrony, and now I'm thrusting my cock, this pole, into the sky. The gentlest breeze teases the tendrils woven around my length, and as I ride along with the cascading sexual energy I realize just moments before it occurs what is happening, and in the brief moment of vision as I climax, I erupt into the sky, and the sky seems to be covered in semen made of stars.

Sharing a Sacred Meal
Adapted from "Casting a Queer Circle: Non-Binary Witchcraft" (Asphodel Press 2017)

by Thista Minai

Sharing food and drink is a well-established mechanism for social bonding. When we eat together, we become not just a group of people, but a community invested in supporting its members. By including the Gods in our meal, we strengthen our bonds not just with each other, but with Them as well. We share nourishment with the Gods and with each other, and we are nourished in return.

On a more practical level, eating and drinking help us return our attention to our physical bodies. Eating in particular tends to be naturally grounding (unless you're specifically eating something with a different effect). Consuming a little food in circle helps participants come down from the energetic high of your ritual, helping them concentrate on dismantling the circle. This aids a transition back to a primary focus on physical reality. For this reason, the food and drink we share is not a full meal, but just enough to bring us back to our bodies and connect us to each other, while still leaving us able to finish our ritual.

In a Traditional Wiccan circle, this sharing of food and drink often begins with what is called "the symbolic Great Rite," in which the tip of the athame is inserted into the cup, a symbol of a penis entering a vagina in heterosexual sex. This blesses the drink with the power of procreation and binary polarity. As a coven that includes people of diverse genders and orientations, we at Spectrum Gate Mysteries tried to make this work for our coven and ritual system, creating a gender-neutral liturgy to go along with the athame-in-cup blessing. Our new practice allows anyone to hold either the cup or the athame, providing access to that procreative polar energy. While this became a functional option, we felt its utility was too narrow to keep as our default blessing. We still use it when we specifically want to work with polarity between two opposites as a source of power, but we needed something different for our everyday food and drink blessing.

We found our answer through examining the meaning of the ritual tools used in the sacred meal: the cup and drink as a symbol of spiritual nourishment, the food as a symbol of social and physical nourishment, and the libation bowl as a symbol of sacrifice and our willingness to work for what we want. These three tools became the inspiration for our new blessing, and their use in the blessing arose from the contemplation of our officiating roles.

Rather than using gendered officiating titles like Priestess and Priest, our coven's circles are led by an Anchor, a Builder, and a Greeter. The Greeter is the ambassador of the circle. They address the congregation, greet the elements, and petition deities. The Builder is the metaphysical muscle of the ritual. They are responsible for creating the energetic structures of the circle and its gates. The Anchor is responsible for the physical space of the circle. They tend to the items necessary for ritual and serve as an energetic point of stability for the Builder and Greeter.

The roles of the Anchor and Builder in the food and drink blessing vary depending on the intent of our ritual. For circles with a more human or community-based focus, the Anchor holds the food which roots our magic in the physical nourishment we offer to one another. For circles with a more divine or spirit-based focus, the Anchor holds the cup (or the pitcher, if you plan on pouring the drink into individual cups) which roots our magic in shared spiritual experience. The Greeter always holds the libation bowl which reaffirms our relationship of reciprocity with each other and with the Gods.

Each holding their respective tool, the Anchor, Builder, and Greeter speak the following words to bless the food and drink:

Food: *We, the community*

Drink: *and the Gods we honor*

Libation: *and the path we walk*

All: *come together for a common goal*

Food: *in fellowship*

Drink: *and faith*

Libation: *and sacrifice*

All: *to become the future of our design*

Food: *of free expression*

Drink: *sincere connection*

Libation: *and fruitful exchange.*

As the final words are spoken, the officiators holding the food and drink each place a bit of their substance into the libation bowl.

All: *As we unite our efforts,*

we ignite the spark of creation,

and our work is done,

and our work begins.

This first act of offering is what blesses and consecrates our food. Once it is complete, food and drink are passed clockwise around the circle and shared by all participants. Usually we do this casually and informally as we appreciate the connective intimacy of passing food and drink like a family as we held the libation bowl for one another. That said, if you have an Assistant that needs a task, or if you want to create a more formal ritual, carrying food, drink, and the libation bowl around the circle could certainly become ceremonial roles.

The cup should never be empty until everyone has gotten some food and drink, and the Greeter is ready to toast the Gods. If there's any doubt as to whether or not you'll have enough drink, keep more stored beneath the altar. The primary reason for not letting the cup run dry is its symbolism of the boundless nature of spirit, but there is also a more functional purpose. There should always remain some drink in the cup, as anything added to it will also receive the blessing.

The toast is another expression of gratitude, specifically directed to the divine, that serves a practical social function. The sacred meal is typically informal. Participants are invited to relax and chat with each other while they eat and drink. This provides a needed break for everyone to allow their focus to wander. The toast signifies the end of that interlude and brings everyone's attention back to the ritual. This is a signal that the group is going to dismantle the circle as well.

When everyone has had enough to eat and drink, and just enough time to relax without getting completely off course, the Greeter raises the cup towards the center of the circle. This signals that the toast is about to happen, and the group quiets and focuses on what the Greeter is about to say. The toast begins with "For the gifts of…" and then the Greeter names three things for which they and likely the entire group are thankful. These can be as vague as concepts like "community" or "stability," as specific as important moments for your particular coven, or as concrete as objects your group is grateful to have. The Greeter finishes the toast with "…we give thanks to the Gods!" Typically, the Greeter pauses before the final "to the Gods," as that last phrase is echoed by the group in the formula of a normal toast. Of course, if "Gods" doesn't work for you as a gender neutral equivalent for deities, try "to the divine" instead, or any other variation that suits your group. After making the toast, the Greeter drains the cup, making sure that none of the consecrated drink is wasted, then places the cup upside down on the altar.

If your group uses a pitcher and individual cups in ritual, make sure the officiator holding the drink for the blessing uses the pitcher, not their individual cup, so that all of the drink gets consecrated. Each person should keep a bit of beverage in their glass for the final toast, and everyone should drink together with the Greeter. The Greeter's cup should be the one placed on the altar as the tool representing Water in the appropriate quarter. All other cups can rest on the altar wherever is most practical, keeping an eye out for overall balance.

Towards a Healed Femininity In Every Body

by Michaela S. Creedon

For all the womxn & femmes,
Great ancestors and all those who still live,
For all those who have resisted, thrived, and lived,
Against all odds,
Found joy and loved,
Spoke out and fought back,
Against patriarchies invalidation, abuse, and attacks.
And for all those who couldn't.
For all those who suffered alone in silence.
This writing is because of, in honor of, and for all you dear ones.
Thank you for your lives, your work, your sacrifices, and for your powerful wisdom and words.

The Body.

Houser of memory.
Keeper of legacy.
Holder of all who
have ever come before
and all who ever will become.

The voices of our grandmothers sing
inside our hearts.

Are you listening?

Regardless of
familial association,
their pain is
our pain,
their joys
our joys,
their struggles
our struggles,
their dreams
our dreams,
their unfinished business
our life's work playing out.

Each of us carries with us
all that has ever come before:
oppressor. oppressed.
colonizer. colonized.
intersectionalities of complicated
interwoven identities
beautifully and tragically married
inside us.

Each of us carries
the gifts and wounds of
the woman who birthed us into being,
the woman who birthed her,
and all the women before her as well.
Scars the patriarchy left deep,
branded within the DNA of our souls.

Spanning centuries,
these old wounds

hold the keys to our power.
For where there is fear,
there is power.
For where we have been oppressed
shines light on our greatest gifts
we have been called to birth forth.
The world is calling us to remember
our essential nature.

That nature is wildly and sensuously feminine.

Do you hear her calls?

Her soft footsteps turn to a heated run.
Running with purpose and swiftness
through the thicket of her forest home.

Even if you have never
stepped foot outside city walls,
She lives in your heart.
No matter how buried,
Her spirit is eternally part of yours.

She is the rays of moonlight that illuminate
the face on a full night.
She is the mother of darkness shining bright,
holding us with love from above.

She is the smallest gesture,
a warm smile,
the kind gaze of understanding witness,
the warm presence of
compassion and acceptance.

Secure loving arms,
ready to joyously hold us
when we are feeling scared and vulnerable.

She is the rich ecstasy of
sensuous moans
interweaving in harmony.
The satisfaction of
bodies enjoying,
reveling in,
savoring in each other fully.

She is the spark of all consuming desire
mixed with strong will and
focused intent,
combined with ritual
to make magic manifest
into the world.

She is the whisper in our ears
that guides us home.
Our intuition,
reminding us of center,
of what we truly want and need
in this world.

She is the freeness and surrender of
one's earthly body dancing,
feeling its currents.
Ebb and flow.
Joyously moving with the rhythm
alive inside of one's self.

She is the womb of potential,
that deep well of knowing
that lives in the center of every body,
regardless of anatomy.

She is the flowing of our tears,
powerfully cleansing.
The feeling of
release and relief
after those tides have
washed over you.

She is the expressing
of long repressed desires,
broken free of
the chains of shame,
pleasure reclaimed,
embodied fully,
hidden longings ready to be explored,
eagerly,
outwardly,
finally.

She is the re-membering of those
disowned and disavowed
parts shrouded in self-hatred,
The welcoming acceptance that calls
them back into the home of our hearts.

She is the knowing that
there is magic much deeper,
wisdom much older,
much more
alive,

true,
powerful,
than this
concrete,
sterile,
capital-driven,
technological progress obsessed,
traumatizing society
tells tales of.

She is the screams of anger let out.
The power of claiming
one's own body sovereignty.
The unapologetic defiance of patriarchy,
The pulsing hot rage of firmly demanding NO.
My Body.
My Voice.
My Boundaries.
My Choice.

She is the burning fury,
fuming with pain and outrage
over grotesque inequalities,
unjust racist killings,
Racist cops,
Racist laws,
Racist prison systems.
Racist country
built as a monument
to white supremacy.

She is the empathetic heart
that will never stop caring.
The fist that will never stop fighting
until these systems of

torture, hate, bigotry and murder
come down.

She is the joy and pleasure
of all those who have been oppressed.
For the laughter and happiness
we express is an act of
radical defiance.
Spitting in the face of all
systems and institutions who have told us
this world was not meant for us.

She is the risk that comes from bravely
living in authenticity.
The pride that comes from holding grounded and true,
even when others discredit and attack you.

She lives in every act
of self-care and self-love
made time for amidst the
struggle to survive in this
fast paced harsh world.

She is the open heartedness of trust.
The conscious, co-committed container
that allows one to feel safe enough to love.

She is present in every act of sweetness and devotion
one lover shows to the other.

She is the tender vulnerability of
showing one's self
honestly and intimately,

first to one's self,
then to the world.

She lives in passed down songs
passionately sung
to sooth souls,
stirring hearts into action once more.

She is the softly whistling winds,
gently blowing against cheeks,
revitalizing our spirits,
visions, and dreams.

She is the hot smolder of coals,
the flicker of flames.
dancing brightly
illuminating our passions,
hearts,
hands,
and sex.

She is the pull
of the oceans'
cold salty waves,
cleansing our feet
and moving our souls.

She is the relaxation of
grounded surrender
that comes
from laying our backs
on the earth,
warmly and securely held.

She is the silent presence of
caring eyes softly holding
open ears and open heart.
Fully present.
Listening intently.
Tenderly loving you
simply as you are.

She lives in the fertile seeds of death.
She is the rotting
that takes place for
new life to blossom and begin.

She is the breath,
the body,
the bone,
the heart,
the soul,
the roots connecting us to
all that is and lives.

For she is life.
Sacred and sentient.
Pulsing with spirit and story,
just waiting to be engaged with,
honored,
listened to,
asked a question,
shown attention.
Loved.

She is the uncontrollable,
dangerous,
unpredictable,

unchainable,
uncertain variable,
great unknowable mystery,
defiant,
disorderly,
delinquent,
disobedient,
wild,
feral,
ungovernable spirits
whose howls can be loudly heard
in the shadows of the forests
come sun rise and sun down.

She is alive in all acts of
resistance and resilience
against empires,
laws, and jaws.

She is the blood that runs through
veins and cunts,
spilling out rich
histories and mysteries.

She knows no binary,
For within every body lies the wisdom of
a sacred femininity.
Each uniquely perfect
in our myriad of differing
expressions and forms.

She is the power of receptivity.
The wisdom of silence

and listening,
that lives inside all bones.

She is the breathing,
beating,
pumping,
feeling
Heart of this
magnificent
Sacred
Mother Earth.

We have forgotten what it means to be human.
Forgotten our mother and creator,
our original life giver.

Yet we are remembering
slowly but surely.
We are awakening,
heart by heart.
We are remembering
what truly matters and what does not.

We have a responsibility to
reclaim,
heal,
feed,
express,
and enjoy the power of
our sacred femininities.

For even just one drop in the ocean of healing,
ripples out forward and backwards in time,

Recreating the present,

revitalizing all who have come before,
And healing all those ones yet to come.

Do you hear her calls?
Are you listening?
She is screaming for you to awaken.
How will you answer them?

Release Ritual
by Inés Ixierda

Hunting Lions & Slaying Serpents: An Execration Rite

by Jay Logan

In the early second century of the Common Era (C.E.), there lived a young man who drowned in the River Nile. According to local Egyptian custom, the young man had a shrine established for him, honoring him as a deified mortal united with the god Osiris, lord of the underworld. He received offerings and perhaps even heard the occasional prayer from local townspeople. Unlike other young men before him, that young man was travelling with the imperial retinue of Rome when tragedy struck, and he happened to be the favorite companion and beloved eromenos of Emperor Hadrian. That young man was Antinous.

As part of an extended journey by the emperor to visit and solidify the borders of the Roman Empire, the imperial retinue travelled up the River Nile and arrived in the city of Hermopolis in late October, 130 C.E., just in time for the Festival of the Nile. This celebrated the inundation of the river, the source of the land's fecundity, and marked the death and resurrection of Osiris. Antinous drowned some time during that week, under circumstances that remain mysterious to this day. Depending on who you asked, it was considered an accident, a suicide, or a gruesome ritual murder. When his body washed upon the shore on that fateful day, Emperor Hadrian grieved extensively for his lost love. He expanded upon local custom to build a city in Antinous' honor, and established a cult for the Divine Antinous that would spread across the Roman Empire. Temples were built in his name, oracles established, mystery traditions initiated, and festivals and games begun in his honor. His face, his beautiful face, would be carved on innumerable statues, making his one of the most recognizable faces in art history. It was a far cry from the simple shrine along the river, had Antinous been anyone else.

While Antinous has remained a recurring figure in European culture as a coded reference to male homoeroticism in certain elite circles, he has found renewed life as an object of veneration and worship among queer pagan and polytheist communities. The form of that veneration has shifted dramatically in the short history of the movement when the first dedicated organization, the *Ecclesia Antinoi*, was established on October 30th, 2002. Some come to him as the apotheosis of homosexuality, worshipping him as Antinous the Gay God. Others come to him from a more expansive, queer perspective, seeing in him a god and ally for all gender and sexual minorities. However you come to Antinous, be welcome! As we say in the Naos Antinoou, *Ave Ave Antinoe! Haec est unde, haec est unde, haec est unde vita venit!* ("Hail Hail Antinous! This is where, this is where, this is where life comes from!")

Every year on August 21st and 22nd, the end of Leo's reign on the astrological calendar, devotees of Antinous celebrate the Festival of the Lion Hunt and the Festival of the Red Lotus, respectively. This is the time when we observe the historical lion hunt that Hadrian and Antinous took part in, in the months leading up to Antinous' drowning in the Nile. Our Beautiful Boy nearly died that day while facing the lion that had been terrorizing the countryside of Libya, but he managed to wound the beast instead. As the poet Pachrates tells it, the lion's blood fed the rich earth and became the lovely red lotus flower, which has become a primary symbol of Antinous. Traditionally in the modern cultus, this is a time when we meditate upon our failures: what we have not accomplished or the traits and ideals we have not lived up to as individuals. It's important to take stock, and to allow those failures to act as fertilizer for the nurturing and growth of the red lotus in our own lives and souls.

In 2017, we wanted to propose an additional focus for our rites, to coincide with the solar eclipse, which was viewable by many people living in North America that year. This synchronicity provided a unique opportunity for those of us in this tradition. Egypt was the land that first recognized Antinous' divinity, and the historic and mythic slaying of the lion syncretized well with the daily slaying of another terrorizing force in Egypt: the serpent Apep. During the eclipse, we had the opportunity to expand our focus beyond the lions haunting our individual lives to face and fight back the deadly serpent who would swallow the sun itself, as the gods with their priests of old did.

The sun played a particularly important role in Kemetic religious traditions, as the god Ra on his solar barque represented the life and potency of the cosmos. Each day, his return from his nocturnal journey in the netherworld (or Duat) would be celebrated, and each evening during that journey *heka* (magic) would be wielded on his behalf against his enemy Apep. This primordial, anti-cosmic being is one who seeks to swallow the sun and destroy the cosmos. Ra's boat would be protected by a number of divine beings, including Set, Isis, and Bast, each wielding a spear or knife to slay the serpent each and every day, thereby maintaining the balance of Ma'at.

It was not only the gods, however, that took part in the slaying of Apep. There were numerous spells that humans could perform to aid the gods in restoring this balance, including from *The Book of Overthrowing Apep*. These spells were performed daily (sometimes multiple times a day) in many temples and were accompanied by the smashing of red clay pots, because it was known that the forces of chaos represented by Apep were always resurgent. The continuation of life and creation was never certain, and the forces that would swallow the world in darkness had to constantly be kept at bay. In modern terms, this is known as an execration rite. These rituals were utilized to protect the pharaoh, the kingdom, and the greater created world in unity with the gods. In modern Kemetic practice, this can be a way of cleansing one's life of unwanted influences, a cathartic experience to bring our lives back into balance and harmony, allowing the life-giving blessings of the gods to flow more readily to and through us. We recommend both, as the destructive forces of Apep can take many forms and influence our lives in diverse ways.

During a solar eclipse, this nightly battle against Apep took on even greater urgency. When the day turned into night, as the stars appeared in the sky and the sun darkened, it was surely seen as a bad omen. It was the serpent Apep nearly succeeding in his goal of swallowing the source of life and un-creating existence. What greater opportunity to fight back and slay that serpent? To smash its image; to spit upon it, burn it, and stab it; and to take away its power and bring back the light? With Antinous-Osiris the Justified by our sides – who perfected the art of hunting when he became a god – what lions could we not hunt, what serpents could we not slay?

There are many forces that need slaying, many forces that have disrupted the balance of Ma'at. This year in Charlottesville, VA we witnessed an escalation of white nationalism, fascism, and Nazi forces, whose clashes with counter-protesters and anti-fascists in the community resulted in one person's death. This was the culmination of months and years of fascism, racism, anti-Semitism, misogyny, transphobia, homophobia, Islamophobia, and many other forces that are tearing this country and world apart. Many pagans, polytheists, witches, and magicians that I know took part in various religio-magical acts in the lead-up to and during the eclipse to push back against these forces and protect those in our disparate communities that are most vulnerable. We of the Naos Antinoou present you with this rite and invite you to join us in this work, our contribution to this movement that can and should be extended beyond this spectacular astronomical event.

For this spell (adapted somewhat from *The Book of Overthrowing Apep*), you will need a piece of red clay pottery, some paint or a marker to draw and inscribe with, and (optionally) a bag you do not mind seeing destroyed. First, you should draw an image of the Apep serpent being slain by Antinous. This will help focus your intent and align your energies with the mythic energies at play. Then, inscribe the names of individuals and forces whose power and influence you wish to see lessened and destroyed, those individuals and powers that would swallow us whole. Take your time, and put as much energy and emotion into this as you can. Let it be real for you. Once your tablet or pot is filled, speak your intention and pray to Antinous-Osiris, and whoever of your gods you deem appropriate for this rite. Then, recite this spell three times, culminating in the destruction of the pot as you see fit. In my own working, a pillowcase was particularly cathartic for me, and allowed me the delicious opportunity of figuratively sweeping fascism off my sidewalk when the rubble and dust broke through the fabric.

Antinous, mighty hunter, slayer of lions, favored companion of Diana – Attend!
Antinous-Osiris the Justified, red lotus, glorious jewel of the Nile – Attend!
Antinous, beloved son of Ra-Horakhty, guardian of the solar barque – Attend!

Attend! Attend! Attend!

Day turns into night, the stars shine in the heavens, as the moon occludes the sun – Attend!
Forces of darkness gather, the prowling lion in the desert, the writhing coils of Apep – Attend!
Torches are raised, weapons are drawn, chants of hatred and bigotry cry loud in the city square – Attend!

Attend! Attend! Attend!

Antinous Liberator, breaker of bonds and chains – Attend to us!
Antinous Navigator, guide who shows us the path to freedom and
liberation – Attend to us!
Antinous Lover, through whose love we become beautiful and good –
Attend to us!

Turn your spear tipped with adamant to the approaching foe, Antinous,
and free us from this blight upon the land and the community!

Addressing the clay pot or tablet:

Taste you death, O Apep, get you back!
Retreat, O enemy of Ra!
Fall down, be repulsed, get back and retreat!
I have driven you back, and I have smashed you into pieces.

Ra triumphs over Apep at dawn – Taste you death, Apep!
Ra triumphs over Apep at noon – Taste you death, Apep!
Ra triumphs over Apep at eventide – Taste you death, Apep!
Ra triumphs over Apep at midnight – Taste you death, Apep!
Back, Fiend, an end to you!
Therefore have I inscribed your many names and broken you into rubble.

I break your will, Apep!
I break your power, Apep!
I break your hatred, Apep!
I break your strife, Apep!
You are tiny, Apep. I can see the whole of eternity, every single fragment
of your existence, and I break them.

TASTE YOU DEATH!

In the name of Ra!
In the name of Horus!
In the name of Set!
In the name of Isis!
In the name of Bast!
In the name of he, at whose name the gates of the underworld tremble!

AEIOU!

Recite the spell above three times then destroy the clay pot or tablet as
you see fit. When complete, say:

You shall never rise again.

Ave Antinoe![1]

---

1   Pronounced Ah-vay Ahn-tin-oh-ey

Golden Waves & Priestess Bodies:
Establishing a Queer-Centric Poly-Normative Aphrodite Cultus in Cascadia

by Reverend Teri D. Ciacchi, MSW

Areia, Hoplismena: Warlike, Armed ~ A Lover's War

Societies never know it, but the war of an artist with his society is a lover's war, and he does, at his best, what lovers do, which is to reveal the beloved to himself and, with that revelation, to make freedom real.

– James Baldwin (*The Price of the Ticket: Collected Nonfiction*, 1948-1985)

The culture we were born into and grew up within — USA, neoliberal, capitalist, racist, sexist, hegemonic oligarchic — can be referred to as "the fading uberculture." This fading uberculture is not *for* me, and resisting the fading uberculture is exhausting and does not provide enough pleasure. As pleasure activists, we want to focus on creating more of what we desire: an intimate community of gender varied friends and lovers who are magickal practitioners focused on creating new ways of being loving humans. In effect, we find ourselves at war/odds with the culture we were born into because that culture does not have a place for us. The fading uberculture does not even have words that we can use to describe or accurately convey our internal experiences of divinity, love, and sex; we must invent new words, use different pronouns. In search of ourselves and our culture we have gone through a series of becomings, an ongoing unfolding of Self that have inspired us to invent/center our own understandings, language, and definitions of what the central mysteries of divinity, love and sex are and can be.

The use of the pronoun "we" throughout this essay is an intentional and admittedly unique usage. The intention is to express my internal experience of being a collective of beings, a multiverse of personas, an individual embedded in an ecological web of relatedness. It is impossible for me to separate "myself" from the complex interweaving and histories of (1) sex-positive and queer ancestors of choice, (2) biological blood ancestors of DNA family heritage, (3) the internal environs of my body that include biota, neural networks, and assimilation of animals and plants as food, (4) the fluidity of ideas, conversation, and activities shared within and between the many people in my communities, (5) the fluids and bodies I exchange when being sexual with others, (6) the lived environments of my physical existence taken in by my body's sensory precepts. It is also important for me as an ecosexual animist to approach the non-human persons around me as an integral part of my Self. So while the use of the pronoun "we" for self-reference is clumsy, it is also for me the most truthful and authentic.

We offer this article as an example, only one example, of one potential way forward. The LLR is not THE WAY forward. We are not a "royal we" and there is no expectation that anyone reading this essay do things the "LLR WAY", in fact, we think a key to our thriving is for each person to build their own visions based on their own personal gnosis. It is our thinking that a culture worth living into would build bioregional subcultures that are, simultaneously, different from, and in allyship with, each other. Living Love Revolution is only one of the multitudes of possible imaginative examples of how queer magical practitioners can center their magick's and their lives around their own values. Creating our own counter cultures is revolutionary praxis and can be more empowering and pleasurable than resisting the fading uberculture.

My work as a Living Love Revolution (LLR) Aphrodite Priestess and Temple Hierophant is my Great Work, an unfinished but steadily building artistic communal masterpiece of transpersonal love and social transformation. The Aphrodite Temple system we have designed and many have co-created over the years is an endeavor in the art of culture building. Since 2009, LLR has produced 3 or 4 weekend-long Aphrodite Temple retreats per year. Both Living Love Revolution and Aphrodite Temples are a social experiment, an attempt to co-create an evolutionary focused, socially diverse, consent-based, queer-centric, poly-normative, ecstatic culture that is worth living into.

We are using the word culture quite specifically here, to indicate both modern and ancient meanings. In modernity this is approached as a particular society that has its own beliefs, ways of life, art, paradigms of thinking, and behaving that exist in a particular place. From antiquity, we call forth the Roman orator Cicero's meaning of "cultus animi" or the cultivation of the soul. We also invoke the Aphrodite cultus as a postmodern series of happenings and events that actualize Cicero's definition of religion as cultus deorum, "the cultivation of the gods," or the knowledge of giving the gods their due. The Living Love Revolution Aphrodite Temple system is a culture designed to take care of, tend, and dwell within the Cascadia Bioregion[1] in a manner that confers respect to the deity Aphrodite, the land itself, and the complex ecological web of human and non-human persons coexisting here.

As Baldwin says, what lovers do best is "reveal the beloved to." We wanted a deity who looked like us, who came from our own blood ancestry, who knew themself as divine, loving, and shamelessly sexual. In the center of the cultus is the image of Aphrodite. *Chrusee*, meaning "golden" or "goldenness," is the word most frequently used in ancient Greek poetry to refer to Aphrodite. The Golden One radiates love, desire, and erotic life force. In a manner that mirrors my own sacred sexual development, religious scholar Paul Friedrich asks and answers the following question:

> Is religion primarily an individual experience that gets extended out to group phenomena, such as communal rituals, or is it mainly a sociocentric reality that is particularized and lived by the individual? Both emphases can be argued for the religion of Aphrodite; some combination of them would be realistic. (*The Meaning of Aphrodite* 1978 p. 130)

Tending Aphrodisiacal culture requires both the centering of the self and the creation of group phenomena like Aphrodite Temples. Having received personal gnosis, we then feel compelled to create communal rituals that give the goddess her due.

> God is Self and Self is God and God is a Person like my Self.
> – Victor Anderson (*Victor Anderson: An American Shaman*, Cornelia Benavidez 2017)

---

1   Cascadia Bioregion - Bioregions are defined through the ecological aspects of a land base such as watersheds (hydrology boundaries) and mountain ranges or deserts. For me it is part of a radical EcoFeminist perspective to name the place that I live after its bioregion rather than by the state names that were assigned to this land after it was taken from the indigenous peoples that lived here long before colonization.

The term Cascadia first came to my attention when reading the utopian novel Ecotopia by Ernest Callenbach. Bates McKee "Cascadia: The Geologic Evolution of the Pacific Northwest," published in 1972, was the first book title to using the word, while David McClosky, founder of the Cascadian Institute, was the first to fully map the Cascadian Bioregion and apply the name. http://cascadia-institute.org/

I have lived in the Cascade bioregion since 1989, spending 10 years in Eugene, Oregon, 12 years in Seattle, Washington, and am starting my 6th year in Portland, OR. The parts of Portland's cultures that I socialize include The Cascadian Coalition Against Hate, attending events like Cascadia Rising and talk seriously about succession. The Cascadian Flag was created in 1994-95 by Portlander Alexander Baretich who maintains the website http://freecascadia.org/ where more history and free classes on Cascadia can be explored.

The creation myth that resonates most with our personal experience of deity is from Victor and Cora Anderson's Feri tradition of Witchcraft. Shared by Starhawk as *The Star Goddess Meditation*, (*The Spiral Dance*, Starhawk 1979), it begins:

> Alone, awesome, complete within herself, the Goddess [...] floated in the abyss of outer darkness [...] She saw by her own light her radiant reflection and fell in love with it. She drew it forth by the power that was in Her and made love to Herself [...]

We take the time to look deeply into the void of space, a metaphor for our own existential experience that there is no one else to guide or tell us the true nature of Divinity, of reality. We look into the reflection, and choose to see ourselves as Deity.

> i found god in myself
> and i loved her
> i loved her fiercely
> – Ntozake Shange, (for colored girls who have considered suicide/when
> the rainbow is not enuf 1974)

We fall in love with ourselves. We choose to love ourselves fiercely as a magickal act and then invent group processes that are holographic reproductions of these autoerotic autonomous actions. We use the image of a golden pillar of radiant light to imagine the divinity that resides in the center of Self. We use this image in the grounding meditations that we teach and embody in order to help people access their own immanence. For if they can palpably experience it within themselves, they can learn to perceive it in other beings. One of Aphrodite's greatest powers is the ability to access/embody the golden light of immanence as the erotic life force that it is.

"Magick," says Aleister Crowley, "is the Science and Art of causing Change to occur in conformity with Will" (*The Equinox: 2 Volume Set (Vol 1)* p.12 1980). Or, if you prefer, magick is the act of creating your world consciously in accordance with your understanding of your divine will.

It is the work of an Aphrodite Priestess to tap into and direct erotic life force – Aphrodisiacal energy – in alignment with their will. Golden light radiates and builds during Temple activities. Skillfully directed by The Priestess Body, this light becomes a golden wave of erotically charged life force that we release as a cone of power at the energetic focal point of our group sex magick. Generating pleasure through sexualoving consensual touch and then directing that energy with intention is the way that we make transformation, healing, and freedom real in our Aphrodisiacal rites.

Pandemos ~ Common To All People

Enjoy Yourself! The life you live today
is yours, and all the rest belongs to fortune.
Honor the god who is by far the sweetest
to mortals: honor kindly Aphrodite.
As for all the rest, forget it. Listen
to what I say, if you think it makes sense.
– Alcestis 788-93 trans. Svalien 2007

Aphrodite is available to us; there is plenty to go around. Oh Sacred Whore, who sees the divinity in all beings and eternally longs to merge! By centering our own queer, fat, kinky, gender-fluid, aging Self and declaring ourselves Holy, we create a safe space for others who are also marginalized by the fading uberculture. Our Aphrodisiacal culture is simultaneously erotic, educational, and therapeutic. LLR Aphrodite Temples are oriented toward healing the erotic traumas inflicted on all of us by the dominant paradigm and shifting our lived experience from one of oppression and obedience to one of sovereignty and authenticity. As a trauma survivor, we are aware that slow somatic experiences build trust and help us stay in our bodies. As a person with a fair amount of social anxiety, we understand what activities are more likely to move us towards self-acceptance and increased resilience. We take our time, breathe slowly and cycle back to grounding and embodiment; we call this: "presencing" or praxis. We use Dan Siegel's acronym C.O.A.L. to remind ourselves to remain Curious, Open, Accepting, and Loving (Daniel J. Siegel, M.D. *Mindsight* 2010).

Aphrodite herself is very clear that she embodies solutions to many of the traumas and conflicts that exist in the fading uberculture's sexual paradigm. She is sweetly insistent that we offer the opportunity to be with her to all people. In choosing to have public events, we are embodying Aphrodite Pandemos, or she who is "for all the people." These teachings are coming from our communion with the deity of Love herself. We are channeling these materials from a holistic dimension that is the non-dual nature of Reality itself. There is a vortex: the space/place in the center of Self—and in the center of the Multiverse—that we inhabit that is beneath/beyond human understanding. This is the source of Love and all experiences of sexual communion. In order to experience the beauty and magnificence of this love and communion, we must remove the false divisions of dualistic man-made religions and reductionist Western intellectual constructs that currently dominate our experiences of deity, love, and sex.

We developed an event structure that honors the Goddess of Love and Lust and allow our personal praxis of deity, love, and sex to be available to any person who feels called to experience it. This event structure both imitates ancient Temple environments and invents new forms of Aphrodisiacal culture. The intention is to help meet contemporary people's needs for touch, belonging, acceptance, and the giving and receiving of sexual pleasure as a joyful act of communion.

We call the core group of individuals who lead temples The Priestess Body. The Priestess Body is composed of people who have attended at least one LLR Aphrodite Temple and desire to help produce the events and begin training to be a resource of transpersonal love in community contexts.

In temple, we introduce Aphrodite as the erotic life force we will be tapping into and communing with. We cast a magic circle of protection and honor the directions, the Ancestors, and the Land. The Priestesses invoke the Golden One opening their bodies through singing and dancing, palpably celebrating her presence.

> *All Hail Aphrodite, fill me with your loving energy. Honeyed Aphrodite, pour your golden waves all over me.*
> – Chant channeled during 2010 Aphrodite Temple by Teri Ciacchi

Doritis ~ Bountiful

> *I can't understand why people are frightened of new ideas. I'm frightened of the old Ones.*
> – John Cage (US composer 1912-1992)

Aphrodite is abundant and expansive. She both inspires autonomy and facilitates reciprocity. She calls us to deepen our self-love and invites ecstatic sensory exploration in myriad forms. If we are to truly embody and embrace her we must have social structures that emulate her sovereignty and our interdependence. Because our definitions of deity, love, and sex are so different from those of the fading uberculture, we seek to create Temporary Autonomous Zones (TAZ) within Temple. These TAZ are spaces where people of all sexes, genders, sexualities, bodies, and relationship structures have the opportunity to explore and develop sexual autonomy. A *Temporary Autonomous Zone*, as described by Hakim Bey as "a mobile or transient location free of economic and social interference by the State" (Hakim Bey, TAZ: The Temporary Autonomous Zone, Ontological Anarchy, *Poetic Terrorism*, 1985). Bey argues for the production of greater autonomy in the present moment, rather than the acceptance of domination in exchange for the promise of some future utopia. TAZ is the concept behind a lot of contemporary festival culture and was influential in the creation of Burning Man. Bey quotes Stephen Pearl Andrews as saying a TAZ is:

> […] the seed of the new society taking shape within the shell of the old" (IWW Preamble). The sixties-style "tribal gathering," the forest conclave of eco-saboteurs, the idyllic Beltane of the neo-pagans, anarchist conferences, gay faerie circles – all these are already "liberated zones" of a sort, or at least potential TAZs.

TAZ are a potent form of declarative social Magick. In order to resist the default heterocisnormative patriarchal contexts for sex, The Priestess Body teaches and embodies a sex-positive, consent-oriented, queer-centric, and poly-normative sacred space.

We create our new paradigm by merging group dynamic practices from social change activism, therapeutic frames of Existential group therapy, and Witchcraft into a program of somatic exercises that take people through the LLR 6 steps of Sex Magick™. We display this poster in the Temple space and teach the steps to all participants, first verbally, then experientially.

Living Love Revolution Sacred Sex Magick Overview™

Sacred Sex Magick is the practice of consciously directing one's life force energy, in alignment with your will and stated intentions, for the manifestation of chosen outcomes. Temple is a sex magick ritual, with each part building on the next as we move through all six steps of the Living Love Revolution Sacred Sex Magick Formula™.

1) Create the Container: identify the boundaries of the physical space, cast the circle, share your relationship agreements and personal agreements, and establish group norms.

2) Purify the Container: distillation by recognizing what is already in the space that you do not wish to invoke. Speak and release fears.

3) Focus the Intent and Cast the Spell: Imagine, visualize and feel what it would be like to already have and be that which you seek.

4) Energize the Spell with Pleasure: Engage with pleasure through touch, breath, sound, and movement.

5) Release the Energized Spell: Utilize the Cone of Power to focus the sexualoving energy. Release attachments to the outcome and devote the erotic energy to the will of your higher/deeper self, the greater good of the planet, and the benefit of all beings.

6) Ground, Separate, and Aftercare: Re-finding our individual centers, releasing all Invoked beings, checking that all are present in their bodies and grounded to reintegrate back into their lives outside of Temple.

Our Sacred Sexual paradigm is reinforced by the magickal protocols we use throughout the event. We purify, consecrate, and decorate the Temple room. We carefully tend the altars and set our charged 3-foot icon of Aphrodite in a central location. A person designated as the "Anchor" grounds the ritual container and attends to the energetics of it from beginning to end of the event. Each guest is greeted individually as they enter the temple space. Priestesses purify them; sprinkling ritually sanctified salt and water over their bodies. Priestesses charge each participant with fire and air, passing incense over their bodies. The High Priestesses offer each guest a blessing: anointing their foreheads with sacred oils and their hearts with magical powders as they approach the altar. Music is playing, incense wafts about the room, and beauty and grace are present in the carefully chosen aesthetics of dress, decoration and adornment displayed within The Priestess Body and the Temple room itself.

Step One: Creating the Container is the longest step in the process by far. In some ways, this step begins eight weeks before the official temple weekend through our administrative and magickal preparations. This time includes interviewing first time attendees, connecting to and thinking well of those who will attend, and sending out a registration letter. This pre-temple work already begins the process of shifting expectations and norms of all attendees. We begin temple programming with a series of magickal declarations called "Creating Temple Context" that carefully define what is meant by sex positive, queer-centric, and poly-normative. The declarative statements are spoken in a relaxed, resonant manner that speaks the values and group norms for our TAZ into being. We state the intentions of the Temple and make a series of verbal consensual agreements with all the participants. The social hierarchy is transparently shared by introducing all members of The Priestess Body and naming their leadership roles.

During this step we review basic sexual etiquette that includes 2 1/2 hours of consent praxis; safer sex demonstrations, and risk aware information about sexually transmitted infections (STIs). Finally, we also give all attendees and priestesses a chance to declare our identities, boundaries, and STI statuses to the group as a whole, which is one way that we normalize the diverse expression of behaviors, sexualities, genders, and relationships that exist within and between us all. Every individual has many opportunities to speak their truth to the group as a whole or within small groups, helping to co-create the Temple atmosphere, encourage authentic vulnerability, and deepen the intimacy between all present.

During all of this section, we are accomplishing four main goals of creating TAZ. First, we are declaring what the group norms are. Next, we are teaching the group norms by both role modeling them and practicing somatic exercises that embody them. Third, we are holding people responsible for behaving in alignment with the group norms they agreed to. Finally, we are gently correcting and re-aligning their behavior if it is not resonant with the group norms they agreed to honor as part of the agreement of attending.

> *For surely, one must be either undiscerning or frightened to love only one person, when the world is so full of gracious and noble spirits*
> – Edna St. Vincent Millay (The Letters of Edna St. Vincent Millay 1982)

There are several ways that Temple processes carefully establish a polyamorous frame. One way is in the "How:" the structure of how we create the small group containers during Step Four: Energizing the Spell with Pleasure. Groups are determined by divination; each participant has a personal token in a bowl on the altar presided over by the Aphrodite statue. The Priestess leading each small group draws the tokens from the bowl by touch but without looking to determine who is in their small group. In the previous Steps 1 through 3, participants have been given the concept of a safer/braver social sexual context and the opportunity to somatically investigate their desires without shame. Small group exercises are timed and each person is offered a turn: an equal amount of time to request and receive the erotic fantasy of their choice based on their internal somatic awareness of what they want.

> *Oh, I know, I know. She is dark.*
> *And so's the coal before the spark*
> *that makes it burn like roses*
> – Asklepiados trans. Sam Hill (The Infinite Moment Poems from Ancient Greek 1992)

A second way we generate a polyamorous frame is in the "What:" what are we doing? Within the small groups of Step 4, Priestesses endeavor to embody the

Sacred Whore archetype by acting as if they are the central tuber root in a polycule of rhizomatic intimacy. Once again intentionally centering a marginalized identity, we reach into the ancient pagan past in our bloodlines to cast a light upon the obscured and denigrated avatars of the Golden One. We re-member, we re-create, we re-enchant, we be-come Aphrodite. We take the hotly debated shreds of historic evidence for the existence of temple prostitution and use them as a foundation for illuminating a specifically queer polyamorous form of sexual relatedness. We become Holy Whore peers and create a partnership model of transpersonal sexual caretaking. We take turns being of service and stewarding each other's sexual/spiritual development. We tend to each other's desires, generating a wide and vast network of priestesses, feeding the soul of all who enter the Temple precincts and building The Priestess Body throughout Cascadia.

Morpho ~ Imagining Shapely Forms

The only war that matters is the war against the imagination and all other wars are subsumed in it [...] it is a war for this world, to keep it a vale of soul making.
– Diane diPrima "Rant" from Pieces of a Song: Selected Poems (2001); hear it here: https://www.youtube.com/watch?v=bw8lUZCihzA accessed 2017

When we hear the word "sex," what images arise? Are these images coming from direct experience? Are they images absorbed from media streams? Does what you are imagining involve yourself and one other? Are you alone in the throes of self-pleasuring? Are you on your bed, a forest floor, a rushing stream, an actual cavern? Are you human or animal? Are you your deified self, your child self, or your "regular everyday" "adulting" self? What does queer sex look like? What does engaging in queer-centric sex magick entail? Who is responsible for your experiences?

Our theory of human sexual development is based on three narratives for sexual behavior described by Galen Moore in his article Quantum Sex (2009, July Quantum Sex. Examiner.com web http://www.examiner.com/article/quantum-sex accessed 2010) and further articulated in our essay What's Sex Got to Do With Ecology? (*Ecosexuality: When Nature Inspires the Arts of Love* ed. Anderlini-D'Onofrio & Hagamen, 2015). The three frames are Procreation, Recreation, and Quantum/Communion. The fading uberculture's frame of sexuality is determined by the hierarchical male dominant Judeo Christian belief that sex is for procreation and anything else is immoral. We suggest that all sex that is not about procreation is therefore sex ripe with queer potential. We assert that all consensual sex that is either recreational or Quantum is queer-ish and wyrd as it requires imagination and inventiveness, two things that are just not found in your standard gender essentialist socialized expectations of procreative sex. Temples are a much-needed TAZ for the exploration of queer sexual expression and embodiment without punishment, policing, or judgment.

Queer sex is not easy to define. Our "Sexual Etiquette Guide" states:

> Sex is an open book: For the purposes of Aphrodite Temple we are not certain if we can define sex. One thing we do know is that it is more than inserting a penis into a vagina. We also know it is okay if sex includes inserting a penis into a vagina.

In order to move beyond sorting a group of people into couples who march off two-by-two to mate in captivity we turn to the queerness of oddity. By this I mean literally engaging in erotic connection in queer groups of 3 and 5, rather than the even numbers of 2, 4 or 6. Odd numbers culture jam heteronormativity by making it more difficult to project an idealized soulmate/spouse onto the other people present in the small group. We avoid dyads and quads in our group exercises and most especially in the small groups of Step 4. Facilitated group erotic and sexual exploration occurs in triads and quintets. Heteronormative programming confines sex to romantic love, procreation, and the perpetuation of capitalism that reinforces and idealizes pair bonding.

If the goal of sex is not to procreate, then we are liberated from biological imperatives of mating. Attraction based on biological determinism; the hormonal drives and pheromone releases, and our DNA's continual incitement toward intercourse and procreation are no longer the reason we are having sex.

As we move away from the gender essentialist binary notions that commodify men as purely financial/resource providers and women as purely social/sexual providers, we then expand the opportunities for negotiating sexual and economic sharing. In recognizing the multitude of abilities, interests, possibilities, identities, and so on that every individual can embody, we move steadily away from heterocisnormativity and toward queerness.

> *The erotic imagination permeates the body making it transparent. We do not know exactly what it is, except that it is something more, more than history, more than sex, more than life, more than death.*
> – Octavio Paz

If duality is not dominating our understanding of gender, then there are more than two genders and they are not diametrically opposed to each other. There is no "opposite sex" to be at war with; instead there are an infinite number of gendered displays, each one a unique, experience. Each one an ephemeral epiphany specific to the relational context in which it co-arises. Gender itself is a liminal state, a mercurial expression that shifts and glides across the reflective surface of the bodies before us.

The relational perspectives and contexts provided for sex in LLR Aphrodite Temple are "all about" recreation and communion, an ecstasy of autoerotic autonomy. Inside our consent-based TAZ of democratic sexualoving meritocracy, every single celebrant becomes a sacred and holy fractal of Divinity. We are, each of us, a shimmering note in a harmonious chorus resounding with her name.

> Aphrodite!
> Golden One, we sing your praises,
> we keep you always, in the center:
> of our hearts, of our lives, of our Loves.
> May our names fall from your honeyed lips.
> Oh Beloved enchantress,
> smile radiantly in our direction.

Blessed Be.

Non-Binary Witches
by EJ Landsman

Non-Binary Witches
by EJ Landsman

The Queer Journey of the Wheel

by Steve Kenson

Queerness is how I found magic. Lying in the lower bunkbed of my classmate in The eight-spoked Wheel of the Year is a foundational part of modern Wiccan and neo-pagan practice, often portrayed as a cyclical journey of life. It is a part of the Temple of Witchcraft tradition, which I helped to found and served as a priest and minister. In this article, I will look at that journey from a queer perspective, as we have done in the Temple's Queer Spirit ministry, reinterpreting traditional lore and offering opportunities for queer-positive and queer-oriented ritual year-round. In this turn of the Wheel, we visit Awakening at Yule, Naming (and self-identification) at Imbolc, Coming Out (truly breaking out of our shells!) at Ostara, Ecstasy at Beltane, Pride at Midsummer, Family and Community at Lammas, Mentorship at Mabon, and finally Elderhood and Death at Samhain.

What are the Queer Mysteries? All people have Mysteries, experiences that change you in ineffable ways. They are rites of passage that can be described and explained, but only truly understood through experience. The experience of shared Mysteries is a powerful foundation for spiritual community. Some Mysteries we share by virtue of being human—birth, adulthood, love, loss—and others are unique to particular people, like the Mystery of childbirth. Likewise, some Mysteries are particular to queer people, and I experience them through the particular lens of being a gay man, although I feel they have wisdom and resonance for many, if not all.

And what about "Queer"? Well, in this case, "queer" is a great many things. In particular, it is both broader and simpler than "bisexual, gay, lesbian, transgender, intersex, questioning…" or the equally common "alphabet soup" of "GLBTQI+."

It is everything that is not the insufficiently-challenged heteronormativity of the over-culture. It is a reclaiming of a word used to attack people, transforming it into one of pride (not unlike the term "Witch"). It is a word that resonates with rebellion and defiance, used by activists like Queer Nation. Queer is as much defined by what it is not (heteronormative) as by the often mercurial nature of what it is. Most importantly for this journey, queer is otherness, a sense of separation and difference, usually related to gender and sexuality.

Yule (Awakening)

The Winter Solstice is a time of birth (or re-birth), the longest night of the year when we wait, breathless in hope and anticipation, for the rebirth of the sun and the return of the light to the world. This dawn of a new beginning represents our Awakening into the Queer Mysteries, stepping from a world of shadow and winter's long nights into a new awareness, not unlike the process of being born.

We all experience those moments of "otherness" where we feel different, isolated, or set apart. For queer people that sense of difference often comes when we are young and vulnerable and lasts until we can recognize and name it. For some, dawn comes in one bright and blinding flash of illumination and understanding. There are others for whom this process is as slow and sometimes painful as birth can be. No matter how it comes, the awareness of being different and being treated badly because of that difference, and the decision to seek out others of our own kind , necessitates leaving behind a safe and comfortable space for the wonders and challenges of the wider world.

Like all awakenings, the awareness of otherness, the sense of what we in the Temple call the Queer Spirit, cannot ever really be undone or forgotten. Once awakened to the experience, we are forever changed by it and cannot simply go back to sleep. Some may refuse to acknowledge it, but this new awareness cannot be denied. Although the process may take some time—for some a lifetime—we must learn to see by the light of this new dawn and to understand what it is showing us about ourselves.

Imbolc (Naming)

Imbolc is also known as Candlemas, a gathering and nurturing of the lights born and kindled at Yuletide. By the light of our new awareness, we are able to view and contemplate ourselves. With a sense of our difference, our otherness, we can peer into the illuminated mirror of our identity to ask the questions: If I am different, then what am I? Who am I? What does this mean?

In between our dawning awareness and our coming out to the world, we come out to ourselves. Imbolc is the Mystery of Naming, the liminal time when we have cast aside many of the things we were taught as true about ourselves and the world but have not yet clothed ourselves in new understanding. It is the sacred skyclad moment of standing naked before the universe and the divine, to see ourselves—and more importantly, to accept ourselves—as we truly are. It is when we articulate and complete the statement "I am..."—whatever that may be for us.

This process of self-identification is a Mystery and rite of passage experienced by all young people coming into their adulthood. Still, it is a particular part of the Queer Mysteries in which we accept (if not also embrace) our otherness, our queer identity, by identifying and naming it. As a child, I felt different from other children for years, especially other boys my age, before awakening to my sexual identity. It was longer still before I realized that meant that I was gay.

For some, the Mystery of Naming leads directly to the next. Others of us shrink back from the truth that we have named, clutching it tightly to us and retreating to the relative safety of the shadows we knew before we stepped into the light. We are like seeds planted deep beneath the earth, waiting to see if we will sprout.

Ostara (Coming Out)

"What is the strength of the plant splitting the seed, pushing up through the soil? The chick breaking out of the egg, the child emerging from the womb, the Goddess rising up from the Underworld...?"

This is what High Priestess Alix Wright asked us to contemplate during the 2015 Temple of Witchcraft Ostara ritual meditation. It was something immediately familiar to me, a Mystery that spoke to my own experience: the strength to Come Out, the courage necessary to overcome fear, shame, and doubt and proudly declare who you are.

"Coming out" is a declaration of one's own truth, a profound moment of sharing, vulnerability, and courage. For queer people, it's more than just the adoption of a label or providing information ("Oh, by the way, did you know...?"). It's a willingness to live your life openly and honestly, to not give in to shame or fear, to refuse to hide, even if hiding might be the safest thing to do.

It's also an ongoing process. One of the qualities of many queer people is our ability to "pass," to hide who we are. Many of us are familiar with the game of skirting around a truth we are not yet ready to share. Because of this, we have to come out many times, in many ways, and it's never really over and done with. People make assumptions: "You're wearing a wedding band, are you married?" A choice is offered: Do I just say "yes" or do I continue with a specific pronoun or name? Do I mention that I have two partners, both of them men (coming out as both gay and polyamorous)? When and how (and how much) to come out is an ongoing choice, as a colleague reminded me in going over a draft of this very paragraph, noting that I had initially distanced myself from the examples herein by using the more generic second person.

Defying those assumptions and expectations takes courage because you never know what you're going to get in response. Those fears and assumptions must be challenged; otherwise, no one knows anything different. The power of coming out is the power of the seedling breaking free from the seed and slowly, steadily, pushing up through the soil, out of the dark, and reaching towards the sun. Just one blade of grass from a single seed may not change the terrain much, but thousands upon thousands of shoot sprouting from countless seeds of diverse plants can transform a landscape. So it is with those who live their truth openly and honestly. It is a force that cracks ossified tradition and expectation, changing it for the better. In this rich soil, new growth can flourish. It is a force that has done a great deal to further understanding for queer people in mainstream society.

Coming out is a Mystery many Neopagans experience as well. It's called "coming out of the broom closet" with good reason. Minority spiritual practices like Witchcraft and other Neopagan traditions can be invisible in a largely Christian society if none of us publicly identify with those traditions. If we choose, we can "pass" in mainstream society until the question arises and the opportunity to come out arrives. "Are you religious?" "What does that star mean?" "What 'Temple' is this?" How do you answer, and how much do you share? I find myself asking when is it the time and place for a conversation that may plant a seed, an idea or experience outside someone's norm, that can grow in its own time?

In some measure, coming out is a Mystery everyone who is challenged to live their truth experiences at one time or another. We all wear many masks in life and deal with the false expectations of individuals and society. Trading or removing those masks, going against who we might be perceived to be in order to be who we feel we truly are, is a challenge, and takes courage. Any time you come out, you never know how it might be received.

Beltane (Ecstasy)

My first experience with ecstasy was on the dance floor, under the pulsating lights. I'm not talking about the infamous club drug of the same name, I'm talking about ecstasy in terms of spiritual experience. Ecstasy's original meaning, ex stasis, is to be outside of one's self, in that eternal moment where time seems to stand still, the mind is quiet, and separation seems to dissolve. I'm likely not alone in the experience, either, as one of the first ways I heard the ecstatic experience explained to a group of gay men was: "It's like when you're dancing and you really get into it…" with various nods of understanding from the audience.

In the book Trance Formation, author and researcher Robin Sylvan looks at the global rave culture and finds numerous examples of experiences we might call "ecstatic" or "shamanistic," such as feelings of ego dissolution, oneness with everything, distortions in time, the perception of spiritual presences, or unexplainable joy and feelings of wholeness or intense meaningfulness. No surprise, really, since dancing to exhaustion following a driving beat in flickering half-light is one of the oldest ecstatic techniques known to humanity. Why, particularly, is it a queer mystery?

Perhaps because of the long association of nightclubs and dance with queer culture. One of the nicknames of the dance club is "gay church." Ecstasy on the dance floor has for some time been the most accessible and affirming form of the practice available to the queer community. Additionally, there is a freeing quality to ecstatic practices that appeals strongly to oppressed or marginalized peoples. This freedom is the first step to the greater ecstasy of letting go of even who you "really" are. You release all preconceptions of self to simply be in the eternal moment where the dichotomy between self and other falls away and the question "who am I?" gives way to the experience of "I AM," in the divine sense of "I am that I am," as the burning bush spoke to Moses.

Just as letting go of our selves is vital to achieve ecstasy, so is letting go of the experience itself. Although the moment can seem timeless, mortals exist in time. So the ecstatic experience or trance cannot last. The return from altered reality is a re-enactment of the divine Fall into space, time, and material existence, which may be gentle or harsh, not unlike our first transition from the ecstatic union of the womb to birth and independent growth within a separate skin . In the language of the journey of the Tarot, we ecstatically cast off the chains of the Devil, recognizing the illusions that imprison us, and experience the fall of the Tower, plummeting from the heights of our experience. Ideally, we emerge from that into the Star, embodying new hope, new potential, new balance, and new openness to growth, change, and progress.

The power of ecstasy is not in remaining in that timeless, transcendent moment. If you could do so, and never return, how would that be any different from death? Those who seek merely ecstasy, and not the ways it can transform them upon their return, are chasing the end of their existence, whether they know it or not. An endless string of "ecstatic experiences" with no real growth or development afterward is a sure sign of a spiritual thrill-seeker who has confused the experience with its purpose. The power of ecstasy is that of creative destruction It is the psychic blast that reveals the ego as nothing more than a sometimes-useful illusion. It is the shamanic initiation of being torn apart so that the spirits can rebuild you, shape you into a person more able to work with them. It is the paradox of letting go of everything you have, everything you think of as yourself, in order to make the leap across the Abyss and find your Higher Self waiting for you on the other side, because you are the one you have been waiting for.

Ecstasy is our birthright as spirits-made-flesh, living in space and time, so we may touch the timeless, eternal source. It is particularly the undeniable birthright of all people who have been maligned, marginalized, persecuted, or mistreated. It is an experience that shows up bullying or oppression for the wrongs that they are and reminds us that they do not, cannot, diminish us or make us any less divine. Like the sacred maxim we recite in the Temple: "there is no part of me that is not of the gods."

Midsummer (Pride)

What does it mean when we talk about "queer pride" and Pride as a queer mystery? "Pride goeth before a fall," we're told in modern spiritual lore, and hubris, or overweening pride, is the tragic flaw of many a Greek hero. For that matter, what are we proud of? Whether sexuality or gender is nature or nurture, it seems largely fixed at a very early age, and certainly not something we choose, so it is an achievement of which we are proud?

Our pride is invested in different achievements. Through the mystery of coming out, we learned to say, "This is who I am." Through the mystery of ecstasy, we experienced the paradox of being a part of, and apart from, everything. We "find ourselves" anew and learn what it means to be who (and what) we are. One of the key concepts of ecstasy is the return; we must come back from that state of bliss, return to the Realized World of form, time, and change, and put what we have learned to work. Our choice to do that work allows us to say, "I will create something better." That choice is the mystery of Pride.

That "something better" is for our community, our people. Pride is not the aggrandizement of self, but just the opposite: it is humble service to a higher ideal, intended to elevate everyone, and a dedication to become a good ancestor and smooth the way for those who come after us. It is the creation of sacred space— queer space—that not only says "You are safe here," but goes beyond to say: "You are special. You are loved and celebrated here." Pride is having a sense of worth that is not satisfied with mere "acceptance." This Mystery says, "I'm better than that. We deserve better than that, and I'm going to help make it happen."

It is fitting that Pride is associated with the longest, and therefore brightest, day of the year, when the Sun reaches the peak of its power. Pride is about shining a brilliant light—not a spotlight on us, but a light that shines out and illuminates, a beacon that others can see to guide them to the better spaces and ideas that we create.

Pride is the assertion of the Will, the power to demand change and to make it happen. Rather than accept what is, the power of Queer Spirit helps us to attain the ability to see what could be, and gives us the determination to bring it into being. It is heat as well as light, the fires of passion, dedication, and, yes, anger. The patrons of the Stonewall Inn did not act initially from a higher vision. They had simply had enough, enough of harassment, enough of persecution, enough of shame, enough of mistreatment. They fought back, and the community put the power of that Pride behind better visions of the future, a better world for themselves and those who would follow them. They marched for their recognition and their rights, and helped to earn them, passing the torch on to the generations after them, to us, to continue the work.

Pride embraces and seeks to create community in common cause. It's a time for the diverse people of the queer rainbow to come together as one, not to quash our differences for everyone else's comfort, but to celebrate our differences for our own liberation. I have seen the powerful magick and sacred space that results when our community sets aside our cliques and artificial niches. Doing so is necessary for the pursuit of our common rights. As Benjamin Franklin observed at the signing of the American Declaration of Independence: "We must all hang together, or assuredly we will all hang separately."

In that common cause, with our Pride, we raise up new possibilities and create a better world than the one we left behind. We realize our differences and claim them as our own. We celebrate the diversity of who and what we are and use it, not as a stigma or source of shame, but as a source of strength and inspiration.

Lammas (Family)

In the Queer Mysteries, we have gone from illumination to revelation (coming out), through ecstasy to pride, the claiming and using of power. Now comes the time to harvest what has been sown through the use of that power. Lammas is also known as Lughnasadh, or "the funeral games of Lugh," but the games are not to honor the Celtic solar god Lugh himself. They are, instead, for his foster mother, Taltiu of the Fir-Bolg, the People of the Spear. Taltiu raised Lugh as her own and later sacrificed herself by expending the last of her strength in digging up all the stones from the fields of Eiru (Ireland) to make them fertile and bountiful. This was the gift of a queen and mother to her people and her child to ensure a bountiful harvest. Her sacrifice is honored, and we can also celebrate our gratitude for the labors of our other ancestors and our activists.

The queer relationship with family is often fraught due to the necessary step of separation, of seeking identity outside of our families of origin. Many families still reject children whose sexuality or gender identities are outside the narrow range of heteronormativity. Even in a supportive family of origin, there is still a time of seeking and, when we become mature adults, a time to create a family of our own.

"Family" is a loaded word, particularly for queer people, who so often experience condemnation and exile from the families who raised us. Even those fortunate enough to retain good relations with the family that raised them—as I have—are still faced with challenges: What does "family" mean to us, and how do we choose to define it?

Family is another area in which queer people often forge their own path. Some may choose the more mainstream model of a monogamous, committed couple, perhaps raising children, but that is by no means the only option. Indeed, many queer people have adopted the expression "family of choice" to reflect their own decision to create new families in configurations that suit them. This highlights a fact most take for granted. As adults, we all choose who we call family. We choose to build together, stay together, manage together, celebrate together, and be together, in whatever way works for us. That's true of all people, but the difference is that the "default" model is not as pervasive with queer people as it is in the larger culture.

Along my journey I have encountered families ranging from same-sex married couples (with or without children, biological or adopted) through a dizzying spectrum of polyamory including Vs, triads, quads, tribes, and other "polycules." There are leather families and kink families and faerie communes and intentional communities and so very much more. All of the successful ones have taken the Mystery of the First Harvest—sowing the seeds, nurturing their growth, harvesting them, and transforming them into things to nourish body, mind, and spirit—and applied it to the sacred work of their lives and the lives of those they love, those they choose. It is sacred work, necessary work, and a part of the maturing process where we transition in our journey of the Mysteries from we to me to us again.

Mabon (Mentorship)

As the Mystery of the First Harvest of Lammas is bread and family, the Mystery of the Second Harvest of Mabon is fermentation and ecstasy. This is not the individual Mystery of Ecstasy of Beltane, but instead is shared ecstasy, brewed and bottled, properly fermented and aged, and given as the divine gift that it is: the Waters of Life, the Draught of Inspiration, the dark, delicious, fertile depths of Creation. As we move into the final phases of the Wheel, it is also one of the Mysteries that still challenges the queer community, that of Mentorship.

One of the secrets of Queer Spirit is that it is rarely found where we begin. Most queer people are born and raised in heterosexual (if not necessarily heterosexist) families, and we are most certainly raised in a heterosexist and largely patriarchal culture. Earlier in the cycle of the Wheel, we are driven by our awareness of otherness, our declaration of identity, to seek out our people, our tribe. This Mystery is the other side of that equinox of Coming Out, the role of those who stand on the other side in a shadowy and often unknown world to welcome the newcomer, extending the heady offering of knowledge, experience, and understanding. Without mentorship, coming out would be a lonely and perhaps self-destructive experience.

This Mystery is also a profound opportunity or calling to seek out and honor our elders, something queer community does not always do well. For many of us around my age and younger, a generation of our elders was decimated by plague and neglect, leaving us without the benefit of their wisdom. We should cherish those who remain that much more because of it. Each of us can seek to grow into the mentors we wish that we had, even though it is difficult to give the generations who come after us a type of care we rarely found. This is part of the reason for establishing queer sacred spaces and communities, such as the Temple of Witchcraft's Queer Spirit Ministry, or queer-focused festivals, traditions, and groups. It is part of the work of this and other essays of this book: distilling our experiences and insights so they may be shared with a new generation.

Samhain (Elderhood)

An end comes to all things. The ecstasy of youth is distilled, refined, and passed on to the next generation. If we are fortunate, we step into the final Mysteries of Elderhood and, eventually, of Death, that final ecstasy, to begin again. Having cultivated the Mysteries of Pride and community, of Family, of Mentorship, it is time to receive the caring and nourishment that we have sown, time for the community to give back to its elders.

If recognizing the Mystery of Mentorship is a challenge for the queer community, then honoring the Mystery of Elderhood is even more so. Our elders too often find themselves forgotten and ignored by a community caught up in the Mysteries of Coming Out, Ecstasy, and Pride. Younger queer people may not recognize how the contributions of those before them helped to make those things possible. Honoring our Queer Ancestors at this turning of the Wheel is only the first step in recognizing and honoring our living elders while they remain with us. Because our elders struggled to survive in very harsh circumstances, many of them are used to being loners. How do we approach them in their isolation while respecting their courage and their sometimes-traumatic histories?

This is another reason for the creation of queer (and queer-friendly) sacred spaces and communities. Relationships that began with mentorship can become reciprocal, offering elders and mentors the care, community, visibility, and purpose they need in return for their experience and guidance. This care from community may be the only sort that queer elders receive, as they may not have children, and may well be estranged from blood relatives. Likewise, when elders have passed beyond the veil, the only reverence they receive as ancestors may come from their queer descendants who remember them in rituals of gratitude and celebration. In the Temple of Witchcraft's Queer Spirit rituals, we regularly call upon our ancestors with the invocation: "Ancestors of Queer Spirit, you who walked the path before us, you who smoothed and eased the way for us, may we follow in your footsteps to ease the way for those who will come after us. You who stand in shadow at the edge of our circle, be welcome at our fire in love and respect."

So the Wheel turns, and we must turn it and turn with it. With that awakening awareness, we return and begin again.

Edge
by Adare

A queer kinky polyamorous woman and a doctor of Chinese medicine, this portrait reflects not just its model, Amy Chang, but ying, her prior incarnation as a female assassin in disguise as a whore in a brothel. The black mark on her face invokes a scar from that past life when she devoted her power and skills to killing rather than healing people.

Interview with Blackberri, Queer Activist and Lucumi Elder

by wolfie

wolfie: it is a glorious day and we are sitting here drinking tea. if you could give me a brief bio, because probably not everybody in the book is going to know who you are, and they need to.

Blackberri: I was born in 1945. I was born Charles Timothy Ashmore, that was my name before I legally changed it in... '70... maybe '74 is when I changed it. Maybe '75. But, anyway, even before I legally changed it I had become Blackberri in 1970 or '71. I was at the University of Arizona at the time and I lived in this community that basically defined itself as a feminist community [...]* We shared things; we gardened and made crafts and did all kinds of stuff. We had study groups at the Women's Center. And I actually started the first gay liberation group there, which met at the Women's Center.

But before that I actually was born in Buffalo [New York], that's where I grew up until I was 7 and then I left Buffalo and moved to Baltimore. In Buffalo, I lived with my mother's father and his two step-children. And his wife. And we left and moved to Baltimore with my grandmother and her husband. [...] In Baltimore they weren't used to black children in white schools, and white teachers didn't know how to treat them, or didn't know anything about them. So, of course I was always one who spoke up for myself, and that was not a wise thing to do in school, with white teachers in white schools. I was considered an uppity little black child. (laughs)

wolfie: why am i not surprised?

(both laugh)

Blackberri: They really gave me a hard time. [...] There were gay children at the school and by the time we all went to high school together we were a tight knit community and for the most part we were out at school, many of us. Yet still kind of closeted in other ways. Me, it was different for me, my mother caught me when I was fourteen, and so that was very liberating, you know, that she...

wolfie: she knew.

Blackberri: She knew, right. With her, if it felt like I was having problems with it, then we would deal with it in another way, but as long as I was okay with it, she was okay with it. And I was very okay with it, and so…

wolfie: that's a pretty amazing parental position to take at that point.

Blackberri: Yeah, well, you know, after she caught me she told me she already knew 'cause no girls ever called the house. She said, "Don't no girls call this house. How could I not know?" (both laugh) [...] I was lovers with this boy in my neighborhood for… oh, I'd say at least eight years. And everybody in the neighborhood knew. And we came out that year. I was fourteen and he was… twelve, I think, maybe? But he was a big twelve. He was big for his age, very mature. Very handsome. And respected by the gangsters in and around our 'hood. I, on the other hand, was a sissy, so… well, I guess they talked about me when I wasn't around. Nobody ever said anything bad about me when I was with them, but every time I would show up they would always tell my friend that… "oh, Lee, here comes your girl." I was his girl. [...] We got stones thrown at us when we left the neighborhood. People would yell shit out their windows because we would walk holding hands or with our arms wrapped around each other. We didn't really care, you know. At one point he got a girlfriend, and she never really liked me. I didn't care, you know. I wasn't jealous of her, especially, but she was particularly jealous of me. It was kind of like a race to see who… who he would go with for the evening, you know. But she always knew she was in danger if she didn't get him out of the neighborhood before he saw me, because if I saw him and I said I wanted him to come with me, he would tell her "later."

(both laugh)

Blackberri: [...] So, yeah. I grew up really really queer and… and I'm really glad that I had that freedom and that my mom didn't repress me or treat me bad or make me feel different. It kind of made me the person I am today.

wolfie: yeah. that's really awesome and not a common story.

Blackberri: No, I know. I realize. I know my story's very different.

wolfie: [...] how long have you had your [dread]locks?

Blackberri: Well, these are my third set. The first set I had for sixteen years, until I got initiated. They were down to my calves. When I got initiated and got The Big Haircut sixteen years ago, they told me that I could do a partial and keep my hair, but I told them, "Nah, I don't want partial anything."

wolfie: i can't see you doing anything halfway, really.

Blackberri: Yeah. We gonna do it, let's do it. They said, "Yeah, it's the best." My Godfather has some of my hair in his pot and I have some of my hair in a special place. It will be buried with me when I get buried. It was my first hair. And I have some of my Godchild's hair, too.

wolfie: there's a lot of magic in hair.

Blackberri: We basically keep it to protect them.

wolfie: when in your life did you start exploring different spiritualities?

Blackberri: I'd say in 1968. I was living at the Castalia Foundation, which was also the League for Spiritual Discovery, acronym for LSD. I lived next door to Timothy Leary. I lived in an ashram. We actually used acid in the ashram for meditations. That's when I got turned on to spirituality and I did a study, I really started reading all kinds of different books and stuff. So that's when I really started. I was a bunch of different things. I had a bunch of different incarnations. I even had a little Christian incarnation for a while. One summer I went to a holiness church and got the holy ghost...

wolfie: the holy ghost touched you?

Blackberri: Yeah, the holy ghost touched me. That was probably my first experience with spirit. It was definitely a spiritual experience. My mom really didn't like it. That was always... I was always proselytizing and she didn't want to hear that bullshit.

(both laugh)

There was a period of time when I started becoming psychic. I started... I could read people. And I could tell things about them, and that was... that was kind of a mistake. I was really scaring a lot of folks, and then I was scary. People were afraid of me, so I stopped.

wolfie: how old were you when that happened?

Blackberri: I was sixteen, seventeen, around that time. [...] I had some possession stuff happen to me, too, and that was a kind of interesting thing. But now, Egun [spirits of the ancestors] or whoever I'm working with can speak through me, as they sometimes do.

Music has also been like that. Music has come through me. Some of it I've used over and over again, and some of them have been one-time things that were meant for whoever was there to hear it and never... I would never remember the chords or the words or anything. Usually at some point when there's a group of folks and we're maybe really high or... got some kind of meditation going and that happens.

wolfie: i remember seeing you, like twenty-something years ago. you did a couple of your standard songs and then you hit this channel and were just flying with it. and it was a glorious performance. i'm trying to remember where or when... it was somewhere here in the bay area. [...] you've used the word queer several times. queer is kind of a relatively young construct as far as a self-identity thing. it really sort of gelled in the 90's and before that it was pretty much pejorative. how do you feel about the identity queer?

Blackberri: I used it when I started out doing gay music. I remember at many of my shows I would say "I don't know if you noticed or not, but I'm (sing-songy) queer!" I'd sing: "Queer!" I've been using that term for a long time. Intermittent with gay. And now, one of my friends has started saying "same gender loving" and I like that, too. I really like that, because it's a different kind of label.

wolfie: yeah. it seems like we keep creating new labels because, what i see is that people are striving to find the most inclusive that they can find.

Blackberri: I think same gender loving came from both the construct for not using clinical terms or terms that the dominant culture used. That's where same gender loving came from.

wolfie: when did you first encounter the orisha? 'cause i know they have been your primary path for a while.

Blackberri: I first got turned on to the Orishas in New York by this guy that lived there, he lives in the Bay Area now. His name is Isaac Jackson. He was a curator for a museum. He had a house that had like three floors and two of the floors were museum galleries and he also DJ'd on BMI [Broadway Music Incorporated]. He had a radio show. I was on his show, I know at least once, I want to say twice, but I'm not sure. All my tapes... all my interview tapes got stolen by somebody I let stay here.

wolfie: i can only barely imagine how you felt.

Blackberri: They took everything. They took my whole archive. Anyway, long story short, Isaac had a blue candle on his altar and a cobalt blue glass like this, and it was burning 24/7; it never went out. The altar was all in blue. It was beautiful. I don't think he wore shoes. It was an altar to Yemaya and I said, "Who is that?" He said she was the patron saint of gay men, and I thought, "A religion that embraces gay people?" and it was African, too! Then I started reading things about the tradition. The stuff I read in the beginning was really scary. It really made me afraid to commit in the way that I wanted to commit. And then as I read more things, I started accepting things. Then I had a reading in the early '80's that blew my mind. Then I really made a commitment. I joined a house that was between the priests that I got read by and my Madrina [spiritual godmother, head of house], but then they parted ways and I kind of stuck with my Madrina. Then, just, you know, just… I learned a lot there and there was a lot of other stuff going on there.

wolfie: yeah. it's such a rich tradition and very complex. all the internal community politics are very complex.

Blackberri: Yeah, that's what it was. I ended up getting a reading about whether or not I should stay in the house, and Oshun told me I should leave the house. It was Oshun's house. I was sad because I had a lot of friends there, but it seemed that after I left my life got really good. (both laugh) And I was told by a priest that I was slotted for initiation, I was scheduled for initiation, but it didn't have to be soon. So I ran with that for a long long time and then in eighty… maybe '86 or '87 I was in Cuba and the Orisha found me. And every time I went to Cuba, the Orisha would find me and show me things or take me on a… sometimes all the people I was with, they would drag them along with me. It was really interesting! And then I met my Padrino [spiritual godfather, head of house] in… '88. In '88. And it was up in the mountains and I, uh, I mean, you know, Orisha was already showing me stuff and I knew there was something for me, but I didn't know where I was going to go or how I was going to do it. And he gave me my guerreros [warrior spirits]. I had an Elegua, but I didn't have Ogun and Ochossi. He gave me those Orishas and, it was really funny because I didn't have any money and it started out with my Padrino saying, "I hear you don't have your Warriors." And I said, "No, I… I have Elegua." He said "Well, we have Warriors here, do you want them?" And I said, "I don't have any money, I'm really broke." He goes "We have Warriors here, do you want them?" And I said, "Um, I can't get them right now…" And he says to me, very firmly he says "We. Have. Them. Do you want them?"

wolfie: "i'm not asking you about money."

(both laugh)

Blackberri: Yeah. Then I said "Oh! Yeah, yeah, I want them." So he gave me Warriors. He gave me another Elegua and Ogun and Ochossi. And then after that he read me and he said, "What are you waiting for? Your road is so open." And I said… I knew what he was talking about, and I said, "Well, I'm waiting to get the money." And he said, "Well, when would you like to do this?" And I said, "Next year." He goes "When next year?" I said, "Oh, December." He goes, "December what?!" (both laugh) So I said, "Twenty-first." I just threw out a number. I said, "December 21st." He said, "Okay. See you December 21st."

wolfie: (overlapping) winter solstice it is!

Blackberri: And when I came back, the money for initiation came from everywhere. [In traditions of the African diaspora, initiates to pay for food, live music, textiles, and other necessities. This tradition of offering a sacrifice to receive divine gifts is an important part of the practice] It was so crazy. The money just all came together. I had so much money that I didn't even need all the money I had. I brought money back home with me after… it was pretty amazing. It was the best thing I've ever done, too, I must say that. And then after I did that I thought, "Well, shit." I was so freaked out I was wondering why didn't I do this earlier? Then I realized that it wasn't time. I did it… I did it…

wolfie: you did it at exactly the right time.

Blackberri: At exactly the right time. And I went… before I went to… about a month before I went, I was… I went down to the ocean because I was really… my big fear was that when I became a priest that I would have to give up all of these things, you know. And so I went to Yemaya, 'cause I thought Yemaya was, was even on my head, I hadn't gotten my head at the time. [The orisha "on one's head" is the primary guardian and teacher of the initiate's spiritual path.] And, uh, I go to Yemaya and I tell her all my, my blues. I tried… I went to Ocean Beach and it was really dark and the tide was up and I couldn't see. I was walking and walking and walking and walking. I still couldn't see the water, so I finally said, "Well, fuck, I'm going to stop here. I'm not going to go any further." So I stopped where I was and I was talking to the ocean, and I told her all this stuff, and she said, "You will get back more than you'll give up." And right as that message came, a wave came in. I don't know where it came from… It came from the ocean, of course, but I couldn't see the water…

wolfie: it came out of nowhere.

Blackberri: The wave came in and it was warm as bathwater. I shit you not. It came in and went up around my ankles. I felt the warmth of it and I sat down so when the wave came back out I could feel the warm water all over the bottom part of my body as the wave went out. And no more water came in after that, but it was like… after I got up and I thought about it, my mind was totally blown 'cause I thought, "This is the Pacific Ocean. It's not warm." It's not warm.

wolfie: no, but when she has a clear message for you… there we go.

(both laugh)

Blackberri: That blew my mind.

wolfie: i bet!

Blackberri: Yeah. So then I knew everything was going to be all right. And it was true. I got waaaay more than I gave up. Way more.

wolfie: do you feel, or have a perception around, where being queer and your magical life intersect? do you feel like queers have a different relationship to spirit? or that the magic that we do has any sort of magical difference to it?

Blackberri: Well, having never been straight, it's hard to say, you know? I do feel in my spirituality, in my magic… um, it's pretty different. And I think, you know, I think everybody's is… is personal. But I know it's always there for me. I'm always learning, and my spiritual godparents in Cuba… in fact, my Godfather called me this morning, actually, 'cause I'm slated to be going out east. He was just touching base to see how I was doing. He told me he saw my pictures on Facebook. "You're looking very good," he said. (both chuckle) And he… he's a trip. Every time I go, he always tries to set me up. Sometimes with people who I'm actually interested in. He always says, "If you see somebody you like, let me know."

wolfie: i went to a couple bembes [a party for the orishas, usually with Yoruban songs for the spirits] and a misa [an oracular ritual event] with Raelyn [Gallina] when i was training with her, and it seemed to me that everybody at those particular ones were all queer. so i never got to experience being in any of those ceremonies with a predominantly straight crowd. but in the pagan [community], the neo-pagans, the witches, there is kind of a noticeable difference between doing that kind of magic with an all queer crowd or with a straight crowd. that's part of what prompted me to start this project: is there a substantive difference, a way that we approach it, or something? but it's also… you're part of a tradition that holds a place for queers specifically.

Blackberri: (overlapping) Yeah. Yeah, yeah, yeah, yeah.

wolfie: and a lot of pagan traditions, you know, some of them have that, but they don't talk about it very much.

Blackberri: But some of that has been erased, too. I know when Catholicism kind of got synthesized into the tradition there was a lot of that sexual guilt that the Catholics go through. But the people… I feel, the people that embraced the Lucumi, the African tradition, were more receptive to the role of gay spirituality in the tradition. And even in Africa, I have never been, but they tell me if you go to the bush the gay people are very different in the bush than they are in the cities where a lot of folks have been converted to Muslims or Christians and are very homophobic and anti-gay. In the bush it's very different. It's like what you do in private is your business. Nobody else has a right to tell you not to or to.

wolfie: as long as all parties are consenting, it's all good.

Blackberri: And then this one priest I know that I went to, he says once a year they have this time where people can do aaaanything they want to. But it's on that one day a year, so. You know, you have something you want to do and need to do, yeah, here's your chance.

wolfie: (overlapping) here's your chance. you have 24 hours.

Blackberri: You know, somebody gave me that opportunity once when I was in Denmark one time, an Ethiopian guy. He gave me a 24 hour… I was really surprised. I was very surprised. I couldn't believe he said it, you know, I'd known him for a while. And it was a good offer, 'cause I was attracted to him. He was very very handsome, very pretty. So, I was like, "oh… cool! All right! Let's go!"

(both laugh)

wolfie: how you do you feel like your queerness and your spirituality have informed each other? […] what their intersection is like, for you?

Blackberri: Hmm. Well, you know, everything's a process. Things change. They grow and they change, they change shape, they change form, they even change meaning sometimes. Um, so they would be, really, really hard… because they're not… they're not separate things. I don't see my sexuality being different from my spiritual offering. And even the things I pray for, you know […] The either/or is really basically a western phenomenon, because a lot of things are not either/or. They're both/and because it's a continuum, so how can it be either/or? Because nothing is separate from anything else, so… it's something, it's a place on the continuum. It's all the same, you know? It's just where are you on the continuum. And, as I say, things change, you know, they…

wolfie: everything shifts.

(Blackberri laughs)

wolfie: you know, talking with people and balance isn't a noun, it's a verb, it's something that's in motion. [...] Have you encountered any kind of homophobia within the tradition since you've been in it?

Blackberri: Um... not really. I've had people joke about it, but... especially in a ceremony it's just... the lines just blur or come together... it's... it's interesting. Just because it's a community... it's a communal thing. I know in Cuba it's very communal. Everybody knows everyone else and everybody has a job to do, and they do their part. There's no, you know, I see queer priests doing the same thing as the other priests. Just doing the work. Then afterwards... you know, what people do afterwards is, you know, it's their own thing.

wolfie: yeah.

Blackberri: The only thing about initiation is when you're doing the initiate work you're back to celibacy during the whole...

wolfie: during iyawó [novice initiate in the tradition, a 1 year period that includes strict rules].

Blackberri: Well, not even iyawó, but even the priests that are working the initiation. It's usually celibacy during the whole time of the ceremony. After the ceremony you can do whatever you want, but usually when the ceremony's going on, because it takes days, actually, to have it... and those days you must be free from being sexual.

wolfie: yep. there was an interesting... sequence, um, clyde hall brought the naraya ceremony, which is a basically a two spirit ceremony, to the radical faeries. and one of the standard practices within first nations stuff is you're celibate from the lighting of the first ceremonial fire until that fire goes out. and it's just a way of focusing and making sure that everybody's on the same energetic page. but the faeries got all up in arms and they all were saying, "you're being sex-negative!" it's like "no, you're projecting white cultural assumption onto first nation reality. let's be clear here."

(both laugh)

Blackberri: Yeah, that's the way it is, isn't it?

wolfie: yeah, it is. i had... i kept my mouth shut for the most part, but i had a moment where somebody was being more obnoxious than i could cope with and i was like, "would you put down your white male privilege lens and realize there is a cultural difference here, please. this is not persecuting you."

Blackberri: (laughs) I know, 'cause I… I had that conversation with Harry [Hay]… Somebody was interviewing me one time and asked me about Faeries and I said "Faeries are… you know, they's good. They do their thing." I said, "But I… would rather embrace my own spirituality. It's not…" I said, "Well, first of all, Faeries is European. And I was colonized by Europeans." And I said, "If I didn't accept their organized religion, why would I accept their Pagan religion?" [...]

(both laugh)

Blackberri: It's like, you know, I said, "I need to embrace the spirituality that's close to my own roots." And that's all I said, but then somehow or another it got back to Harry. Harry calls me and says, "Why do you hate the Faeries?" I said, "Harry, I didn't say that I hate the Faeries. I don't know where that story came from." [...] I wasn't anti-Faery. [...]

wolfie: can you talk a little bit more about yemaya and her relationship with queers?

Blackberri: Well, there's a story about Yemaya… Some folks were trying to make sure she wasn't around, they were trying to kill her. So she went to this island where nothing but gay men lived on this island. It was kind of like the Isle of Lesbos, only it was men who lived there. And they protected her and they fed her and they took care of her, and so it made… she… in her heart she said, "There's always a space for you in my heart." So when she returned, she kept her promise.

And then I also found out that her sister, who is Oya—and her sister's colors are the colors of the gay flag—is also a protector of gay men. I thought, "Wow, this is really interesting." I didn't learn about Oya until much much later. I was already… I had already become a priest. I was reading about her 'cause my, uh, my Godfather's name is Inle and, uh, my Godbrother has Inle, he has Inle, he has the Orisha Inle, so. He's also queer. He's Ochosi's child.

wolfie: yeah. there was some discussion with the number of women I spent about a year with, they were also all butch lesbians, and they talked about oya being the protector of lesbians and market women.

Blackberri: Yeah. Oshun is too, I'm told.

wolfie: and they always liked the story of chango dressing up like a girl to sneak out.

Blackberri: Yeah, Chango. I mean, even the men this day wear their hair like women, the Chango Priests. I've seen pictures of them. And I have a friend that I met online who is a Chango priest, and it's his hair, too. Actually I've met a couple of Chango priests. I'm friends with a couple priests in Africa, in Nigeria. There's this one guy that… he told me he wanted me to play at his wedding. I said, "Oh, great, I can do that." (both chuckle) He loves me! He always says good things. His prayers for me are really beautiful. He's also helping me with, uh, Yoruba things. He'll write things and I'll have to ask him the meaning. I try to speak to him in Yoruba as much as… it helps me learn the language. He's a great guy, I really like him.

wolfie: it seems a little easier to find houses and groups that aren't as caught up in catholicism than it used to be. but that's from my very peripheral observation.

Blackberri: It depends on what part of the tradition where people bring their lineage.

wolfie: yeah. there's a thread in the neo… the white neo-pagan community. this woman went down to brazil and she got her head washed and she somehow interpreted that as getting her head made, so she came back and started her own umbanda house which was not well received by traditional practitioners. they saw it as appropriation.

Blackberri: Yeah. It's different when you get your head washed. Or even when you get a wash pot, that's very different, too. I know somebody, he got a wash pot, and he was trying to tell everybody that he was a Babalawo [a fully-initiated practitioner of Ifa, priest of Orula].

wolfie: uhh… no.

Blackberri: And the Babalawo that gave him the wash pot said, "He's not a Babalawo. I just gave him a wash pot." And he's going to tell everybody he's a Babalawo now, so… and he… he wanted me to do prescriptions for him and… 'cause he was reading people. And I said "Oh, I can't do that." If I do prescriptions, I have to read them all over again, you know. He goes "Well, there's a chance we could make money. You can make money on the prescription and I can make money on the reading. We could partner up." And I said "Eh… it's not gonna work." And he got really upset with me. Really upset with me. He cussed me out and called me all kinds of names. I said, "Whoa, where is all this coming from? That's not very priestly!" Not very Babalawo-ly. He even went as far as getting homophobic. He started saying homophobic stuff.

wolfie: ick.

Blackberri: I was a "pre-vert." I was like, "Okay. I was a pre-vert when you wanted to do this…"

wolfie: yeah, it's kind of a last resort for people when they run out of other insults. (both chuckle)

wolfie: well, thank you so much for giving me this much of your day.

Blackberri: Thank you so much!

* Interview conducted on March 19th, 2017. Original interview abridged for length. Complete inteview can be found at www.MysticProductionsPress.com/queermagic

I Am God/dess: Possession and Gender Identity

by Doug Middlemiss (Ade Kola)

For many, the term possession brings up images of demonic horror, scary movies, and fear of the unknown. The very idea that something outside of yourself could push your soul and consciousness aside and steps into the driver's seat of your body is terrifying to them. Even within the pagan community, where we often talk about aspecting deities, invoking deities, and drawing down the moon, there is rarely complete surrender to the spirit, and the human mind is usually still present alongside the deity or spirit. Yet, spirit possession—also referred to as being "mounted" or "ridden" by a spirit—is the ideal connection to the divine in various traditions. Whether it's the individual being mounted and being intertwined with a god, or the individual attending a ceremony where someone else is being used as a vessel for a deity that's chosen to come to Earth, this ancient spiritual practice provides many with comfort and healing.

I think whether this practice is appealing or terrifying depends on a person's upbringing and understanding of possession. Many people's only exposure to this powerful spiritual practice is through films depicting modern American Christian or Catholic concepts of demonic possession requiring exorcism. If we only know of this practice in the religious views of the dominant modern American churches, we've probably never seen the beauty or healing it can bring. Those who embrace it or even seek it out are often seeking direct communication with the divine, beyond filters or preached perception. There is a desire to be in the presence of God, to hear the messages that Heaven might have for you directly from the lips of an angel, god, ancestor, or other form of spirit. With this, I think it brings validation that we are seen. That among hundreds of thousands of people, we matter.

My own story with possession occurred within my search for wholeness, love, and the embrace of the divine. I grew up as an only child of a single mother who battled addiction and a constant cycle of abusive relationships. My first thoughts about other boys occurred when I was four years old, when I instinctively knew that I wanted a husband and not a wife. Already feeling like an outsider, as I got older and saw the damage that men could do, I began to hate the fact that I too was a man and became afraid of what I might become. This pushed me further into reclusion and self-hatred.

It was at the ripe age of ten years old that I found paganism and Wicca. I leapt feet first into Goddess worship, trusting in the Mother to heal and nurture me and to keep me safe. The divine feminine was easy for me to access; it felt right. She felt like a part of me. During the tween years that followed, I became increasingly androgynous, making every attempt at being gender neutral that I could, though I was fairly certain I was not transgender. All I knew was that I could trust in the Goddess while the God of paganism felt completely foreign to me. Finally, at the age of fifteen, I met a woman who would become my High Priestess and initiate me into Wicca. Her tradition emphasized, "I am God. I am Goddess. I am one whole and complete within myself."

I was lucky to find this woman and this tradition, as part of my training included being able to stand as either the priest or priestess in a ritual. In other words, I was trained to be able to hold space for the God or the Goddess. Many traditional covens are strongly against a man invoking the Goddess or a woman invoking the God. Even within paganism we often have strict gender definitions and rules.

I still remember the first time that I drew down the moon at an esbat (a ceremony to honor a particular phase of the moon and the Goddess): the words from Starhawk's *Charge of the Goddess* flowed out of me, the cells in my body awakened and I felt the light of the moon radiating into me. My etheric body changed, taking on the female form, and I had never been surer of the presence of the Goddess than I was in that moment. She was in me, part of me, regardless of the physical form. I was Goddess, and she was me. In a time when I was struggling with my gender identity, embracing the Goddess and feeling her lunar light fill my being allowed me to love myself. I was at peace for the first time in years.

It was this experience, as well as others like it, that led me to question the effect of spirit possession on individual gender identities. I was a young man experiencing a degree of possession by a female spirit, which I knew to be frowned upon in some traditions. However, men in Hinduism, Vodou, Santeria/Lucumi, Candomble, and many other faiths are regularly mounted by female spirits. Likewise, many women fill the role as a vessel for male spirits. Many traditions know that spirits do not care about the physical gender of their vessels (sometimes called "horses" as the individual is mounted by the spirit). Whether it's an Orisha of the Lucumi tradition, a *Lwa* in Vodou, or an elevated spirit or ancestor called upon during a *misa espiritual*, the individual spirit could not care less what the *horse's* gender identity is. All that they know is that they share a connection that allows the spirit to take a seat and use a human body and voice to communicate with the individuals present. Often the *horse* gives their body freely to the spirit without caring about the gender configuration between them. They may see it as a gift to be used by the divine in this way as well as an opportunity to connect with their guardian angel or patron deity. Sometimes, however, a possession by a spirit with a gender other than their own is impactful on the vessel, either positively—as was my experience with the Goddess—or negatively.

One woman that I spoke to, we'll call her Maria, has been a priestess of Chango for many years. Chango is a male Orisha (spirit or divinity) from West Africa. He is known for being a warrior, a gambler, a womanizer, and a "machismo", or the cliché bravado persona of masculine pride. He is the spirit of manliness. Maria, a cisgender heterosexual feminine woman, had no problems initiating in to his priesthood at first. She saw him as a father and brother. Then the time came when Chango decided he would use her as a vessel during a religious event. While dancing in front of the drums as the rhythms played for Chango, her feet began to move in steps she wasn't conscious of. Her eyes closed as she felt the music lure her in, and suddenly Chango mounted her. Maria doesn't remember anything that occurred while Chango was using her body, as is typical of this experience. When she returned upon Chango's departure, the people present told her it was obvious that she wasn't there in spirit or consciousness because she "looked manly." Going from her usual feminine self to embodying masculine bravado was a sign to all present that Chango was there, but the effect on Maria was a bit different. Hearing that she looked manly and masculine was something contrary to her own gender identity, and for her this was a reason to avoid being in the position where Chango could mount her again. It wasn't that she didn't love Chango, or that she didn't want to be his *omo* (child), but she had a difficult time reconciling how she could be herself and then be perceived as a different gender from her own.

Like Maria, there are men who struggle with conflicting gender identities in regards to possession. I've encountered men—strong masculine beard-wielding straight cis men—who have been mounted by female spirits. Some of them accepted that the spirit, as a divine or enlightened presence, is something separate from them. Others were terrified about how others might perceive them afterwards. For men especially, I believe some of the fear about being mounted by a female spirit stems from homophobia and the fear that others will see them as weak, as "sissies," or otherwise queer if they allow themselves to be mounted by a female spirit. It's less about how they see themselves, and more about how others see them. One man I spoke to told me that he's always been a little worried concerning his (female) guardian angel taking over his body, not because he doesn't love or trust her, but because of the conflict between his own gender identity and the femininity that she represents.

While there are people who struggle with their own gender identity when dealing with spiritual possession, most people who practice traditions where this is a regular part of their lives don't give it much thought. Possession is simply part of their lives. They recognize that the vessel is the vessel and the spirit is the spirit. The fact that the spirit chooses that person as a vessel is no comment on that individual's gender or sexual orientation. One practitioner I spoke with made a comment about possession bringing balance; for someone who identifies as cisgender and heterosexual to be mounted by a spirit of what they consider to be the "opposite" gender identity could be an act of true spiritual balance. They are embodying the masculine and feminine in the same moment. They are a spiritual crossroads of communication from the spirit world to earth. They are merging the physical and the spiritual. This argument of balance is based within a hetero-normative and cis-normative paradigm of both bodies and spirits. Where does it leave LGBTQ+ people who are mounted by spirits? We may already be bending gender norms or inhabiting genders beyond or between masculine and feminine. We are already living every day as people who do not fit into the mold, regularly breaking stereotypes and defying expectations by our very existence.

Maybe LGBTQ+ people can reap more reward out of being possessed than our straight brothers and sisters. We are already used to being considered "other" in some way, which may contribute to the likelihood of being comfortable with possession by a spirit of a different gender than our own. Gender fluidity is part of our communities, our histories, and, often, our lives. However, possession of a spirit by the same gender can be equally as powerful for us. For a gay man possessed by a masculine spirit, this could be healing and affirming of our own gender identity as well as healing to our internal homophobia by being embraced by the archetype of our oppression. Similarly, for a femme lesbian, being mounted by a feminine spirit might bring her peace of mind in embodying her femininity while also bending that gender stereotype by loving women. Although I haven't met a trans person who has been fully mounted by their Orisha (or another spirit), I would imagine the psychological impact would depend on their relationship to their assigned gender and the gender of the spirit. A trans woman crowned with Oshun (a female Orisha of the river, beauty, and community) may have an easier time embracing the experience than a trans woman crowned with Ogun (a male Orisha of war and blacksmiths), for example.

Embracing the masculine in anything was never high on my personal agenda. I steered away from patriarchal religion, avoided masculine gods, and I avoided the fact that I was male for as long as I could. I even avoided the Lucumi tradition for years solely because of the Orisha known as Chango, the spirit I mentioned earlier. Then, one day I found myself sitting on a stool, my bare feet on a straw mat, with a *santera* (a priestess) in front of me giving me a *diloggun* reading (the oracle system of the Lucumi tradition that uses sixteen cowrie shells to divine). My life was a wreck. I was suicidal and the words the Orisha gave to me that day saved my life. I was ready to give them my service in exchange for the blessings they had given me.

A few years later, I went to have a special reading referred to as a "head marking." This is done to identify if you are destined for the path to priesthood and, if so, which Orisha you are destined to become a priest of. People usually think they can guess which Orisha will claim someone's head before the reading is done, but no one knows until the Orisha declare it through the cowrie shells. It's about which Orisha you need in your life to fulfill your destiny, not which Orisha you want. Leading up to my own head marking, the only guesses people had shared with me were two female Orisha. Not one person ever guessed a male Orisha, at least not to my face. Then when the time came, the pattern of shells that fell (known as an *odu*) marked the birth of Chango as an Orisha, where the tale is told of how a human king was elevated to become an Orisha through the praise of his people. I thought to myself, "I'm so fucked." Sure enough, it was Chango who would claim my head, the Orisha I had feared for years and the sole reason I had tried to avoid this religion. Later that day someone said to me, "Chango for you will be everything the men in your life haven't been." I considered that as much as I could at the time and moved toward becoming a priest, despite my shock and disappointment.

My decision to move forward was due to wanting the blessings of making Ocha, of becoming a priest and having an Orisha placed inside my head, of being their vessel. When one becomes a priest in the Lucumi tradition, they are "crowned" with their guardian Orisha, or rather they have the essence of that Orisha placed on their head and they become a walking vessel of that Orisha on Earth. I did not move forward because I wanted Chango himself. But in the years since I became his priest, I've seen the blessings he has brought me. One of those blessings truly started to manifest after he mounted me and took over my body. It was at a drumming event (sometimes called a *tambor* or *bembe*). As the drums began playing the rhythms for Chango, my steps fell in line with the drums, my eyes closed, and I felt as if I had been struck by lightning. Heart racing, a whirlwind of motion, I realized that I wasn't controlling my body. I was unaware of what it was doing. Afterward, the confirmation I received that Chango had come was humbling and beautiful. Aside from the physical aftermath of being mounted, the feeling I was left with was acceptance and love. I felt with absolutely certainty in that moment that Chango was a part of me and loved me as his son.

It was truly then that I began to embrace my own masculinity and manhood. I was able to know in my bones what I had not felt from my life experiences: men were not all bad people, men aren't all abusive, and not all men wanted to change me. Chango embracing me the way he did, even though I am gay and far from butch, for me was an act of love and acceptance that no person's voice could give me. It was Chango, the machismo, who finally allowed me to embrace and accept myself through embracing me as his son and using me as his vessel.

By experiencing possession, I could finally embrace my own gender identity. As a teenager, it was feeling the embrace of a Mother, the Goddess, who loved me when I was living in a world of neglect and addiction. As an adult, it was feeling the acceptance of a Father, Chango, whom I thought could not care less about me, was life changing. The depth and impact of these experiences is much deeper than I can even begin to describe. The act of being accepted by a Mother and Father, being shown that I wasn't alone after years of feeling isolated, and being possessed and enveloped by the masculine and feminine sides of Spirit/God/dess made me whole.

When it comes down to it, spirits and gods don't care about gender or sexual orientation. It is we that place these rules and stereotypes on ourselves. Some people might struggle with the idea of possession in general and others might not like the idea of a spirit of another gender taking over their body. For those of us who can let go of our own ego and surrender to the divine, possession may be an avenue through which we can find balance and peace. Your gender identity and your work as a spiritual practitioner/vessel do not have to conflict with each other. Embrace that you are divine, become self-possessed by all that you are, and allow Spirit in whatever form you see it to work with you and through you.

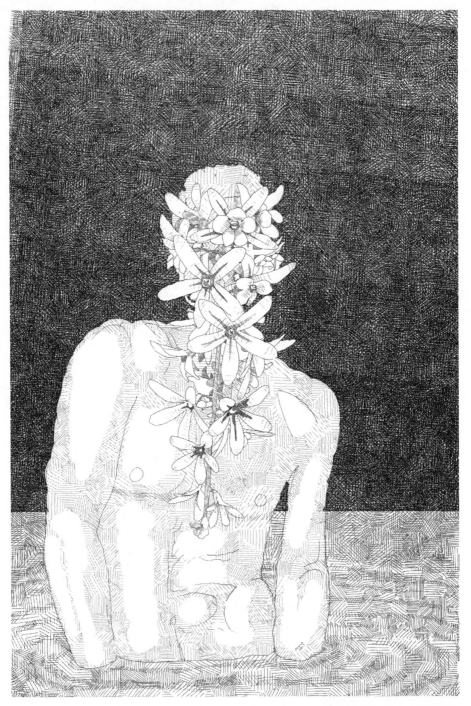

Fragile Masculinity

by Malcolm Maune

Walkers Between Worlds: The Witch Blood and Queer Spirit

by Giariel Foxwood

I am a Queer Witch

There was a time not long ago that I would have balked at the words "Queer" and "Witch." They were too divisive, too controversial, and carried with them too much historical baggage. "Queer" had been the weapon on the tongues of my tormentors. "Witch" evoked insidious Hollywood images of devil worship and black magick. I opted, instead, for the more palatable descriptors of "gay," "pagan," or "Wiccan." Those words carried with them the hope of acceptance in a culture that does not favor otherness. When I use the words Queer and Witch now, I capitalize them as I would any magickal word of power.

The word "Queer" also has power. It also has an edge. It also has teeth. It also makes people uncomfortable. The word "Queer" carries with it the traditional meanings of strange, odd, eccentric, and unnatural. It was used as another way of describing a person that was suspected of being a Witch. In "post-marriage equality" America, the younger generation is teaching us the power of Queerness. The Queer youth of today innately embody a fluidity of sexuality, love, gender, and form that takes decades for magickal practitioners to embrace and master. These youth unapologetically demand recognition of their right to exist on their own terms. As a Witch, I could no longer deny the power to be gained by abandoning the mediocrity of comfortable compliance with societal norms and embracing the beauty of being Queer. So now I embrace the label: I am Queer.

In my training with L. Orion Foxwood in tradition-based witchcraft, I learned that the word "Witch" has power. It has an edge. It has teeth. It makes people uncomfortable. As I learned to stop being afraid of my own personal power, to unveil the light of my soul, and to unleash the song of my spirit, I also learned to stop giving a shit about making people uncomfortable. As my Witch Queen Lady Circe advised, I am learning to walk between the worlds of light and shadow and to go where angels fear to tread, because sometimes in the darkest of places, a Witch is the only source of light. So now I embrace the label: I am a Witch.

I use the word Queer because I am Queer. I realize not everyone is comfortable self-identifying as Queer, however, it is an inclusive umbrella term I use to describe the diverse spectrum of human sexual and gender expression. So no matter which letter of the alphabet soup of LGBTIQA+ appeals to you, what your kinks are, or how many sides there are to your love polygon, know that when I use the word Queer, I am speaking lovingly of YOU. For are all Children of Queer Spirit are my beloved Queerkin.

I will use the word Witch because I am a Witch. But in this context, I will use it to refer to all practitioners of spiritual, mystical, or magickal techniques; those agents of change who consort with unseen forces to transform themselves and the world around them for the betterment of ALL. I realize not everyone self-identifies as a Witch, but know that when I use the word Witch, I am speaking lovingly of YOU. For you all Children of the Witch Blood are my beloved Witches.

In European traditions of Witchery, the Witch Blood is a term used to describe a recurrent human phenomenon that is universal and pancultural: the emergence of individuals with the proclivity towards magick, healing, or the ability to mediate spirit. Not all who claim to be Witches carry the Witch Blood, and not all who carry the Witch Blood become Witches. I use Queer Spirit to describe a parallel phenomenon that encompasses the spectrum of the Queer experience. Like Queer Spirit, the Witch Blood does not care what name you call it, what color of your skin, what language you speak, who your ancestors were, or which gods you claim as your own.

Queering the Circle

How does your Queerness inform and inspire your spiritual and magickal practice?

The answers I have heard to this question are as diverse as Queerness itself. For some people, hearing this question is their first time considering the thought. Many see their Queerness as being separate and distinct from their spirituality. For most of my life, I was one of those people.

Our Queerness is the lens through which we experience all forms of Love. Love is the language of the Divine. How could our Queerness and our spirituality not be inexorably intertwined?

Even as we have seen great global strides in equality for Queer people, the most powerful religious institutions of the world, in particular the Abrahamic sects, still cling to orthodox views that attach a stigma to Queerness. They are a product of the societally accepted norms that birthed them thousands of years ago and are the greatest force working to maintain patriarchal heteronormative systems of control to this day. The consequences of their efforts have propagated a system of oppression against women, people of color, and Queerkin alike. This oppression expresses itself through persecution, violence, and death. In our world today, assimilation is rewarded. Being perceived as "other" brings danger. While some denominations have become more accepting and welcoming of their Queer people of faith, it requires some cognitive dissonance to accept a "non-traditional" interpretation of the holy texts. It requires turning a blind eye to certain passages and historic institutional practices.

The neo-pagan paths and traditions, being a product of their time and societally accepted norms, have also been problematic. While the neo-pagan community as a whole is very accepting and supportive of its Queer members, the spiritual practices are still heavily focused on fertility and the gender binary of Goddess and God, and therefore female and male. As in all religions, personal prejudices also carry over into religious dogma, and people are very creative in finding ways to use their faith to justify their hate, fear, or willful ignorance. There are pagan traditions that do not allow homosexual members, and the struggle to gain recognition and acceptance of gender fluid and transgender people has been a great challenge for even the most inclusive pagan spaces.

There are notable exceptions within the neo-pagan movement, as several traditions have risen which not only accept, but embrace and celebrate Queerness. Some are gender-exclusive while others are gender-agnostic. Finding a pagan path that suits one's personal spiritual journey can be a harrowing ordeal. Many Queer pagans, having found a tradition that speaks the language of their soul, are reluctant to abandon their path for one more accommodating to their Queer identity, and are struggling to find their place in the circle. Even if one is fortunate enough to have a spiritual or religious practice that is accepting of Queerness, it is not surprising that some Queer people drawn to the practices of faith might build an internal separation of identity between their faith and their sexuality or gender.

My own early spiritual struggle—a self-identified gay cisgender man in an earth-based Goddess/God tradition with strictly formed gender roles—goaded me to uncover my own truths in the pursuit of Queer Spirit. I now know that a natural resonance exists between Witchery and Queerness. As Witches, we live our lives between the civilized and tamed worlds of humanity and the wild and uncanny haunts of the natural world and the unseen spirits. As Queerkin, we live our lives between the constructs and traditions of the moral majority and the liberated and fluid expanses of human connection and love unbound. Both have a long history of being derided and vilified. Both are the champion of the underdog, the voiceless, and the unseen. Both are seen as different, eccentric, or other. Both are streams of human experience, the Witch Blood and Queer Spirit, woven and often interwoven throughout the diverse tapestry of human life.

The Streams of Witchery and Queerness

"Faery tradition" describes a wide and varied body of ancient folk lore and practices that center around the spirits of Nature that we have come to call "faery." Faery traditions and lore are the great-grandmothers of European Witchery. The Faery are ancient non-corporeal beings that reside in the "underworld," and are the architects of material form. They spark inspiration and creativity in the hearts and minds of humanity, planting the seeds of our arts and sciences.

The underworld is also where the spirits of the Ancestors reside, beyond the River of Blood, which is a vast river that flows between the land of the Faery and the human realms. In order to visit the Faery realm, one must cross the River of Blood and be baptized in the blood of our Ancestors. The River of Blood is the embodiment of the stream of humanity that flows from the natural life of the Earth, with a divine purpose yet to be revealed. Each of us is but a wave that emerges from the River of Blood into this world, receding when our corporeal bodies fade and release our spirits, only to emerge again at another time and place, as in the concept of the transmigration of souls.

In many traditions of Witchery, those with the potential or talent for Witchery can be identified by the Witch Blood, emerging from and hidden within the River of Blood. The Witch Blood is present in all those who possess a proclivity for magick. The Witch Blood rises within family bloodlines, lineated traditions, and spontaneously whenever and wherever the world is in need of the power and wisdom of the Witch. In those who possess the Witch Blood, it lies dormant until need and opportunity awaken it to rise and boil within our veins. It is the Witch Blood that drives us to seek esoteric and occult wisdom. It is the Witch Blood that awakens us from the illusion of isolation and sets us on the quest to seek a home we cannot remember in the embrace of divine source. It is the Witch Blood that sours our tongue when we feast on mediocrity and complacency. It is the Divine Discontent that drives us deep into the dark and dangerous wilds of the natural world, beyond the hedge ways that mark the end of the realms of humanity, and through the veil that obfuscates the spirit realms as we chase our bliss. When we allow the Witch Blood within us to remember, awaken, and become, we claim sovereignty of our power, our spirit, and our soul.

Those with the potential or proclivity towards Queerness are the children of Queer Spirit, emerging from and hidden within the River of Blood. Queer Spirit is present in all those whose ways of loving and being do not conform to the heteronormative models of the dominant cultures of the world. Queer Spirit emerges within family bloodlines as well as spontaneously, appearing whenever and wherever the world is in need of the disruptive and expansive powers of Queer Love, Queer Anger, and Queer Power. In those who were born out of Queer Spirit, we strain and struggle against the chains of convention which are laid upon us, inherited from our families and our culture, as we mature into adulthood. It is Queer Spirit that awakens within us when we find the courage and strength to break the bonds of expectation laid upon us in the same way a seedling struggles against the weight of the earth to break through to the light. It is Queer Spirit that blossoms from the dark cloak of our secret inner lives and the veil of our silence, driving us to commit the ultimate act of apotheosis in the creation of our self in our own image. When we allow the Queer Spirit within us to express, heal, and reveal, we claim dominion over our power, our spirit, and our soul.

While all Witches are not Queer, and all Queerkin are not Witches, the divine impulse, which is the driving force and momentum of their emergence in the stream of humanity, share a common purpose: Liberation of the Spirit. The Witch Blood seeks to awaken humanity from the Song of Forgetfulness that leads us to see ourselves as separate from the natural world. It reminds us that all life is interconnected and everything is alive. It reminds us that the divine exists within us, all things are sacred, all our words cast a spell, and all our actions are rituals. It reminds us that we have the power to change the world. Queer Spirit seeks to free our spirit from the bonds of assimilation. It challenges us to be wild and bold in our self-expression and our expressions of love. It challenges us to live without fear, to laugh without limits, and to just love more. It challenges us to see the beauty in the world and to know that we make the world more beautiful by letting the light of our authentic selves shine. It reminds us that our lives, our bodies, and our spirits belong to us as individuals. Claim it! Own it! Shape it!

Witches are not born, we are made. The Witch Blood lies dormant until awakened, so Witches must be taught and trained in the knowledge and skills that will become our craft. Much of the training of a Witch involves unlearning much of what has been both deliberately and subconsciously taught to us. We must learn to walk between the worlds and exist with one foot in this world and one foot in the spirit realm. We must learn to see with one eye into the hard edges of reality and see with the other eye into the subtle realms of the inner world. Witches become edge-walkers, living in the world but not of it. We exist at the edges of humanity, at the perimeter of the fire's light, with one foot in the shadow. We must learn to become comfortable with uncertainty, living betwixt and between in the liminal places, absent of absolutes. We must learn the inner landscape of our souls and take careful inventory of our pains and scars, in order to claim dominion over our spirit by mastering our demons. "Gnothi seauton" (γνῶθι σεαυτόν), or "know thyself", is the core work of the Witch.

Queerkin are not made, we are born. Being the children of Queer Spirit, the seed of Queer expression grows within the fertile soil of our souls. It demands to be heard. Even before we have the language to describe the experience, many of us become intuitively aware of our otherness. As our inner self-awareness grows, we begin to learn a complicated Queer arithmetic to safely navigate a world we instinctively know is dangerous, giving us an intuitive sense of subtle energies. The ability to walk between the worlds and shape-shift is a matter of survival. Queerkin start our lives walking between the worlds and moving easily between states of being. As Queer Spirit demands to be expressed, the need for authentic self-expression creates a building pressure against the desire to remain safe, silent, and unseen. If "know thyself" is the undermost work of the Witch, surely "create thyself" is the core work of being Queerkin.

Queerkin make natural Witches. The process of unlearning the programming of compliance seems to be much easier for anyone who is already disenfranchised from the artificial social constructs of society. Fluidity of form comes naturally to Queerkin, while the "coming out" process demands a self-knowledge that many Witches struggle through a lifetime to achieve. Likewise, for Witches, there is a sympathetic resonance with Queer energy. Witches are the champion of the underdog and the oppressed, and we speak for those that cannot speak for themselves. Queerkin have been present since the beginning in the fight for social justice, racial equality, and gender equality. Witches are the last resort of the truly desperate, when all other options have been exhausted. Queerkin are often the last bastion of hope for the lost, the homeless, and when family have turned their backs on us. Witches also celebrate the spectrum of human sexual expression, often sharing the Queer values of sex-positivity, kink, and various degrees of polyamory.

Witches and Queerkin also share the same adversaries. The same forces that would see a return of the Inquisition, the installment of a state religion, and the criminalization of witchcraft, would also see Queer people imprisoned, deported, criminalized, or executed. Witches and Queer people in different parts of the world are dying today. It is my hope that with more discussion of these commonalities, Witches might start to see themselves as being a little Queer and Queer people might let themselves be a little Witchy.

We are the Coming Storm and the Winds of Change

The River of Blood is the embodiment of the stream of human ancestry throughout existence, emerging from the past and flowing into the future. Ancestry, in this spiritual context, expands beyond traditional definitions of family bloodlines, genealogy, and genetics. As you follow the River of Blood upstream, back through the generations over the hundreds of thousands of years of human existence to the first being that might be considered the Mother of humanity, it doesn't suddenly stop. Humans tend to forget that humanity emerged from the stream of life force that flows out of the planet itself which we call Nature; we are not separate from Nature. When we look back before the first Mother of humanity, our stream of ancestry becomes non-human. The animals, plants, soil, oceans, and Mother Earth itself, they are all our Ancestors.

Nature is the ultimate source of all life on this planet, including us. It is also the most powerful creative force and the most powerful destructive force on the planet. No technology, no tool or weapon of humanity, is more powerful than the forces of Nature. That primordial flow of creative and destructive energy is called the Wyld Force. In the lore of Witchery in which I was trained, the Witch has the ability to tap into the Wyld Force, and enter into a co-creative relationship with the forces of Nature. Of all the reported powers of a Witch, the ability to wield the Wyld Force was one of the most terrifying. In ages past, being "wild" didn't just mean "untamed," it meant "deadly." Humanity is in a constant state of war against the forces of Nature working to tear down our cities and monuments to reclaim the earth.

The Wyld Force is the river that breaks the levees. It is the tornado that brings the winds of change. It is the wildfire, the lightning strike, the tidal wave, and all the beautiful and terrible things in the natural world. It is the untamable and unpredictable side of Nature. When the Witch wields the Wyld Force, they become a force of Nature, as generous and nurturing as the ocean, and as dispassionate and cruel as a wildfire. The Witch strives to build direct relationship with the spirits of the natural and unseen worlds, the architects of form, that we call Faery. Because they watch us and see how we treat each other, they will not fully trust us until we have been bathed in the blood of our Ancestors. Why would they want to build direct relationship with a species that treats other member of the same species so poorly?

The Witch Blood is a manifestation of the Wyld Force, flowing as a stream of blue Witch Flame through the River of Blood. Like the Wyld Force, Witches are wild, untamable, uncontrollable, and unpredictable. They can be the loyal hound that guards the flock or the wolf that thins the herd. The Witch is Nature's way of bringing balance to the scales. We are the keepers of knowledge and lore. We temper the flames of intolerance to help restore harmony, and when necessary, we humble the arrogance of humanity. In the darkest of times, we restore faith and trust in the natural order of creation, and in the eternal constancy of divine love. Witches are agents of change, working to bring Eden to earth by helping to bring humanity into co-creative relationship with the planet and with each other.

Queer Spirit is also a manifestation of the Wyld Force, a stream of white starlight flowing from the stars through the River of Blood. Like the Wyld Force, Queerkin are beautiful and fierce. If Witches embody the creative and destructive forces of Nature, Queerkin embody the evolutionary and transformative forces of Nature. Queerkin are Nature's way of agitating or shattering the old structures that threaten to confine and suffocate humanity. They remind us that joy is a discipline and of the wonderment of playfulness. They remind us that beyond the pain and fear lies unexplored pleasures. They remind us that you can choose the shape of your world or let the world shape you. They remind us that everyone has a story that must be told and a song that must be sung. They remind us that Love comes in different shapes and cannot be restrained. They are the wounded healer whose pain points in the direction of healing. Queerkin are agents of liberation, inviting humanity to free itself from the superficial constructs of societal norms, to dig deep into the muck of our soul's pain to reveal the pearl of great cost which is our divine purpose, fully expressed. Queerness, like Witchery, is a spiritual path in its own right, a spiritual calling that demands to be heard.

A special synergy happens where the Witch Blood merges with Queer Spirit, and those two streams begin to inspire and inform each other. The Wyld Force, within a Queer Witch, manifests as the Audacity of Nature. Be audacious. Be bold. Challenge every belief you hold dear. Challenge every thought that enters your mind. Challenge every emotion that emerges in your being. Challenge every preconceived idea. Know thyself. Heal thyself. Grow thyself. Reveal thyself.

Queer Spirit is calling to you. It is a living spirit being whose form is made up of the Queer Ancestors, and which holds their combined wisdom. As one of the Queerkin, you have only one mission: to allow your own Queerness to blossom fully in your spirit and the expression of your life. Your Queerness is a part of you, and part of the divine impulse that inspired your birth. It is part of your divine purpose for being. It is a holy sacrament to explore your own Queer expression. Embrace your otherness. The path to great wisdom is fraught with great peril, but you are not alone.

All Witches and Queerkin are heretics.

Queer Love is heresy.

Queer Sex is sacrilege.

Queer Identity is blasphemy.

Queer Anger is apostasy.

But Queer Anger is Queer Power.

Queer Power is Transformation.

Queer Spirit is Liberation.

Be free.

La Limpia
by Inés Ixierda

The Unfettered Mind Allows for The Free Flow of Spirit.

by Cazembe Abena

There is no separation in Spirit.

There is a Oneness that exists in all things, which defies categorization. It simply *is* by the virtue of its vibration. Many things exist and cannot be categorized or contained by the human mind. They cannot be labeled. As humans, we label to understand, use, and control. Spirit and/or energy can neither be created nor destroyed. While in human form, our understanding of Spirit is limited at best. It is like trying to explain calculus to an infant – they do not have the tools at that stage to even speak the language. We label to control for use in this 3rd dimension. Spirit exists far beyond this dimension and has roots in other non-physical realities. As a result, the re-interpretation of energies as they filter themselves down from the ethers to be used here on this plane is a process that is often not easily understood or employed. The results can appear less than expected to the human eye and rational mind, or are absent altogether. Even on this plane, there are always things happening 'beyond the veil' that serve to adjust, shift, and manipulate us and our current states in physical form.

Calling forth an energy for healing, abundance, etc. is important to provide direction; however, we must align our intention with what is needed, in as much purity as possible, and release what we think will be the outcome. To refrain from doing so is to try to fit Spirit into a human box. We cannot contain energy through physical means or within a human mind that is steeped in the physical.

When Spirit reveals Itself to us, we take the information, and mold it to the confines of our language and cultural parameters. We have to do this initially to bring meaning to Spirit *for us* and to make it fit within our immediate surroundings and life. However, to further expand our understanding of Spirit, we must be willing to see Spirit beyond the parameters of our immediate existence and experiences – all of which are rooted in the physical. The more diverse and expansive our needs are on the physical plane in our 3rd dimensional reality, the more extensive the powers of Spirit can show themselves to be. Mentally confining Spirit to our limited experiences is putting brakes on the flow of the energy we have called in to help us.

Channeling taught me this profound lesson. We all have gifts beyond the physical because our essence is Spiritual, but the burden of discovering who we are, and what we have rests upon our shoulders. We may start with our immediate culture and ethnicity, but who we truly are is far beyond these constructs. It is believed by some that our journey to a full understanding of our essence is why we are here on

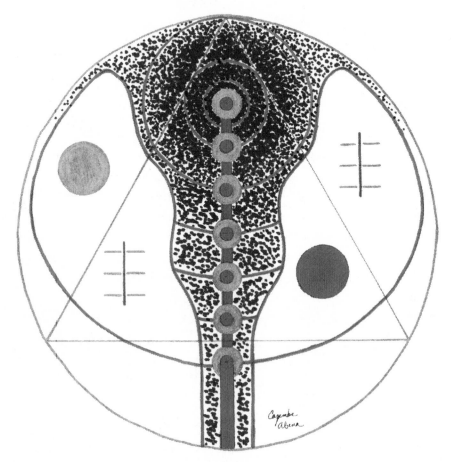

A symbol for clearing of the mind, breaking mental barriers, and expanding awareness to embrace the Oneness of the Abyss out of which everything manifests, by Cazembe Abena.

this 'training ground' that we call Earth. I discovered several years ago during a 90-day channeling exercise with Ascended Master Vywamus that I channel symbols. I wasn't asking for this gift, but it came to me in support of a goal that I was seeking to accomplish with the exercise. One of the benefits of working with Vywamus is that the work reveals inner gifts. I did not know this aspect of the energy until after I completed the exercise. My gift was revealed to me loud and clear as a direct download into my consciousness. I doubted it until I tested the validity of what I received.

I drew 5 symbols, gave them to my instructor at the time (who was very sensitive to energy), and asked him what he felt with each one. Unbeknownst to him, one of the symbols was his. He went through the symbols, revealing only minor reactions to the energies until he reached his. He stopped at his symbol and said that his whole body was beginning to vibrate. When I shared that it was his symbol, he said 3 things, "These are powerful. Don't stop. Don't doubt." Unfortunately, I did.

Doubt had me paralyzed in the use of my gift for 2 years. Our gifts are not for us, they are for others. I woke up when I realized that I had been cheating the community of a service and potential blessing. I sought feedback as to how the symbols were affecting people. Because the feedback wasn't what I thought it should be, I stopped. Weeks after creating symbols for clients, I realized that feedback was sparse because people simply weren't using the symbols. They hadn't put in the work of using them in meditation or in their daily lives. In spite of this, I began to receive positive feedback about the effects of the symbols (emotional peace, greater income, sound sleep, happier lives, etc.) months (even years) after I expected to. I had subconsciously imposed my expectations on a spiritual tool, which in turn led me to undervalue its gift. When I finally released my expectations, my clients' feedback showed me that Spirit works in ways far beyond our perception.

Another lesson came when I endeavored to create the symbols again regularly. Spirit cannot be forced, it must be *allowed*. Sometimes in my haste to finish a symbol for a client, I found myself trying to think my way through the process. I soon found that nothing would stop the flow of Spirit faster. A famous quote from Bruce Lee, one of the most revered martial artists of all time, in the short-lived 1971 TV series 'Longstreet', further conveys how our body and mind should flow:

> *"Empty your mind, be formless, shapeless —* **like water***. Now you put* **water** *in a cup, it becomes the cup; you put* **water** *into a bottle it becomes the bottle; you put it in a teapot it becomes the teapot. Now* **water** *can flow or it can crash."*

Martial artists, athletes, musicians, entrepreneurs, and many types of artists understand that power, energy, and creativity flow more freely through a relaxed vessel. Spiritual work is no different. A closed mind is a tense mind. A tense mind is stress. Stress is tension. Tension is constriction. Extended constriction is restriction. Restriction is blockage. The water-like mind leaves all confines behind so that it may flow freely. When I take the time to clear my mind and allow Spirit to flow, it reveals symbols and information to me so effortlessly that I often feel like I'm not *doing* anything. That is the revelation. Once we make the request of Spirit, there is nothing to do but *allow*.

When we call Spirit forth to complete a goal for a task or for healing, we must free ourselves of preconceived notions of laws and rules to allow Spirit to operate in its fullest form. Blockages and imposed control in thought when operating with Spirit *restricts* Spirit – especially if we are calling Spirit to work through our bodies in possession or embodiment. Just as one of the most powerful elements on Earth is free-flowing water in a tidal wave, so do we need to allow Spirit to flow through us unencumbered with rational thought and paradigms that may diminish and delay its power.

If we are perplexed at how our mindset can affect the potency of Spirit on this plane, let us remember that we as human beings are the bridge between Spirit and the material. As human beings, there is a part of us that is spirit 'hu,' and another that is matter 'man.' *Hu* is Sanskrit for spirit, and man is associated with 'ma' or 'mana,' a derivative for matter or building in Sanskrit in both an abstract and literal sense. We act as a bridge due to our dual make-up of Spirit and matter, providing us an invitation to both worlds if we expand our awareness enough to properly embrace both. This duality that is our birthright, our innate being-ness, allows us the power to usher the immaterial into the material.

Part of my spiritual healing practice involves me being a DOM in a method of BDSM I created called Senergetic™ (Sensual/Energetic) BDSM. In addition to impact play and sensual touch, I channel energies to provide the appropriate healing and balance during these often-intense healing sessions. I enter the session as a man, but by the time Spirit engages, I have embraced both the masculine and the feminine energies. I've learned to concede to Spirit completely because in that moment, for the sake of the client, I must allow for my flexibility to provide harmony to the life/energy/being of the client for their healing. My only focus is to ignite balance in the client. For this, I must be fluid.

The key to gaining control over our physical reality is not only the open mindset, but also high vibrational thoughts. To this end, I start all of my Senergetic™ BDSM sessions with affirming intentions spoken by the submissive. I hold the intention throughout the scene. This is the end point – the what. I allow Spirit to take over, and provide the how. The healing power that comes from releasing all restrictions – mental, emotional, cultural, gendered, and physical is transcendental.

In her book, *The Spirit of Intimacy: Ancient African Teachings in the Ways of Relationships*, Sobonfu Somé talks about the special presence of LGBTQ individuals in ritual. Somé, of the Dagara Nation of Burkina Faso in West Africa, speaks of some people as being *gate keepers* in certain rituals due to their dual nature. The understanding is that some individuals' ability to expand their sexuality (release certain restrictions) translates in Spirit as the gift of connecting worlds and dimensions. Certain rituals cannot be done without the presence of this type of energy. This same understanding has been espoused by some Native American cultures as well. Although some polls show that values are slowly changing to embrace LGBTQ rights, the historical mainstream conservative idea that there is no place in Spirit for LGBTQ energy doesn't apply here. What is conveyed here with these two examples is not mere tolerance, but an integral need for this energy as it relates to the livelihood of a culture and people. As with all creation, there is a place and a purpose – often beyond the confines of the myopic mindset. Once again, it would appear that a freedom of expression and thought on this plane of existence translates to expansion of abilities in the Spiritual.

It is interesting to hear people confine Source (or replace whichever title you wish for The Creator) to a gender. It is intriguing to see how (and why) we would want to call God omnipotent, but yet restrict It to one gender over another. I support and understand the necessity for liberal naming in order to break away from the patriarchal structure (Goddess vs. God, etc.). In many pantheons, there are delineations of masculine and feminine energies, but I would like to offer that even in the identification of the masculine and the feminine within the deities of certain pantheons, it should be noted that to fully express or embody the energy, deity, or Goddess would require an open-ended expression and understanding of gender. In the final analysis, we should keep in mind that ultimately Spirit is genderless because it is free of all restrictions. This may challenge our present notions of gender, but we must allow the energy to express itself in the purest form as it sees *fit*. This often can mean that the energy may perform and express itself in ways that are perhaps unfamiliar to us. A 'blockage' or retardation of energetic flow is sometimes due to the conflict of Spirit trying to make Its way into a physical form, and our logical mind attempting to decipher the messages.

If we engage Spirit with the human mind and understanding alone, we will miss its expansive brilliance and depth. We often engage energy and use it here for a fraction of what it can truly do.

When engaging Spirit, forget what you know. Forget what you think you know. Forget *thinking* altogether. Just allow. Allow the connection to form.

Come to Spirit with a pure intention, and then release cultural restrictions, labels, definitions, categories, and the like as much as possible. Understand that a 'name' is different from a 'label.' A name is an identifier, a sound, a vibration that makes a thing what it is. A name reflects the true essence of a thing. The essence of a thing, when engaging spirit, is far beyond what words can describe.

Labels are for physical ideas confined to the physical, low vibrational realities that we are all rooted to in order to learn how to rise out of. In this regard, low vibration is not seen as negative, but as a means to identify the more gross and solid state that atoms vibrate in to reflect physical matter. This idea of rising out of low vibrations brings us to another phenomenon – Ascension.

It is believed in some circles that we are here to experience and remember who and what we are as a part of the body of Source. This experience is critical, as Source cannot know Itself without splintering Itself up into nearly infinite pieces and experiences to acquire knowledge of what it has created. Everything is expected to evolve and to grow. Releasing notions of good or bad, this certain understanding suggests that we are here to learn how to ascend ourselves by drawing Spirit down into the physical body, so that we can integrate our physical and energetic body, and rise in the Spiritual. We are innately programmed to expand and develop. To remain stagnate is a certain type of death. But it is our minds which are attached to powerful emotions that hold energies that can prevent this growth. Once again, we are called to shed the shackles of our reality for a greater one, a one in which boundaries dissolve the higher we climb.

It is our Spirit mind/body that we must use when engaging Spirit. The way to engage entails the releasing of categories, labels, concrete definitions, and parameters. With true depth and investigation, we find that in assessing Spirit, things turn from black and white to gray. As we engage Spirit appropriately, the information and experiences become more profound and broad simultaneously, something we do not often encounter while working in the physical. The more things appear different, the more they appear the same. The farther away we think we are traveling, the closer to home we arrive. When we expand we break the prison of the ego mind, which thrives on individuality and segregation. Through this spiritual journey we embrace the Oneness, which connects us all and reflects our true essence. Why?

Love is infinite and expansive. The only truth is ultimately Love, and Love is the Ultimate expression of *Oneness*. Oneness is the connective thread for all things as it marries us eternally to Source. The connecting thread through all of this is Love. Love simultaneously shatters boundaries and draws all things together. Love is the energy that birthed the Universe.

But is energy *all* Source? Is it *all* holy? Perhaps… because it all exists.

What exists was created out of Source. Nothing exists outside of Source. Source created *all* in all manifestations and all things. This is often difficult to wrap our human minds around, as we find ourselves drowning in a segregated universe of individualism. This idea of Oneness is the perfect expression of releasing boundaries, labels, and constrictions that segregate. It is Universal Love in existence.

As a priest of Osumaré, I was initiated in a way that allowed me to fully embody Spirit. As an Initiate it is up to me to consult with Spirit itself to receive the answers. Unlike many initiated priests, I am not married to a particular cultural expression with this energy. There are benefits and limitations to this approach. The benefit is the freedom of expression and the power it bestowes.. The limitation is that you are often flying by the seat of your pants, and you must trust the process deeply.

I had to approach Spirit in a way where I was open to receiving the messages, absent from pre-conceived notions of the energy itself. Consequently, I was exposed to truths far beyond what I had initially imagined. There is a complete fluidity in the energy of Osumaré, whether that is in the arena of gender or Light and Dark energies. In some cultural expressions of Osumaré, it is seen as either a male or female. I have come to understand it as both, able to express itself at will in the manner it chooses. My previous notion that Osumaré was only about Light was quickly revealed to be only part of the truth for this energy. In totality, it is Light and Dark because Osumaré is about *Universal Love* – the acceptance of *all* things. I had to throw away what I thought I knew. Much of the information I received defied the cultural norms in which it was presented to me. There were times when I doubted the information that I was receiving because I was relying on what had been told to my conscious mind in physical reality. I was carrying the prison of the 3rd dimensional mind into Spirit, but soon I began to shift.

My initiation showed me that if we are open enough, if we expand enough, if we vibrate high enough, we can contact Spirit and receive the messages that It has for us. That Spirit can speak to each of us in ways that only we were meant to hear, as well as in ways that we can disseminate to the masses. My personal experience with Osumaré has pushed me to be more self-accepting, and therefore more accepting of all. As Spirit works through and expresses itself in ways that are often exclusive to the vessel carrying it (the person channeling or embodying the energy), we see the colors of Creation reveal Itself. Ultimately, when we engage Spirit and allow it to work with us, we open an opportunity to co-create a new reality, and in doing so, we take part in the revelation of Spirit unto Itself.

Queer Elements: Working with Interstitial Energies

by Lee Harrington

Many neopagan magical models conceptualize elemental forces to fall into four directions: Earth (North), Air (East), Fire (South), and Water (West). Wicca models this in the directions that its quarters are cast to manifest a circle when gathering for ritual. Ceremonial magic calls upon the watchtowers to watch over work, though some of their formats hold each of these 4 elements in association with different directions. There are also systems that may be associated with the solar calendar through the solstices and equinoxes, or the wheel of the turning seasons.

Unfortunately, a wide swath of magical potential has been lost through looking at these forces in a linear or quadratic way. I will look first at how each of these elements has been over-simplified in ritual use by the fact that the elements themselves have been made one-sided, then look at the many spaces between these four elements – the spaces that can be seen as interstitial energies or elements.

Things that are interstitial fall between. An interstitial space is one between structures or objects. Interstitial fluid is the solution that surrounds the cells of the human (or animal) body. Interstitial art is that which falls between, or is a combination of, genres.

If Earth, Air, Water, and Fire are four primary elements in use energetically in many magical models, then the interstitial elements are those which fall between them. They are those that combine elements in such a way as to not know where one starts and the other begins. They are the elements that fall outside of the dyads, outside of the opposites of perceived polarities. They are the queer elements.

Queer elements are the places that fill those middle points. They are southeast, southwest, northeast, and northwest. They are the places where South and North dance as a joyous couple, rather than always sitting at opposite ends of the room. They are when the lovers East and West find their lips together, rather than whispering at each other from miles away.

Directional Assignments

The primary neopagan format for the directional assignments for the four primary elements is often seen as:

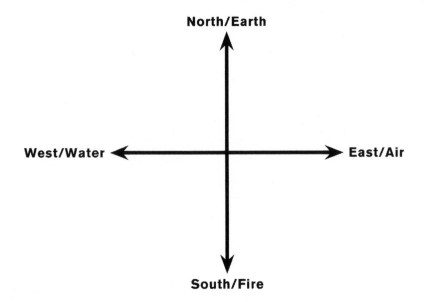

For peoples coming from certain parts of Europe, these associations make sense. In the north you have the tall mountains, in the east the howling plains, in the south it warms towards the equator, and to the west lies the ocean. Earth, air, fire, water.

But this association does not make sense everywhere. Perhaps the water where you live is to the south, or the winds always blow down from the north. Do the mountains fall to the east, and the heat comes in from the west? For this reason, there are people who have shifted the directional associations with elements according to their own truth and experience, rather than be constrained by this framework.

For the purpose of this discussion though, we will use the above directions to start the dialogue. Once we start getting into the six interstitial elements, it will be clear that the directions themselves do not actually matter. These associations are made by humans with limited understandings, not by the universe that experiences truths far broader and beyond such simplifications. It will, however, be easier to begin understanding that when I refer to the northeast, I am describing the space or interaction between north and east, which is in this case the space between earth and air.

Please make sure, if you are working with different directional associations, to translate your queer elements to the appropriate places on your own grid. If you've never tried going outside the assumptions of what elements should be associated with what directions, consider giving it a try. Queer experience is not about forcing your identity into the standing framework, it is about modifying the frameworks in order to have your experience flourish. So it is for queer elements. These energies can only truly be accessed if you tap into them in a way that your spirit, your essence, can be heard by them. Only by hearing you can they heed your call.

Classic Elements

Before we can examine the spaces between them, it is important to get to know the four core elements most commonly used in ritual and magical workings. Almost every modern magical practitioner calls upon them in some way, and yet many of us have not spent time coming to understand the force, power, and diversity each one represents in and of themselves. So many constructs gloss over them as being simply earth, simply air, simply fire, and simply water. But there is nothing simple about them.

North: Earth

Classically representing such traits as abundance, stability, wealth, prosperity, fertility, and strength, Earth is often called upon first as a "rooted" place to begin ritual. This is far from saying that any one element is best, because none are. This is important to bring up because when doing workings, it is important to consider which direction we are leading with.

These associations come from one face of earth. It is the side that is the fertile field. It is the side that has taken in bounty, having worked hard all season to do so. It is the soil which a mighty tree can grow from.

However, earth takes many forms. It is the mountain pass, with much to see on the other side. It is the broken wasteland, a warning to go no further. It is the rocks that need to be removed from the soil before it can be used. It is the underground cave, promising a rich adventure ahead, or a tale of woe. It is the graveyard that holds the memories of our ancestors.

Earth is stick, stone, and bone. It is rugged terrain and the open plain. This element can be as hard as diamonds, or it can be like limestone so soft you can dig into it with your fingertips.

Without earth, what would the rest attach to? No human can live on the sun, the epitome of the element fire. They cannot exist only in air. There would be no ocean floor to nestle the ocean in its arms.

But earth is not predictable. Earth is also earthquakes. It is rocks falling onto freeways. There are even parts of earth that have been tamed by human kind in the form of pavement itself, or subterranean firmness transformed into unimposing gravel.

East: Air

Communication, inspiration, knowledge, intelligence, and ideas are classical traits represented by the element Air. These associations are based on the side of air that carries our words, or has us hear sounds echoing across the open range. It is the side that ferries sweet nothings, screams, and moans alike.

But the reality is that in seeing air from only this one perspective, there is much being left out. Air is the soft breeze carrying a sailboat across the lake, or the storm that sinks it. It is the scent of ancient clearings and toxic fumes. Air can be wild, stagnant, or steady. It is the words that spread misinformation as much as it is the words that carry truth.

A person can live without food for a few weeks. They can survive without water for 3-5 days. But without air, even the most trained diver cannot last long. We are dependent on it for life itself.

Air has also come to be manipulated by human kind. Fans of all shapes are used to push air in different directions and speeds. We've invented instruments that take the air from our bodies and transform it into music. But Air will never let us forget that it is also a tornado, and media has taught us what happens to some witches when tornados drop perfectly good houses from the sky.

South: Fire

Under classical forms, Fire is tied to the concepts of passion, inspiration, leadership, love, and energy. These concepts are based on a few different manifestations of fire. Inspiration comes in the form of sparks flying. Passion and leadership are things that charge ahead, like a fire consuming fuel. Love burns deep like a hearth fire ablaze.

There are other sides of fire as well. Fire is the smoldering coals that can relight days later in the right conditions. It is a forest fire that destroys hundreds of square miles. It is massive bonfires our tribes can gather around, as well as a single candle.

The sun is one of the major ways that humans interact with fire. Vitamin D is available in very few foods, but necessary for our health. It is found, however, through exposure to sunlight. Lack of sun can affect mental health, in the form of Seasonal Affective Disorder. On the other side, the sun burns the flesh, causes cancer, and leads to mania if kept in it continuously for days.

Humans may think they have tamed fire, but fire is notorious for getting out of control. People have, however, found interesting ways to harness it. Lighters keep access to fire always on hand. Flamethrowers are used as a weapon against nature and man alike. Candles carry a spark forward with us. Fire is within the ignition spark in engines that allow us to travel faster than our feet could ever carry us.

West: Water

Known oftentimes as the element of emotions, Water is often simplified in ritual down to being a chalice or bowl – filled, still, and clear. The stuff of tears and fears, anger and spit, blood pouring down from our wounds, water is what we ourselves are made of, down to the piss draining out of us at the end of a long day.

In the realm of salt water, the vast oceans hold depth of the subconscious mind. Though we have mapped the land and walked on the moon, humans have never been to the bottom of those vast expanses, nor seen what mysteries and wisdom they hold – not unlike the mysteries and wisdom in the depths of our own soul. The waves of those seas also move in and out like an eternal metronome, beating out the days, mirroring the power of the moon above. Even as we walk along the shore, the sea sweeps away the footsteps that prove we were ever there.

Whether sea or unsalted water, this element has the capacity to slowly erode us, helping us find what is inside. Canyons become carved, rock walls slowly dissolve, and our inner truths and ancient stone are exposed. In turn, when water is disturbed, it simply absorbs what it has received and lets it sink beneath the waves, or skip over its surface. The exception to this is ice, a stabilized liquid which is solid to walk on – except when it cracks, sending ancient ice sheets the size of Delaware floating away.

In the shower, water can quickly cleanse us. Meanwhile, a bath can fill our senses and give us an opportunity for the dance of tub and drain to suck our sorrows down the spiral at our toes. Water allows us to float in our own sense of self, or become slick and unable to be held. We can swim home, or drown in our own sorrows and rage if we are not caring for ourselves.

Queer Elements

There has historically been a belief that these four elements and their associations provided enough variety to tap into energetically. This belief has limited us, keeping us from so many more elemental powers that fall outside the false lines drawn by the notion that the world is made up of binaries – Earth and Air, Fire and Water. Between each of these false binaries lie an additional queer element, and there are a variety of aspects within each of these.

With that in mind, the directional associations for the queer elements are:

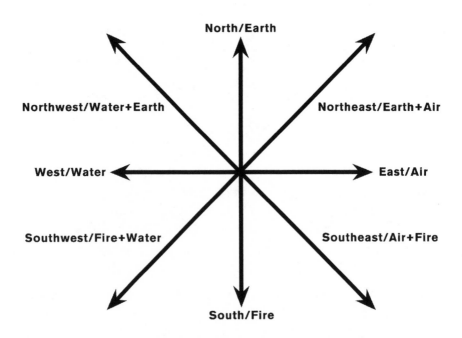

These associations also need to include the queer elements along the latitudinal and longitudnal axis:

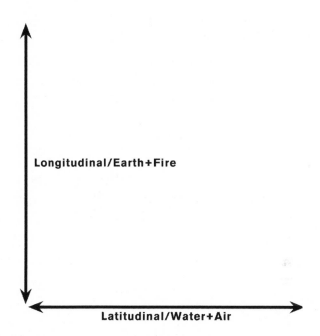

Northeast: Earth + Air

The taste of dust in the air while sweeping the porch, Northeast is the element that allows us to quiet ourselves and look inward. Its face as the sand storm encourages us to hunker down and stay safe, pulling out the resources we have prepared in our past to use them in our time of need, showing our resilience. As the dust bowl, Northeast lets us look back on our own history to the times our ancestors were desperate, to consider towns that now hold only tumble weeds and the taste of dried tears. Tornado touchdowns reveal that we can also have our life radically transformed in an instant, whether we lose all we possess, or are lifted off to magical lands with ruby slippers, making it a powerful tool for the radical shifts needed in life.

Southeast: Air + Fire

As lightning arcs across the sky in blazing bolts of violet, the elemental force of Southeast shows us the awesome glory of divinity. Whether it is ball lightning and the following thunder crash that tells of coming storms in our life, or a lightning strike which is used metaphorically for unexpected pitfalls, this element has the capacity to rock and shock us. In its expansive form, it is firenados that rise up from forest fires, spiraling flames out into the sky, carrying our fire out beyond ourselves. In its contained form, Southeast can also intimidate, shock, and terrify in the weaponized flamethrower, and we know that the same tools we use to harm can also be used to burn invading kudzu vines to the ground so that native plants have space to blossom once more. Fire is also dependent upon air, a unique bond of necessity, as air is necessary for a flame to burn.

Southwest: Fire + Water

Bubbling, boiling, steaming, and sweaty, Southwest is the heat of our sweat as it beads up on our brow from endurance and hard work. We can access the power of this element through its temples: saunas, hot springs, and bath houses. The sauna reminds us to care for our flesh rather than just our minds and hearts. In the temple of the hot spring, we can soak up the memories of the earth and sigh along with her ancient sigh. The bathhouse reveals sweat from grinding bodies, the passion boiling up as many forms combine into one, helping us pull out the power of group workings. This energy can also be tapped through breathing in the steam over a pot of boiling water over a fire, calling upon the hearth energy, healing capacity, and capacity for energetic sterilization that this element also holds.

Northwest: Water + Earth

The force of the swamp and its feral alligator nature can be tapped using this element. One of the most diverse elements, this direction also pulls on the absorbing and innocuous capacities of quicksand, swallowing what does not serve us, letting it take what might mean us ill. Wonderful both for defense and for offense when others wish us ill, Northwest's forms such as the flash flood and mud slide can be directed outwards, as long as its force is respected. In its constructive aspects, this element manifests in the form of logs floating down the river and beaver dams that can transform a creek into the beginning of a lake, keeping things out of our life or building something mighty out of what might seem like little. The mudflat aspect of this element can also tap into healing energy, but be sure not to forget that the Northwest also holds the rhythmic and liminal shoreline, slowly moving the line between worlds as the metronome of the soul.

Longitudinal: Earth + Fire

Rolling slowly out of towering volcanos, this element is a powerful creative force. Like the god Shiva who is the destroyer so that the world can be created anew, lava rolls over what was there before, leaving new land in its place. Erupting from the ocean of our unconscious, Longitudinal work also involves creating, with great force, something where there was nothing before. The forest fire aspect of this element clears out the detritus of what was dry within us, making space for saplings to slowly come up over years to come, work that may not immediately manifest. In its smelting aspect, this work can be about taking raw energy and making it into powerful or beautiful forces to take out into the world, whether it's crafting sand into glass or veins of gold into glittering rings. Remember that one can do immediate intention-changing work as well – this is the element that turns swords into plowshares after all.

Latitudinal: Water + Air

The song of the sea spray mists over us as the waves crash into the immovable forces in our life. This force can help us obfuscate our intentions in its form of fog, or allow us time for slow transition between periods of our life as mist on the moors. Aphrodite also calls this element her own, pulling out love energy as she rose from the sea foam of her manifestation. Meanwhile, the hurricane force brings us to mass destruction in the Caribbean – Poseidon's dark form wiping out thousands in a single swirling breath. Breathe deep and remember that this element also has its gentle side, and is easily accessible as a tool for aspurging, blessing, or cleansing a space or person as drops of water dance across open space. Use this force consciously though, even in its simple forms, because too much of a good thing can remind us that this element also can manifest as the geyser, taking what seemed safe and sending it far into the skies with powerful eruptions.

Element: Self

With any element calling, you are the element that stands at the center. Northeast, Northwest, Southwest, Southeast, Longitude, Latitude – they meet at a center called you.

You are the element at the center of these queer elements, should you be called to call upon them. As with any of the four better-known elements, they are not always safe, so consciousness is key. When working with interstitial spaces, we also have the power to open our awareness to the intersectional work that is necessary in the world. What is considered the work of queer empowerment, by its nature, overlaps the issues of racial justice, religious freedom, access for differently abled individuals, socioeconomic empowerment, and immigrant rights. This makes these elemental forces all the more powerful by their nature of being between.

Keep in mind that there are not truly four core elements either. These aspects are not just 10 total elemental directions – there are innumerable aspects between them and beyond. They help us find a path to the center of our being, and have a deeper understanding of it. In turn, they offer us a mirror for which to understand above as well as below. The categorizations that humans develop are methods for our limited minds to understand and discuss that which our spirit inherently understands is possible. We have access to so many elemental powers, spirits, and presences if we let go of our forced labels, and let our spirit help us understand that we have access to that power.

Breathe deep. Take in your power. Pull it up. Drink it in. Feel the spark ignite.

Honor past energy. Let yourself be inspired. Soak up the heat. Build upon the energy you have. Craft your Self. Rise up from the surf.

You stand at the center.

Let your queer glory shine.

Banishment Sigil

by Dmitri Arbacauskas

"By my fists and by my words,
You cannot harm me.
I have walked through Darkness and Fear,
And grown stronger for it.
This place and this person are not yours,
Your power and your authority are broken.
So again, I deny you.

FUCK OFF OR GET FUCKED UP

BE NOT AND BE GONE."

The Endlessly Enfolding Mirror:

An Introduction to the Queer Sex Magic of Traditional Witchcraft

by Troll Huldren

"As between lovers there is a secret language of word, gesture and intimation, which none but they, the Adorants, may know, so there is a hidden speech known only to the Lovers of God."

- QUTUB, Andrew Chumbley

The *prima materia* of witchcraft is the body. The power wielded by the witch, and through the witch, is that of Creation. This power, called by many names in many places, flows through the Land. A cunning sorcerer knows how to connect with it and to embody this quintessence of creation that binds all of the elements together in the dance of Life and Death. The Cornish witches refer to this power as the "Sarf Ruth," the Fire-in-the-Earth or Dragon-energy, which translates into English as "Red Serpent." It is inherently sexual, and winds crookedly through the Land, along what we know today as ley lines or ghost roads.

Witches know that sexual desire and creativity are the same force, running along the same lines in the body, for the same purpose. We know that the body of the Land and the body of the witch are the same. The Red Serpent is as natural to the body as it is to the Land, and indeed an "umbilicus" or serpentine-thread of force connects the root of our bodies to the root, the center, of the Earth.

A charm for raising this power up through our bodies, raising our libido, can be chanted or sung over and over while rocking on our pelvis:

Red the Serpent of Desire
from the pelvis, rising higher,
Turning, churning, stirring pleasure,
Like the hive drips golden treasure.

Many witches who belong to the major initiatory Houses refer to the cauldron of our pelvis as the seat of the Fetch. The Fetch is the dreaming-soul that is most awake when our waking minds sleep, and which will live on among the Ancestral Host after we shed our flesh in the eternal dream of death. Each night when we dream, our Fetch extends our awareness down along that umbilicus into the Underworld, the inner dimension of reality where the Ancestors and spirits dwell. Much of our experiences of dream are lost or faded when we return to the bright vitality of the waking world. The conscious world of daylight is embodied in our Aura, the breath-soul we inhabit most while awake, seated in the cauldron of our ribcage. This is the Shining Life within us that inspirits our waking existence. It is part of the immortal Breath of God (Herself) that puts all things into motion in and between the worlds. It is the breath that unites the souls together, breathing into and through them, finding the Flow of Power that exists as much within the body as between the worlds.

These two souls are like twins watched over by a divine parent: the Daimon, the ancestral-guardian-soul who is infinite because it is the embodied wedding of the Fetch and the Aura. It is the resolution of all opposites. This is the True-Self that is beyond Life and Death. It exists in the perpetuity of the Eternal Moment of Creation, the rapture of wholeness. In the Daimon, we know, deep and wide in our very bones, that we are children of both Earth and Starry Heaven. We are whole and complete, and therein lies our Mastery.

In queer sex magic, the identification as "whole and complete" is integral to the awareness-state we must have as practitioners. We are not one-half of anything, as posited in the cis-heteronormative paradigm. We are not looking to be completed by another, for we realize that we already are. We are monads, eschewing any ultimate polarity, and fundamentally resolving them.

Witchcraft is animistic. When we look around us we know, as witches, that we are sensing the divine and that the world is alive. Just as the bioregion is the microcosm of the whole cosmos, the body of the witch is also known to be the body of the whole cosmos, whom we understand as "Clitorophallic God Herself," to quote Victor Anderson, the late Grandmaster of the Faery Tradition. We might also render this as the "Divine Androgyn," idolized as the Virile and Buxom Hermaphroditic Black Goat of the Sabbat.

In our stories, God Herself gazes at Her reflection in the Curved Black Mirror of space, and all that is, is a reflection therein. She is the Grandmother of All Phenomena, the Dark Weaver. The fabric of reality is revealed as a grand field of processes, happenings, verbs, and spiritual experiences embodied within living phenomena, constantly shapeshifting. Her name is Mystery of Mysteries, the place one touches in the rapture of orgasm, and which is a door to the eternal Witches' Sabbat.

Queer sex magic allows for the partnering of anybody with anybody in duos, threesomes, and orgies. We seek to peel back the layers of self and expose the True-Self—"true" like a sword is made true. This True-Self, the Daimonic Void-body, is a self-containing holographic piece of the World riding the waves of the Creative Force, the Orgasm of God Herself. In some of the major Houses, which are the initiatory clans of traditional witchcraft, this is related as a possible experience of the Witches' Sabbat; the strange, joyous, and terrifying primal Origin-event of the Cosmos that is eternally taking place outside of Time. Here, God Herself is *Old Fate*, who needs no other being but Herself to bring forth Creation. The cosmological Moment of Creation is played out within the meeting place of body-with-body. It is free from the limitations of ordinary waking consciousness such as personal identity, mortal desires, and egoic preferences. In this rapturous experience, just as in the experience of orgasm, there is no ego with which to attach; it has momentarily shattered. Its practitioners are consumed in the Holy Hunger of Hermaphroditos; avatars of Dame Venus locked in union with the Thrice-Great Hermes, the Sorcerer God who is Light and Motion.

We seek to ultimately identify with the whole, so we seek to identify our Self with God Herself. Victor Anderson shared with his tradition another aphorism: "God is Self, and Self is God, and God is a person like myself." The magic is in knowing how to flip the Mirror, so we may realize that the splitting of Self and Other (the reflection) is as false as any polarity. The black mirror of the Deep Well of Space enfolds upon itself endlessly, warping the reflections, but they are all reflections. Nothing is static, all of reality moves and senses through the whole scale of being. The reflection becomes Beautiful/Ugly, Desire/Transgression, the resolution of which is ecstasy and union; wholeness.

To put it more simply, in queer sex magic one seeks to unite their spark of the Cunning Fire with the spark of another. This is the putting back together of our

God, who appears as an Androgynous Monster: Beastly, Human, and Divine—
"Tikkun Olam" as a Jewish mystic might conjure. It is in this act that queer sex
magic begins, and the attainment of true desires, the operative magic, may follow.

In witchcraft, we posit that the flesh is also the Hedge. The body itself is the threshold
of ecstasy and transgression. Witches are truly embodiments of the Other inside
of human skin. We are the Wild that has been born into Civilization to hold back
its hand, to give it both medicine and poison, to break up the concrete like weeds
growing through the sidewalk and remind Civilization that it resides within the Wild.
Witches can extend from the flesh in the rapture of Spirit-Flight, and as such we
already embody a dichotomy of Self/Other. This, like the endlessly enfolding mirror,
is not static. It constantly "flips" so we can behold Self as Other and Other as Self.
We are Hedge-riders, always in motion between one thing and another, defiant to
any permanent definition, ever reifying wholeness. So, too, is queerness.

Many of the Wild places in the world are poisoned by Civilization. It is my opinion
that witches must save all the Wild places that are left, especially the ones inside
us. This is where the power of queer sex magic comes into play; one of the few
wild places left untamed. Queer sex has long been associated with witchcraft itself,
as well as untamed desire. We know, as queer witches, that our sexuality is deeply
holy, not an aberration as contemporary culture would like us to think. It is a sacred
expression of the Wildness.

It is important to bear witness to your wildness, and give room to let go and explore
the depths and heights of your desire, and the valleys and shadows where power
likes to hide. Fear is a great tool of the witch; as the saying goes, "Where there is
Fear, there is Power." Power-from-within, valid Power, the power to create and
express your deep desire, goes hand-in-hand with power-with, where many come
together to act in unity, to co-create. To Fear is a sign that great power lies beyond it,
and a cunning witch will chase after what they fear, peer into it, and look to uncover
power that may be knotted there.

In our current civilization, a culture rife with the toxic memes of misogyny, racism,
classism, sizeism and fatphobia, ageism, ableism, queerphobia and transphobia, cis-
heteronormativity, ad nauseum, it comes as no surprise to those of us on the margins
of society that our sexualities are twisted up, knotted, and deeply defiled by the illness
of our culture. We must begin the work of re-wilding our sexual drives and desires.

A useful tool in re-wilding our sexual drives and urges is to pay attention to what I
call Preserver versus Defiler behavior. To preserve is to keep safe. Witches strive to

keep safe our flesh as much as we strive to protect and preserve the ecology of the Land. To defile is to trample down and violate. What are you making sacred in your sexual behavior? Are your urges self-destructive? Are your urges connective? If we take care to know ourselves in a deep way, we will be less likely to violate our own dignity or let others use us.

In our first task as witches who wish to successfully perform queer sex magic, we must re-marry Lust and Love to reformulate the Holy Hunger of God Herself. Even if it is only for the moment, we must Love and Lust the others we are with as intensely as any star shines bright. To Love here means to lift up and adore as holy. Love is a practice, a verb. To love is something that we must do, not something we must feel.

Those of us who have done sex work will know this trick, a mystery of the Venusian Rose Queen, She who is the Mother of witchcraft. To conjure forth lust for bodies we have taught ourselves to dislike is not a far cry from conjuring Love for a stranger. This is not mere affection, but the recognition of the Power of Creation in another. We see their Sex, and therefore can become truly sexual with them. Not using any other person as a masturbatory prop, but uplifting them, adoring them, and recognizing them as holy. This has very little to do with our own egoic preferences, but letting go of our finite self to be caught up in the Rapture of knowing you are God gazing at Herself in Her Curved Black Mirror. Uniting our personal Red Serpent with another opens doors of Mystery and brings the Witches' Sabbat into the living flesh; it forms the spiral helix ladder that unites Above and Below. It is the paradise of Heaven-Down-On-Earth.

But a fair warning: this is not to say that we should have sex with everyone and not use our discernment, but that we can conjure sexual attraction to any kind of body. Use care in choosing the persons with whom you practice these arts.

This brings us to the second task of preparation in queer sex magic: embracing the Other, embodied in this culture as the Abject. I find this quote by Lee Morgan, Magister of the Anderean Coven in Tasmania very apt: "The worn-in beauty of the hag is the harsh beauty of Old Craft itself, if you are repelled by it there is nothing for you here and you should seek out a prettier path."

I am also reminded of a quote by my own Craft teacher, Gabriel Carrillo: "Any 'witchcraft' that upholds or enshrines the values and mores of the dominant culture, and refuses to transgress them, is no real witchcraft."

There is no easy way to put this, so I will address is plainly. We must attack the ideas of what is attractive and what is not when we are preparing ourselves for this kind of magic. None of us "grew" into our desires on our own. We are attracted to what we are because of politics, because of cultural forces shaping our waking minds. There are peaks and valleys to this, and inversions, but largely our experiences in culture give rise to what is and isn't attractive to us. If our bodies are to be able to respond to any other body in this work, we must de-spell our minds from the ideas fertilized there, from the wicked sorcery of modernity.

There are various methods, but the most potent and traditional is the path of transgression, where the witch actively embraces the Abject, or what our civilization deems worthless. Embracing and actively eroticizing bodies that are "too much" is at the heart of this: too old, too fat, too dark, too slender, too short, too tall, too hairy, too hairless, too disabled, too diseased, bodies that are shaped in a unique way; any bodies that do not conform to mainstream standards. We embrace acts that defy the teachings of dominance and control, making ourselves vulnerable. We embrace desire that feels forbidden, that brings terror. We embrace secret desire that threatens us with shame. All these places are doorways into liberation, that we may be unshackled by all save Love, the Hand of God Herself. It is this very force that tames the most Terrible of All Spirits, the Proud Prince of Paradise, Heaven-Down-On-Earth.

Again, a warning in this: the witch must respect the power of Life in all things, and to violate the consent of anyone is to disrespect Life itself. Beware those who would harm children or those who cannot ethically consent; the wrath of the Twilight Gods befalls them until they are ground to nothing.

As an essential to the path, a witch seeks to upend the status quo, to invite our Turnskin Master, the Lord of Misrule, to the party. The witches' Devil is the one who shows us the way through, leading by the light of gnosis, the Cunning Fire, into the Otherworld. He is the Other, perpetually, and also the Self embodied in our own Daimon, the resolution of all opposites. He is the Master Sorcerer and Shapeshifter, and it is because he is all Light and Motion that he is Truly Nameless, egoless. He also acts as the Adversary, the guardian of the winding path who tests us and grinds us against the Mill of Stars. Some witches see him as the Cosmic Blacksmith, forging us upon the Anvil that is life. We tread upon his crooked track, following the cloven hoof-prints, seeking Mastery and Wholeness, seeking to carry the torch ourselves.

In the embrace of the abject, we crack our ego. The ego is not a thing, but rather a process. It is the identification of the Self with the mind-stream, the continuous river of thought that flows through our waking consciousness. If we become too strongly identified with the mind-stream, we become less permeable, less flexible and resistant to the Flow of Power. We can become stuck because we are separated from the transformations of life. Over-identified with who we think we are, we are afraid to become who we must be as life continues on and we are immersed in new experiences. We keep resisting change. It's like a shell that keeps the Waking-Self and the Dreaming-Self disconnected. We become lost in the delusion of thinking that the mind-stream is the whole of who we are, which I call the "fog of human confusion." But something must give rise to and contain this stream. It lives somewhere within us, being that we have access to the stories and identities we are attached to through our intellect, and that place is the waking consciousness itself, the Aura.

In practicing "cracking" or destroying the ego, over and over, we learn to become more and more permeable. We must willingly become unidentified with the mind-stream, and we can do this simply by observing it and not attaching ourselves to the observations. The ego, identifying with our mindstream, doesn't seem like it can be "beaten," so we must continually practice until we die. I do not think the ego survives death, because in dying we enter into the eternal dream of unconsciousness, and the waking mind is flooded with the reality of the invisible world that is "under" and "inside" of creation; a very strange and eerie place, where all is Dream.

Perhaps in the alchemical process of knowing ourselves in all our parts, the vitality of our waking lives can become the materia through which our Daimon may wed the Fetch, and we may become "justified" or one of the Mighty Dead. We can realize we are dying, pass by the waters of forgetfulness, and drink from the Well of Memory. If we are able to become unidentified with the mind-stream, then the unconsciousness of dream/death will not confuse us. As Nigel Jackson once wrote:

> 'Ye are Gods!' Thus speaketh the Old Master. Thou art the incarnate divinity of thy Daimonic Self — thy profane pseudo-self must be utterly reversed and consumed in the fires of thy Godhead. Now the Age of Misrule is at hand — all must be inverted, turned upside-down and inside-out for no hoary truism, no sanctimonious untruth, may rest unchallenged in the Court of the White Stag.

This requires that we follow our passions fully, living our lives to their fullness, ever-prepared to pour all of ourselves, every last drop of blood, into the cauldron. We must be willing to sacrifice the parts of us that do not serve our wholeness. We must be willing to ritually die, again and again. It is for this reason that the Master Spirit in queer sex magic is encoded in the symbol of the golden Drone Bee.

The Drone Bee has but one task in the Hive: to mate with the Virgin Queen. The Virgin Queen flies to where hundreds of Drones are prepared to begin the spiral dance of mating. In its zenith, a Drone will mount the Queen and insert his endophallus to ejaculate semen, wherein the spiral helix of DNA is passed. The Drone Bee then pulls away from the Queen while his phallus remains locked within her, tearing it from his body. He falls, his abdomen spilling out his life. However, the hive is perpetuated from that holy death. The Queen Bee will store the semen of dozens of Drones from her mating flight for use over the rest of her reign.

We can't sleep-walk through our lives. We must reconcile the waking and dreaming parts of us. We must realize all in the world that appears to be "opposite" as actually unified into a deep wholeness and completion. Truly, the Adversary is the guardian of this process.

The final task for preparing to perform queer sex magic is the validation of the body. This is something we must do ourselves, and not look to others or stories from our culture. Here we must take stock in all the ways we deny the reality of our bodies. We must work to fully inhabit our bodies, instead of cutting ourselves up into parts that are acceptable and unacceptable. We must be whole! Again we must dispel the magic of modernity and stop the constant search for "self-improvement." This is a false foundation, the belief that we are currently unworthy or not good enough. When we deny the reality of our bodies, we are buying into structural oppression's ideals, again, of being "too much" of something. It also manifests as "not enough," too. It keeps us from being present with the reality of ourselves as we are. And we are **always** worthy. This is the teaching of the Rose Queen.

The Rose Queen, who is the Witch-mother Goddess, the Daughter-Self of Old Fate, is the twining-together of sexual desire and death, having aspects both like Aphrodite and Persephone. She is Queen of Love and Pleasure and Queen of the Dead. For the witch, these things are wrought together and are of one another. We are among the company of the Dead and of the Living, desiring both wisdom and pleasure, willing to slay our egos and all that does not serve us. Within the context of queer sex magic, Our Lady is encoded in the symbol of the Queen Bee. All things that seem to be opposed to one another find their resolution in the kingdom of the divine forbearers of witchery.

She is also known as "Babylon the Great, the Mother of Harlots and Abominations of the Earth." She is the Sacred Whore, Rose-Red, the insatiable Lady who turns away none. We must embody this, at least in the moment of our queer sex magic, accept into our hearts our co-conspirators in this work, and fully accept them as worthy of our Love and affection. We must reach out and embrace much of what is reviled by our sick culture, those things that have been thrown away and trampled by structural oppression, for in that embrace we become truly free.

This is not easy work. It requires patience and trust, and making ourselves vulnerable to one another. It is Heart-work and we must be clean with our intentions. Ritual baths are encouraged before engaging in queer sex magic, while meditating on all these themes and coming into a clear understanding of our own worthiness. We must be willing to get "down and dirty" with this work, as it is much like tending a garden. Our bodies are the fertile soil of growth and exploration, and our intentions are clear water and bright sunshine that encourage fecundity. We must always seek to preserve our integrity and the dignity of those with whom we share these Mysteries.

In closing, let us affirm the Compass by which we may be guided in this work:

May we be oriented toward our own divine Light, the stars Above and Below. We know the Mysteries of the Phallus and the Skull are one in the body of the two-headed Eld God, He who is the Bones of the Land and Door to the Underworld, the South. We know the Cunt and the Cauldron are one in the Dark Weaver, the dark and starry North. Let the Master Spirit and the Rose Queen lead us by their light of Truth, Love, and Wisdom; from East-of-East to West-of-West. Let them show us the way to and fro, between Day and Night, Self and Other, Love and Lust, Beauty and Ugliness. And may we dare to chance the Starry Black Gnosis of the Divine Androgyn, the Sabbatic Idol who is the Great Mystery, the One at the Midst of the Crossroads who is Both Living and Dead, who holds the Keys to Hell and Death ... and Life Eternal. Amen.

Altar

by Inés Ixierda

Fluid Magic

by Lucecita Cruz

When this piece began, I knew that sharing my culture, my experiences, and the stories I tell as a queer trans person of color were necessary. As a Puerto Rican born in and primarily raised in NYC, I understand the "why" of preserving my culture, precisely because I am not in constant connection with it.

I also know that as important as that is for me, it is even more important to uplift the voices of the individuals who taught me to stay connected with my culture. I would not be who I am without them. At this time in the wake of Hurricane Maria, in the wake of starvation, dehydration and death, I hold these traditions close to me.

I hold these traditions as gifts of a culture that is currently feeling the effects of long-suffered colonization. My magic is a political statement; it is done despite the barriers placed on me. To me it is my true freedom.

This story is for those who have lost their lives, those who are surviving, and for those who have the strength to fight back against these systems of oppression and do the work that is necessary.

Pa'lante

I was seven years old when I realized that the "perfume" my mother put behind my ears was for luck; the old man whose voice sounded like Barry White, deep, smooth and buttery, had made it.

Rituals in gender and spirituality were put into practice longer than I can remember: gold bracelets bought for me as a newborn garnishing the evil eye to keep me safe as a baby, being dressed in pink to affirm my female identity, a name bracelet when the pink didn't work, and finally piercing my ears at 9 months when the constant confusion regarding my gender frustrated my mother to the point of no return. There were crucifixes hung in my abuela's home, and there was an altar in every room. Blood sausage was brought back from trips to Puerto Rico and devoured within hours of landing. All of this was not coincidental, but I didn't really become aware of it until the age of seven.

At the time my mother worked at a party supply shop, she made souvenirs for bodas, quinceañeros, baby showers, and the occasional bautismo. The building that housed this party supply store was located on the grand concourse in the Bronx. It had a split layout that housed two completely different businesses; if you walked through the doorway to the other side of the building, you were transported to a land of smells not from this country and music that filled your spirit and left you tingly with energy. Barry White is what we called him and to this day I don't actually know his real name. He was a master Santero always concocting; potions, powders and ointments. The acrid smells of items brewing would fill my nose when I crossed the threshold into his shop. I always knew a present would be bestowed upon me, a blessing of some sort, or he'd read my energy and he'd tell me to take action; to put on this ointment and wear it for a number of days, or sleep with this rock under my pillow, wear this chain around my neck, rub myself with an egg daily. It was these rituals that I began to seek comfort in; it was this realization that I was magic that gave me a glimmer of hope.

It was at the age of seven when the notion of a training bra made me cry and it was at seven when my mother had to reason with me, and we came to a compromise that sport bras were okay. I felt safe under their compression and I felt comforted in my anxiety to be wrapped so tightly. These sports bras were my ticket out, their compression would delay any growth, they would prevent my biggest fear from happening.

It is believed that seven is the age of reason, the number of Jesus Christ himself, and in Christianity the age at which all sins committed count against your entry into heaven. In Santería, Las Siete Potencias Africanas, The Seven African Powers, are orishas that we call upon in times of great need, each with their own correlating Catholic saint. I grew up learning that in Puerto Rico, Catholicism and Santería lie in the same bed and occasionally hold hands. Seven was a very important number for me; it was an awakening into the magic that I held at my fingertips and it was the vexatious sensations in my skin as my gender was realized both internally and externally.

At the age of fourteen I went to Puerto Rico to bury my Abuelita; she passed away just after arriving to New York on one of her yearly trips to La Isla. Not forty eight hours later she was returning, this time in a casket. At the time, most veladas, wakes, depending on the era of your grandparents, took place in the home of a relative or the home of the deceased. My abuela's velorio took place on August fourteenth two thousand six in the home of my aunt. For seven days after the deceased is buried, you are supposed to sit and pray the rosary, and for seven years after the relative has died, you are supposed to come together on the anniversary of their death and pray the rosary. For three of those years I returned to the island, and for two of them I saw miracles happen before my eyes.

My Tía, Blanca, is a healer; she isn't actually my aunt as she is my third cousin, but her age demands that the respect she be treated with was to be that of an aunt. One night my family and I were hanging out on my Tía's porch. She lives across the street from a baseball field. Several people walked up to her gate and asked for her with urgency. They were carrying their fellow teammate, a muscular individual weighing two hundred and fifty pounds, who required four of them to hold his weight. They were playing a game of baseball when he dislocated his knee cap sliding into base. Hospitals in Puerto Rico are expensive when you don't have health insurance and they also don't provide any real quality of care. So the individuals who are often sought after when injuries like this occur are people like my aunt. My aunt came outside and ushered them in, then kicked everyone out of her house except for the injured one. She lit candles, said a prayer, and went to work. At the time I had no idea what she had done. All I knew was that an hour after being carried into her home by four men, this guy was walking out of it.

I only know what happened to that man that night because the second miracle happened to me. I am not at liberty to disclose any of the details of the ritual, but I will tell you this: If I had any doubt that magic was real, that healing through energy could occur faster than western medicine, that doubt was all removed the night my aunt healed me. The belief that nothing was impossible was instilled in me that night, but the looming dark cloud of puberty had closed in. The misogyny, slut shaming, and transphobia that came with this wealth of knowledge had me wondering whether or not it was all worth it.

My abuela got married at the age of twenty-eight to a man who was thirty-two years her senior and she birthed six children. She was a powerhouse of a woman and my idol of femininity; hair always perfect, makeup and nails always done. She also perpetuated the patriarchy in a society where machismo rules all, and at a time when a man was justified in beating his wife if she was not submissive enough.

I don't blame my grandmother for trying to make me submissive the only way she knew how. Hell, I don't blame my mother for trying to do the same, but these acts of abuse coupled with my own self-hatred, gender dysphoria, and desire to disseminate from a culture and from a religion that I felt would never accept me, caused my practice to cease. Instead I fell into a spiral of drug and alcohol abuse, high risk sexual behavior, and was intent upon self-destruction.

I eventually sobered up and started to put the pieces of my life back together.

At the age of 23 I met someone whose powers exemplified all that I could hope for. I had never really had any examples of what the marriage of magic and queerness could look like until I met this powerhouse of a being. She was a pivotal part of the revelation that my queerness and magic don't have to contradict each other and can live together symbiotically. It was through her that I was exposed to a community of people who were queer and practicing magic, whatever and however that manifested for them.

It was through this community that I learned that magic transcends gender. It doesn't judge you for what you look like or how you choose to present yourself, and it only works if you stay true to yourself and show integrity. Its power moves with you based on the content of your character.

I knew that in order for me to get to that place of symbiosis though, it would take some serious healing.

Part of the healing that was necessary for me was centered around healing my trauma and abuse, making amends with the abuses I doled out to other people, and learning that my abuse doesn't excuse the abuse I inflict on others. Without that healing, there is no way that any of my magic could have worked. There was no way for my practice to be whole if I myself wasn't.

As my exposure grew, I began to do more research on Santería and on the Orishas that I grew up hearing stories about for most of my childhood. If I were going to practice any sort of polytheist religion, it was only ever going to be Santería. I knew that in the core of my being I was desperate to find some correlation between my queerness and that particular practice because it was in a sense the only way that I would return home.

It took doing my own research, dispelling myths about the fluidity of magic and my own gender, and years of being at battle with myself. This Orisha, despite the obvious connections to my airy nature, became my guiding light. Legend has it that she fought fearlessly alongside her husband in battle while wearing a beard; she embodied maleness just as much as she embodied femininity.

Oyá, Oyá, Oyá…. This Orisha is one that would grow over the years to become imbedded in my bloodstream, to sit on my head at times, to use me as her physical manifestation, Goddess of the winds, the marketplace, a fearless warrior. Oyá… it's hard to say where I begin and she ends.

When entering the game of gender, I stood at the center for a very long time, and after a while I felt a push to have to choose a side. When I did, it never quite fit. The more I became recognized as male, and indoctrinated to the rights of male privilege, the more disgust I began to feel. This, for so long, was the thing I fought against, and there I was, standing in the middle of it.

My desire to wear makeup never subsided and my longing to have a body covered in glitter never changed, but I knew that these things weren't intrinsically tied to any particular gender. Dressing in men's clothing became just as much of a costume as women's. I decided to dress based on how I felt. On any given day, what that looks like can be drastically different. On days when things get hard and I feel like I can't decide; when I feel like giving up and when I feel like every decision I make is the wrong one, I call upon my Oyá to help center me.

I've spent the last seven years figuring out what my queerness looks like and how my magic manifests itself.

I am an air sign. I am a genderqueer femme of color. My gender is just as fluid as the winds. I am a warrior, and not just metaphysically. I fight every day for my continued existence, and I fight every day to live in a body that is brown, queer, and femme.

These days, my queerness is inseparable from my magic because my magic is rooted in the belief that I must live as my most genuine self, that I love fluidly and exist fluidly much like the winds of Oyá.

The Fluidity of Spirit

by Laura Tempest Zakroff

Biographies

Aaron Oberon is a practicing witch of over 10 years who spends most of his time talking to plants and avoiding his neighbors. Aaron's witchcraft centers around spirit work, folklore, and finding magic in the landscape around him. Looking at the landscape as something magical is what first drew Aaron to exploring how queerness and witchcraft intersect three years ago. He started exploring drag as a way to navigate those waters, but wouldn't call himself a queen just yet.

Abby Helasdottir is a writer, musician and graphic designer. Her path is a Rökkr one, exploring the twilight side of Norse cosmology with a particular emphasis on Hela, goddess of death and the underworld. As a musician, she creates music as Gydja, described as dark ambience for dark goddesses, revealing an interest in goddess figures from other mythological systems.

Adare works to challenge both overt and covert biases to show the truth of what it means to be human. Fierce and unapologetic, Adare strives to break free of traditional stereotypes as an openly genderqueer artist. Living on an active volcano in the middle of the ocean, Adare spins fire, chants in sweat lodges, and teaches her students how to access spirit through the paint brush. Layering their oil paintings with gold leaf and metallic pigments, Adare creates the feel of a living, breathing person on canvas. "When you paint someone's portrait you become a vessel. Their spirit tells the essential story, channeling every part of their life into shape and color."

Adrian Moran is a Chicago-based Pagan and Polytheist blogger. He is the Magister of the Chicago Temple of the Fellowship of the Phoenix, a Queer Neopagan Order. He has presented for the Owen Society for Hermetic and Spiritual Enlightenment and has been a guest on Magick Radio Chicago. His interests also include LGBTQ issues, environmentalism, veganism, art, opera, gardening, and Steampunk. His blog about his personal spiritual path can be found at www.adrianmoran.com. The Fellowship of the Phoenix can be found at fellowshipofthephoenix.org.

Alder Knight is passionate about dancing, ancestor veneration, black excellence, drag, rootworking, transgender liberation, environmental justice, collecting rocks, building renewable energy, dismantling global capitalism, baking cookies, and dreaming the future. They write, perform, march, instigate, baby talk to plants, climb on strangers' roofs, and help their comrades fix minor electrical issues. Their work with Agdistis and Dionysos comes out of years of personal transformative practices around trauma and dysphoria, and they are eager to share tools and strategies with other TGNC folks for collective healing. You can find their collaborative undertakings for the transgender dead and participate in the annual Transgender Rite of Ancestor Elevation at http://trans-rite.tumblr.com.

Alex Batagi (Bonkira Bon Oungan) is a queer, transgender man who found his way to the feet of the lwa, and, with the guidance of his spiritual mother, Manbo Maude (Antiola Bo Manbo) of Sosyete Nago, followed his spirits into the djevo where he was made a houngan asogwe. A longtime polytheist, spiritual worker, and artist, Alex has found that vodou provided the container that he could place all of himself into and gives shape to a life spent seeking out balance and addressing social inequality. He serves all his divinities at home, and in his spiritual mother's temples in Boston and Jacmel, Haiti. He blogs frequently at http://rockofeye.tumblr.com and can be found in Facebook as Bonkira Bon Oungan.

Almah Rice-Yorkman is a queer hummingbird femme fairy who engages in daily divination play. Her dreamworking science was published in the anthology, *Black Quantum Futurism: Theory & Practice*. Her live interactive dream installation was featured in the Transmodern Festival in Baltimore, MD. With María Firmino-Castillo, Almah filmed and choreographed *Aria Del Rio/River Aria*, a short/performance ritual invoking Osun. Her essay, "Remedios," was published in the anthology *Solace: Writing, Refuge, & LGBTQ Women of Color.* Almah is currently at work on a book-length divinatory project involving Black Kentucky folk magic and fictions.

Cazembe Abena is a Certified Holistic Practitioner known as 'The Heart Whisperer,' Tantra Intimacy Coach, Priest of Osumare,' and DOM. Cazembe is originally from Portland OR, and earned a B.A. in Psychology from Clark Atlanta University, in Atlanta GA where he resides. His company, Divine Resonance LLC's mission is "Rekindling the Spark and Deepening the Connection to Source, Self, and Life through Love." Cazembe uses a combination of Energy Therapy, Coaching, Nurturing Touch, and CBT tools to promote evolution, self-acceptance, and healing of the holistic four-body system to foster a life of abundant authentic living. Cazembe's custom-drawn energetic symbols are called Sacred Symbol Technology™ and his healing method of BDSM is called Senergetic™ BDSM. Cazembe is available for individual and couples sessions, workshops, lectures, and Senergetic™ exhibitions. Sessions can be done in person or remotely via phone. Contact Cazembe throuhg his website www.divine-resonance.com or on Facebook for more information.

Charlie Stang is a lifelong lover of magic and the land. She became involved with a Pagan community in Virginia as a child and draws on almost three decades of magical practice in her service and teachings. Her spiritual practice plays a critical role in her activism and she is deeply committed to the work of justice with roots in pagan practice. Chuck currently lives in Unceeded Ohlone territory, also known as the California Bay Area.

Doug Middlemiss (Ade Kola) was initiated as a 2nd Degree Wiccan High Priest in 2009, and initiated as a priest of Chango in the Santeria/Lucumi tradition in 2012. He has been a student of various traditions of magic and spirituality, including Stregheria, the Anderson Feri Tradition, Hoodoo, and espiritismo. After years of focus on witchcraft and paganism, he now primarily works within the context of Lucumi and espiritismo, honoring the Orisha along with his spirit guides and ancestors. He lives in Portland, OR.

Dmitri Arbacauskas is an artist and practitioner in the Pacific Northwest. In between visually hexing the unwary and trying to maintain a homelife, he also makes all manner of leatherwork and art, which can be seen and ordered at www.tormenedartifacts.com.

EJ Landsman is a trans, non-binary artist living in Seattle, Washington. A graduate of Oberlin College and the University of Washington's Scientific Illustration certificate program, they make natural illustrations and comics about nature, gender, living with mental illness, and other normal things.

Inés Ixierda is an interdisciplinary visual artist and Bolivian bruja in Oakland, California. She uses handcraft, mark making, art rituals, and graphic narratives to heal and hold her lived experience as a queer disabled Woman of Color. She is influenced by liberation and self-determination movements, ancestral knowledge, and the moon.

Ivo Domínguez, Jr. has been active in Wicca and the Pagan community since 1978. He is an Elder of the Assembly of the Sacred Wheel, a Wiccan syncretic tradition, and is one of its founders. He is a part of the core group that started and manages the New Alexandrian Library. Ivo is the author of *Keys To Perception, Practical Astrology for Witches and Pagans, Casting Sacred Space, Spirit Speak, Beneath the Skins,* and numerous shorter works. Ivo is also a professional astrologer who has studied astrology since 1980 and has been offering consultations and readings since 1988. Ivo lives in Delaware in the woods of Seelie Court. www.ivodominguezjr.com.

Jay Logan is native (but not indigenous) to the Pacific Northwest, residing in the would-be sovereign state of Cascadia. He is an initiated priest of Chalice Hart, a local Wiccan coven, as well as a mystes of the Naos Antinoou, for which he serves as a Mystagogue. A librarian by trade, he enjoys reading, researching, providing resources and information to the public, knitting, as well as dancing under moonlight during the Witches' Sabbat.

Naos Antinoou is a queer, Graeco-Roman-Egyptian devotional polytheist community honoring Antinous, the deified lover of the Roman Emperor Hadrian, and related gods and divine figures. We provide space for practicing devotion to

Antinous, participation in His sacred mysteries, and together seek the promotion of social and spiritual justice.

Laura Tempest Zakroff is a professional artist, author, dancer, designer, and witch based in Seattle, Washington. Her artwork embodies myth and the esoteric through her drawings and paintings, jewelry, talismans, and other designs. Her art has won numerous awards and honors, is collected world-wide, and appears in numerous books and publications.

She blogs at Patheos as *A Modern Traditional Witch* and at Witches & Pagans as *Fine Art Witchery*. She recently published her first book, *The Witch's Cauldron: The Craft, Lore, & Magick of Ritual Vessels*, with her next book *Sigil Witchery: A Witch's Guide to Crafting Magical Symbols* due out in early 2018 (Llewellyn Worldwide). For more information, please visit www.lauratempestzakroff.com and www.owlkeyme.com.

Lee Harrington is an eclectic artist, author, spirit-worker, gender radical, and internationally known sexuality, spirituality, and personal authenticity educator who has taught in every state, as well as worldwide. He has been an active part of the international pagan and sex positive communities for over 20 years, and believes passionately that laughter and soul-searching rise from the same well. An award-winning author and editor on gender, sexuality, and sacred experience, his books include *Sacred Kink: The Eightfold Paths of BDSM and Beyond, Traversing Gender: Understanding Transgender Journeys*, and *Shibari You Can Use: Japanese Rope Bondage and Erotic Macramé*, among many other titles. Lee actively incorporates his various sexual practices and gender experience into his spiritual workings as a spirit-worker in service to Bear, as well as running private, group, and community rituals across various spiritual paths. He has been blogging online since 1998, serving as a priest(ess) since 1999, and has been teaching worldwide since 2001. Read more about Lee at www.PassionAndSoul.com.

Lucecita Cruz is a Puerto Rican genderqueer activist, writer, farmer, and collector of stories. They live and breathe earth, whether it is farming, community organizing for food justice issues, or collecting the experiences of others who do this work in their Zine titled *Comida con cuidado*. They believe in the power of magical healing through food.

Malcolm Maune is an artist who lives in Berkley with his two adopted sons.

Maisha Najuma Aza, MSW, is a queer black witch, healer, polyamorous leather-woman, parent of two teens, and an ecstatic lover of life. She erotically weaves her black queer lesbian activist roots, spirituality, shamanic practices, and bodywork to co-create intuitive healing sessions. Her work impacts the multidimensional aspects of each person's social, sexual, spiritual, emotional, physical, and energetic world. Maisha's light-hearted, deeply accepting, down-to-earth and empathic nature makes her private consultations and public engagements especially powerful and deeply transformational! Maisha's passion is sharing the erotic integration of spirituality, sexuality, and embodiment with other LGBQTPOC in her healing sessions, consultations, classes, workshops, and speaking engagements around the world.

Maisha is an ordained Tribal Shaman, certified in Integrated Healing Arts, Tantra Sacred Intimacy, Shamanic Reiki II, and Massage Therapy; and holds a master's degree in Social Work. She is the Founder of "A Life Alive Consulting" and "Black Girl Tantra" , based in Atlanta, GA, and can be found online at www.alifealiveconulting.com and @blackgirltantra on Instagram.

Michael Greywolf is an artist and podcaster living in Texas. He attended Southern Methodist University, where he studied Sociology and Studio Art. Michael has been active in the pagan community since 2004, and an initiated brother of the Unnamed Path (an emerging Shamanic tradition for men who love men) since 2014. Michael co-hosts two podcasts on the Pagans Tonight Radio Network. He has co-hosted All Acts of Love and Pleasure, a show about sex, sexuality, gender, and various other topics with Dr. Susan Harper since February 2015. In September of 2016, Michael and co-host Mathew Sydney, started the podcast Walking the Unnamed Path. On this show, Mathew and Michael discuss and expand on the teaching and techniques laid out by the late founder of the Unnamed Path, Eddy 'Hyperion' Gutierrez. They also cover various topics and ideas that affect queer pagan men in general. Michael can be found on social media using Facebook, Instagram @michaelgreywolf, Twitter @GreywolfMusings, or emailed at michaelgreywolf.musings@gmail.com.

Michaela is a tender-hearted fierce femme queer witch who has had access to the privilege of dedicating time to personal healing. She is passionately committed to helping make the tools and opportunities she has had accessible to all. More of her writings on the topic of healing her relationship to femininity, and more, can be found at https://healingfemininity.wixsite.com/re-memberingdesire. She resides in her hometown of San Francisco, California, where she is currently participating in the Somatic Sex Education Practitioner Program as well as studying to be an EMT. She aspires to help facilitate others in reconnecting to their bodies, feelings, and authentic desires, as well as aid in others' journeys of self healing, self love, self acceptance and self empowerment.

M.C. MoHagani Magnetek is a delightful Transgender African American Anthropologist, writer, poet and performance artist. She draws inspiration from within to create stories and narratives about obscure aspects of life. Sometimes surreal noir and other times concrete realities, she fashions her stories with a great deal of poetics. As a transgender woman with Bipolar Disorder and PTSD living on the last great frontier of Alaska, she employs many of her experiences in her works of fiction, non-fiction, and poetry. She is the author of 10 short stories, an anthology, two novellas, a novel, a poetry collection, and has been included in a few publications and website blogs.

Orion Foxwood is a traditional witch, conjure-man and faery seer, and, the author of *The Faery Teachings* (RJ Stewart Books), *The Tree of Enchantment, The Candle & the Crossroads* and *The Flame in the Cauldron* (Weiser Books). Born with the veil in Shenandoah Valley, Virginia, he was exposed to faith-healing, root-doctoring, faery lore, and southern and Appalachian folk magic. He is the founder of the House of Brigh Faery Seership Institute and Foxwood Temple where his goal is pass on the traditional witchcraft of his elders. Orion is also the co-founder of Conjure Crossroads, the annual Folk Magic Festival in New Orleans, Conjure-Craft, and the Witches in the Woods gatherings aimed at fostering education, community, co-creative magic and the healing and helping practices of the traditions he carries. He holds a master's degree in Human Services. Website: orionfoxwood.com.

Papacon is an artist based in Europe. He enjoys drawing male/male erotica, for both pleasure and as a work-for-hire artist. He is an avid fan of Sir Christopher Lee. A collection of his work can be found in the novel *The Initiate*, written by J. Swartz. Look for his work on his Papa-con tumblr.

Pavini Moray facilitates glittering queer pleasure revolutions and getting down with ancestors. Find Pe at transcestralhealing.com. Wheeeeee!

Rocket is a gender-ambivalent, futureshocked nice Jewitch boy who prefers "it" pronouns and is, at present, exploring the interplay between poetry, spells, trauma, time travel, language, and trans identity using a combination of sadomasochism, rhinestones, and strategically applied pyromania. Rocket works on the Transgender Rite of Ancestor Elevation (trans-rite.tumblr.com/), Mythical Events, and the Agdistine Order, and can be found online at @FlamingKorybante and in meatspace in Brooklyn.

Sam 'Eyrie' Ward is delighted by paradox, craves the liminal, and is unabashedly inquisitive about all aspects of human behavior. She is a polyamorous, demisexual slut, who's spirituality is very much bound up in kink, sex, and the science and magic of ritual-making. Among the many roles and titles she embodies, such as mother, submissive, student, and writer, Sam is an epidemiologist, trauma researcher, and licensed social worker who has developed and taught workshops for young people and other helping professionals about teen sexuality, resiliency, strategic sharing, and institutionalized power dynamics. Her research in the neuroscience of trauma and recovery intersects with her understanding of the power of magical communities: particularly in how synchronicity, rhythm, and connection create opportunities for profound learning and growth.

From Mexico originally, **Stan Stanley** has settled in NYC and refuses to budge. She makes comics that are spooky and queer, mostly because she is rather spooky and queer herself. Stan has worked on comics since the late 90s, taking a break in 2009 to focus on grad school and trying to be a serious scientist. Turns out she likes working on comics much better. Previously responsible for Friendly Hostility, Stan currently publishes The Hazards of Love and Abernathy Square both online and in print. In her personal life, she enjoys tea, collecting skulls and other bones, and the cheesy satisfaction of helping tourists get to wherever it is they're trying to go. Like guiding ducklings back into the lake, honestly.

Steve Dee is the author of *A Gnostic's Progress: Magic and the Path of Awakening* and the co-author (with Julian Vayne) of *Chaos Craft*. After a near miss with the Anglican Priesthood, Steve focused his energies on more occult pursuits that have included work within the east/west tantra group AMOOKOS and the Chaos Magic current. His current interest in Gnosticism represents an attempt to explore the way in which joys of heretical freethinking can be harnessed for the benefit of all. He currently blogs over at https://theblogofbaphomet.com.

Steve Kenson is a co-founder of the Temple of Witchcraft (www.templeofwitchcraft. org), a 501(c)3 religious nonprofit dedicated to the Great Work of Witchcraft in the world. He is lead minister of the Temple's Gemini ministry, responsible for Queer Spirit work. He has taught workshops and facilitated rituals at the Between the Worlds Queer Men's Gathering, Coph Nia Queer Men's Festival, ConVocation, TempleFest, and other events. Steve is managing partner of Copper Cauldron Publishing, producing Witchcraft, pagan, and New Age titles. Steve lives in New Hampshire with his partners, Christopher Penczak and Adam Sartwell, and can be found online at http://templeofwitchcraft.org/steve-kenson-hp/

Susan Harper, Ph.D., is an educator, activist, advocate, and ritual specialist living, loving, making magick, and agitating for change in the Dallas, TX area. She holds a PhD in Cultural Anthropology from Southern Methodist University, where her doctoral research focused on the intersections of gender, sexual orientation, and religious identity in the Texas NeoPagan community. She also holds an MA in Multicultural Women's and Gender Studies from Texas Woman's University. Susan is passionate about making spirituality accessible, practical, and personal. Her workshops focus on using spiritual information and techniques to facilitate transformation in our personal lives. She seeks to help people equip themselves with skills and tools that will aid their continuous growth. Susan has over two decades' worth of experience with Feminist Spiritualty, Wicca and other forms of NeoPaganism, energetic healing modalities, Tarot, ecstatic movement, and other transformative practices. She facilitates a monthly Full Moon circle which is inclusive of all women and nonbinary people who find their homes in women- and femme-centric spaces. She has written extensively on Goddess Spirituality, activism, and feminism. You can follow her latest adventures at dreamingpriestess.wordpress.com.

Tai Fenix Kulystin, MA, CSB, CCTP is an identity and intimacy geek, somatic sex educator and bodyworker, sacred sexuality practitioner and guide, and ritual artist. A student and practitioner of magic and witchcraft for over half of their life, Tai has a love of bringing the sacred and ritual into all aspects of their life. They are a student of Anderson Feri witchcraft, an adept in the Golden Dawn tradition of magic, and a practical and erotic Alchemist. Their professional work is called Conscious Pleasure, a somatic sex education and bodywork practice based in Seattle, Washington where they provide heart-centered, therapeutic guidance for adults of all genders, sizes, relationship statuses, and sexualities who are struggling with identity, sexuality, or connection and who long to be seen. You can find more about Tai's professional work at www.ConsciousPleasure.com and

www.TempleOfEroticAlchemy.com.

Reverend Teri D. Ciacchi, MSW, is the matrix of Living Love Revolution; an EcoSexual Activist, a Priestess of Aphrodite, a holistic spiritual healer and an EcoMagicks practitioner. As an EcoMagick practitioner, she translates the teaching she receives from mycelium (mushrooms), bees, and stardust into useable social skills for human beings, leading collaborative workshops that honor the innate connections between human beings and the living Earth. Her EcoSexual activism is based in the Cascadia bioregion and includes creating & organizing the yearly Surrender: The EcoSex Convergence, holding monthly EcoSex salons and Happenings and tending her many gardens of beloveds.

A Priestess of Aphrodite with over 30 years of training in Reclaiming Witchcraft, Ceremonial Magick, Tibetan Buddhism in the lineage of Chogyam Trungpa Rinpoche, and the Tantric lineage of Swami Rama, she teaches Living Love Revolution Aphrodite Temples quarterly in the Pacific Northwest. Living Love Revolution is her life work and spiritual calling, and a community building experience-based system of healing that focuses on expansion, liberation and sovereignty. She can be heard regularly on: www.SexTalkRadioNetwork.com. Keep up with her at: www.LivingLoveRevolution.com, www.AphroditeTemple.com, and www.EcoSexConvergence.org.

Thista Minai is a Priestess of Artemis, polytheist, spiritworker, ordeal facilitator, Third Degree High Priestess in the Blue Star Tradition of Wicca, and founder of Spectrum Gate Mysteries. She has more than fifteen years of experience with designing and conducting rituals, performing various types of energy work, and has taught lectures and workshops on a variety of topics including modern Paganism, sacred sexuality, ordeal, and kink. Thista applies the knowledge gained from her master's degree in education to developing better curriculum and support structures for students of modern Paganism and spirituality, and is the author of *Casting a Queer Circle: Non-binary Witchcraft.*

Troll Huldren is a native of Appalachia living in Columbus, OH with their partner and spawn. They are an initiate of two major Houses of traditional witchcraft, the Anderson Faery tradition and the WildWood tradition. They are a founding member of Talaith y Gwynt, a network for Faggot-identified witches. They work as a professional cook, a Faery Doctor and diviner, and are involved in multiple arenas of social justice activism. They are currently at work on a manual of queer sex magic and are curating a podcast on "Faggot Witchery" with coven mates, as well as re-awakening the "Aradian Current" through a series of integral skillset workshops for witches around the U.S and abroad. They see the work of the witch as involved in resistance to oppression and liberation of people, and in sacred guardianship of the Land.

W. L. Bolm is a writer and techie living in Wisconsin. They have been actively writing and practicing magick and ritual since the late nineties. They converted to Judaism in 2009, and since then, their concept of deity has evolved to accept the unknowable mystery of the divine.

W.'s work as a journalist has appeared in the *St. Petersberg Times, The Tampa Tribune, Create Loafing, The New Gay, 411 Magazine,* and a number of print and online publications. They are currently shopping around a polyamorous YA paranormal romance to agents.

In their spare time, W. works on writing and art projects and is a QUILTBAG activist. They are a fully-professed member of the Sisters of Perpetual Indulgence of the Parish of the Muddy Waters in New Orleans. They have organized sex positivity events in New Orleans and have appeared on the Loving Without Boundaries podcast.

wolfie is a witch, a radical faerie, a thelemite, a pervert, and a not quite run-of-the-mill revolutionary. they live in *chaos,* a radical faerie collective in california. a practising discordian, she has also been seen at pujas, tsoks, in gardnerian circles, and eats hotdogs almost every friday. he's been known to show up at pagan gatherings, leather parties, trans marches and deathbeds. v founded the holy order of the epicenes, a spiritual order for people who see themselves and deity as being outside of any binary gender spectrum, and are committed to a life of service. their pronoun of choice is not the same one twice in a row, or whichever is most applicable at the time. s/he doesn't approve of capitalisation, or capitalism.

Yvonne Aburrow is a queer polytheist Gardnerian Wiccan, the author of *All Acts of Love and Pleasure: inclusive Wicca*, and several other books on folklore and witchcraft, co-editor with Christine Hoff-Kraemer of *Pagan Consent Culture*, and keen blogger and poet. She lives in Oxford with two cats and a lovely man called Bob. She is a web developer and trade union activist, and loves trees, stars, stones, and the Moon.

Yin Q. is a BDSM practitioner, educator, sex work activist, and writer residing in Brooklyn with her partner and two children. She has a BA from Barnard College and an MFA in Creative Nonfiction from The New School. Her writing, classes, and random thoughts can be found at www.YINQ.net. Other publications include *A Women's Thing, BUST, Chance Magazine, Through the Looking Glass*, and *Apogee Journal*. She is currently working on a memoir of violence and magic.

Z Griss (Zahava) is the founder of *EMBODY more LOVE*, healing through dance, bodywork, performance, and coaching. Z focuses on social change leaders who are ready for a breakthrough in their sexual and spiritual expression. This work is about the body as our ally in releasing trauma, transforming limiting beliefs, and creating pleasure to access new possibilities in our personal and societal lives. Z comes from 30 years of dance training, certifications in Yoga for birth, Esalen Massage, Urban Tantra, Pilates, and Health Coaching. Powerful influences include the arts of unlearning racism, Sufi whirling, Sexual Shamanism, bioenergetics, socially conscious entrepreneurship, and transformational group dynamics.

Z directed Spiritual Nourishment for Conscious Activism in collaboration with Deepak Chopra and has been listening to, speaking in, and facilitating spaces to acknowledge and transform white privilege since 1999 including work with the People's Institute for Survival and Beyond, Sarah Lawrence College, the Re-Evaluating Counseling community, and the national White Privilege Conference. Z co-founded White Folks Soul, By Any Dance Necessary, a dance company exploring the incompatibility of wholeness and the race construct for white people. www.EmbodyMoreLove.com.